INDIGENOUS CHURCHES

THE GOAL OF BIBLICAL MISSIONS

By

BOB C. GREEN, B.A., M.A., D.Min

August, 2015

REL006201: Religion: Biblical Studies - Topical

ISBN 978-0-9962591-7-0

All Scripture quotes are from the King James Bible.

Address All Inquiries To:
THE OLD PATHS PUBLICATIONS, Inc.
142 Gold Flume Way
Cleveland, Georgia, U.S.A.

Web: www.theoldpathspublications.com
E-mail: TOP@theoldpathspublications.com

1.0

DEDICATION

This book is dedicated in honor of Bob and Anita Steele of Bristol, Virginia and Wade and Mary Jane Hawks of Mount Airy, North Carolina. Of all the individuals and churches that have prayed for us, encouraged us and supported the ministry over the past forty-eight years, these folk have done so the longest, with the greatest faithfulness.

Patsy and I soon learned in 1968 that we were not alone in serving the Lord. The Lord has used dozens of additional individuals that though they were not wealthy, some were widows, etc. and churches small and great to make it possible for us to continue to labor in the ministry of planting indigenous churches. Though not named here, the Lord has recorded to their accounts in heaven the fruit that abounds to His glory. The Lord will give honor to whom honor is due at His Judgment Seat.

FOREWORD

Writing a book is no easy task. I can assure you that I have agonized much in prayer whether to even attempt to do so. I certainly do not presume to know all there is to know about planting indigenous churches, but the Lord Jesus Christ has graciously allowed me to gain what knowledge I possess through forty-seven years of observation and personal church planting experience both on the foreign field and in the USA.

I owe a great debt to the Lord for salvation and His all-sufficient grace in my life. As is generally the case, He has used me in the ministry in spite of myself. I am also indebted to the second most important person (the Lord being first) in my life, my wonderful wife of 50 years, Patsy. She is truly a gift from God.

The list of people to whom I am indebted must include missionary Bruce Bell for the influence that he had in my life and ministry. Much of what I learned about planting indigenous churches while in Central America came from serving as his assistant in the Bible Institute "IBERO" and as Co-founding pastor of the Miramonte Baptist Church in San Salvador, El Salvador. The Lord brought Bruce and Karen Bell into our lives very early in our ministry. I admit that at that time I was floundering as a church planter.

There are many precious people to whom I owe a debt of gratitude, pastors, missionaries, friends, prayer warriors, family members, etc., but none are more special to me than the Hispanic nationals with whom Patsy and I have had the privilege of serving. The national preachers and pastors that serve in the churches, that we either started or that have grown out of churches which we were involved in starting, have been used greatly of the Lord. Their success in the ministry glorifies the Lord and is a source of great blessing to us. I am so thankful to God for them and their families.

I count it a great privilege to have been called of God to serve in the ministry of His Word but I am especially thankful that He has assigned me to serve in missions in church planting. "Missions" is the heartbeat of God, the central theme of the Bible and the mission of the church. The purposes of the believer and the local church begin with the glorification and exaltation of the LORD. We exist for His glory. As is said in John 15, He is glorified when we bring forth "much fruit." Fulfilling our mission will bring fulfillment of our main purpose – to glorify HIM. Each servant of God stands or falls according to God's standard, not man's. It can be said:

"A missionary's success should not be measured by how much is being accomplished while he is on the field but by what fruit remains when he is gone."

Dr. Bob C. Green
July, 2015

TABLE OF CONTENTS

DEDICATION **3**
FOREWORD **5**
TABLE OF CONTENTS **7**
FRUIT THAT REMAINS **13**
PREFACE **15**
INTRODUCTION **17**
Defining the Indigenous Church: 17
Indigenous vs. American 18
CHAPTER ONE: WHY ESTABLISH INDIGENOUS CHURCHES? **21**
CHAPTER TWO: HINDRANCES TO THE PLANTING OF INDIGENOUS CHURCHES **25**
THE MISSIONARY CREED: 30
CHAPTER THREE: IMPORTANT CONSIDERATIONS: **41**
CHAPTER FOUR: HOW TO BEGIN A NEW CHURCH ON THE FIELD **49**
Planting Indigenous Churches Begins With Evangelism 49
San Miguel vs. San Salvador 57
CHAPTER FIVE: DISCIPLESHIP **69**
RESPONSIBILITY DEFINED: 70
Discipleship Considerations: 75
CHAPTER SIX: THE ORGANIZATIONAL SERVICE OF THE NEW CHURCH **83**
The Purposes of the New Church 83
The Pastor of the New Church 84
Involve the Nationals in the Ministry 85
Set Biblical Standards 85
Work to Make Them the People's Standards 86
Review 87
CHAPTER SEVEN: PRODUCING THE THREE KEY ELEMENTS OF INDIGENEITY: A. SELF-GOVERNING **91**
Spirit-filled Leaders 94
Pastors, Elders, Bishops & Deacons: Qualifications 95
The Deacons 97
CHAPTER EIGHT: B. SELF-SUPPORTING **109**
The Keys 110
CHAPTER NINE: C. SELF-PROPAGATING **117**
CHAPTER TEN: THE CONCLUSION **123**
APPENDIX ONE: **125**
Various Church Documents 125
A Sample Doctrinal Statement 125
A Sample Constitution 127
PREAMBLE 127
ARTICLE I – NAME 127
ARTICLE II – PURPOSE 128

ARTICLE III – ARTICLES OF FAITH 128
ARTICLE IV – CHURCH COVENANT 131
ARTICLE V – MEMBERSHIP 131
SECTION 1. RECEPTION OF MEMBERS 131
SECTION 2. PROCEDURE FOR MEMBERSHIP 131
SECTION 3. DISMISSAL FROM MEMBERSHIP 132
SECTION 4. DUTIES OF MEMBERS – 133
ARTICLE VI – ORGANIZATION 133
SECTION A. 133
SECTION B. 133
SECTION C. 133
SECTION D. 134
ARTICLE VII – MEETINGS AND ELECTIONS 135
SECTION A. 135
SECTION B. 135
SECTION C. 135
SECTION D. 135
SECTION E. 135
SECTION F. 136
ARTICLE VIII – AUXILIARY ORGANIZATIONS 136
ARTICLE IX – AMENDMENTS 136
ARTICLE X – DISSOLUTION 136
A SAMPLE DOCUMENT: 136
ESTABLISHING THE CHURCH AS A NON-PROFIT RELIGIOUS CORPORATION 136
ARTICLE I 136
ARTICLE II 137
ARTICLE III 137
ARTICLE IV 138
ARTICLE V 138
ARTICLE VI 139
APPENDIX TWO: 141
TEACHING GIVING 141
APPENDIX THREE: 145
A SAMPLE MISSIONS POLICY 145
MISSIONS POLICY 145
Missionary Profile 157
APPENDIX FOUR: 159
FAITH PROMISE OR GRACE GIVING TO MISSIONS 159
The Faith Promise or Grace Giving Plan functions like this: 160
The blessings associated with this type of giving are multiple and abundant. 161
Why should a person obligate himself or herself to give an offering "Faith Promise?" 161
The Cards 163
APPENDIX FIVE: 165

SAMPLES OF VARIOUS FORMS 165
A Sample Church Membership Covenant 165
Sample Letter Calling for an Organization Council 166
Date of letter 166
New Testament Baptist Church 166
Any Street 166
Any Town in the World 166
Agenda for a Recognition Council 167
Recognition Service Order 167
A Covenant for the Leaders and Workers of the Local Church 168
APPENDIX SIX: ACTUAL STATEMENT OF FAITH (SOF) AND BYLAWS OF A LOCAL BAPTIST CHURCH 171
TABLE OF CONTENTS 171
STATEMENT OF FAITH 177
ARTICLE 1—NAME AND PURPOSE 177
SECTION 1.01—NAME 177
SECTION 1.02—PURPOSE 177
ARTICLE 2—STATEMENT OF FAITH AND COVENANT 177
SECTION 2.01—STATEMENT OF FAITH 177
I. THE HOLY SCRIPTURES: THE BIBLE 177
II. THE TRIUNE GOD: THE GODHEAD 181
III. THE LORD JESUS CHRIST--HIS VIRGIN BIRTH 182
a. His Bodily Resurrection: 185
b. The Lord's Descent: 185
c. His Bodily Ascension: 185
d. His High Priestly Work: 185
e. His Bodily Return: The Second Coming: 186
IV. GOD THE HOLY SPIRIT 186
V. THE CREATION OF THE UNIVERSE 188
VI. THE CREATION AND FALL OF MAN 188
VII. THE CHRISTIAN'S TWO NATURES 189
VIII. THE CHRISTIAN'S SERVICE 189
IX. SATAN AND FALLEN AND UNFALLEN ANGELS 190
X. THE FALL OF MAN 192
XI. THE RIGHTEOUS AND THE WICKED 192
XII. SALVATION ONLY THROUGH CHRIST 192
XIII. THE NEW BIRTH 194
XIV. JUSTIFICATION 195
XV. SANCTIFICATION 196
XVI. THE ETERNAL SECURITY OF BELIEVERS 196
XVII. THE ASSURANCE OF THE BELIEVERS 197
XVIII. THE CHURCH 198
XIX. THE CHURCH'S GREAT COMMISSION 199
XX. THE CHURCH'S TWO ORDINANCES: BAPTISM AND THE LORD'S SUPPER 199

XXI. BIBLICAL SEPARATION 200
XXII. CIVIL GOVERNMENT 205
XXIII. ISRAEL 205
XXIV. THE RAPTURE—THE BLESSED HOPE 206
XXV. THE TRIBULATION 206
XXVI. THE SECOND COMING OF CHRIST 207
XXVII. THE ETERNAL STATE 207
XXVIII. THE BIBLICAL DISPENSATIONS 208
XXIX. Civil Government. 210
XXX. Human Sexuality. 210
XXXI. Family Relationships. 210
XXXII. Divorce and Remarriage 211
XXXIII. Abortion. 212
XXXIV. Euthanasia. 212
XXXV. Love. 212
XXXVI. Lawsuits Between Believers. 213
XXXVII. Missions. 213
XXXVIII. Giving. 213
SECTION 2.02—AUTHORITY OF STATEMENT OF FAITH 214
SECTION 2.03—COVENANT 214
ARTICLE 3—MEMBERSHIP 215
SECTION 3.01—QUALIFICATIONS FOR MEMBERSHIP 215
SECTION 3.02—DUTIES OF A MEMBER 216
SECTION 3.03—PRIVILEGES OF MEMBERSHIP 216
SECTION 3.04—DISCIPLINE OF A MEMBER 217
SECTION 3.05—TRANSFER OF MEMBERSHIP 219
SECTION 3.06—TERMINATION OF MEMBERSHIP 219
SECTION 3.07—AFFILIATED CO-LABORER 220
ARTICLE 4—OFFICERS 221
SECTION 4.01—CHURCH OFFICERS 221
SECTION 4.02—DESIGNATION OF CORPORATE OFFICERS 221
SECTION 4.03—ELIGIBILITY FOR OFFICE 222
SECTION 4.04—TERMS OF OFFICE 222
SECTION 4.05—ELECTION OF OFFICERS AND CALLING A PASTOR 223
SECTION 4.06—PASTORAL OVERSIGHT OF OFFICERS AND STAFF 224
ARTICLE 5—DUTIES AND POWERS OF OFFICERS 225
SECTION 5.01—THE PASTOR 225
SECTION 5.02—THE BOARD OF DEACONS 226
SECTION 5.03—THE MINISTER OF RECORDS 228
SECTION 5.04—THE MINISTER OF FINANCE (TREASURER) 229
SECTION 5.05—FINANCIAL SECRETARY 231
SECTION 5.06—ASSOCIATE PASTORS 231
SECTION 5.07—DUTIES OF ALL OFFICERS 231
SECTION 5.08—INSTALLATION OF OFFICERS 232
ARTICLE 6—MEETINGS 232

SECTION 6.01—MEETINGS FOR WORSHIP 232
SECTION 6.02—MEETINGS FOR CHURCH ADMINISTRATION 232
SECTION 6.03—SPECIAL MEETINGS 234
SECTION 6.04—MOTIONS 235
SECTION 6.05—FISCAL YEAR 235
ARTICLE 7—MINISTRY OF EDUCATION 235
SECTION 7.01—PURPOSE 235
SECTION 7.02—CHURCH PARTICIPATION 235
SECTION 7.03—STAFF MEMBERSHIP 236
SECTION 7.04—STATEMENT OF FAITH ACCORD 236
SECTION 7.05—UNITY 236
SECTION 7.06—TEACHING 236
SECTION 7.07—CHRISTIAN WALK 236
ARTICLE 8—ORDINATION 237
SECTION 8.01—ORDINATION QUALIFICATIONS 237
SECTION 8.02—ORDINATION PROCEDURE 238
SECTION 8.03—REVOCATION OF ORDINATION 239
SECTION 8.04—LICENSE 239
ARTICLE 9—INDEMNIFICATION 239
SECTION 9.01—ACTIONS SUBJECT TO INDEMNIFICATION 239
SECTION 9.02—EXPENSES SUBJECT TO INDEMNIFICATION 240
SECTION 9.03—LIMITATIONS OF INDEMNIFICATION 240
SECTION 9.04—TIMING OF INDEMNIFICATION 241
SECTION 9.05—EXTENT OF INDEMNIFICATION 241
SECTION 9.06—INSURANCE 241
ARTICLE 10—COMMITTEES 242
SECTION 10.01—STANDING COMMITTEES 242
SECTION 10.02—SPECIAL COMMITTEES 242
SECTION 10.03—ACTIONS OF COMMITTEES 242
ARTICLE 11—DESIGNATED CONTRIBUTIONS 243
ARTICLE 12—BINDING ARBITRATION 243
SECTION 12.01—SUBMISSION TO ARBITRATION 243
SECTION 12.02—NOTICE OF ARBITRATION 243
SECTION 12.03—LIMITATIONS ON ARBITRATION DECISIONS 244
SECTION 12.04—ARBITRATION PROCEDURES 244
ARTICLE 13—CONFLICT OF INTEREST 244
SECTION 13.01—PURPOSE 244
SECTION 13.02—DEFINITIONS 244
SECTION 13.03—PROCEDURES 245
SECTION 13.04—RECORDS OF PROCEEDINGS 247
SECTION 13.05—COMPENSATION 247
ARTICLE 14—AMENDMENTS 247
ADOPTION 248
ARTICLE 15—TAX-EXEMPT PROVISIONS 248
SECTION 15.01—PRIVATE INUREMENT 248

SECTION 15.02—POLITICAL INVOLVEMENT 249
SECTION 15.03—DISSOLUTION.. 249
SECTION 15.04—RACIAL NONDISCRIMINATION 249
SECTION 15.05—LIMITATION OF ACTIVITIES 249
ARTICLE 16—PROCEDURES FOR ARBITRATION 250
SECTION 16.01—SCOPE OF ARBITRATION 250
SECTION 16.02—SUBMISSION TO ARBITRATION 250
SECTION 16.03—TERMS AND CONDITIONS OF ARBITRATION 251
SECTION 16.04—CONDUCT AND RULES OF HEARING 252
SECTION 16.05—DUTIES OF ARBITRATORS 253
SECTION 16.06—DECISION OF ARBITRATORS 253
SECTION 16.07—PARTIES TO COOPERATE 254
SECTION 16.08—COSTS AND EXPENSES 254
SECTION 16.09—AMENDMENTS... 254
SECTION 16.10—ADOPTION 254
SUGGESTED FORMS AND DOCUMENTS TO USE FOR THE MINISTRY.... 257
LIST OF SCRIPTURE REFERENCES IN THIS ACTUAL SOF AND BYLAWS259
INDEX OF WORDS AND PHRASES IN THIS ACTUAL SOF AND BYLAWS 267
SAMPLE GUIDELINES FOR NURSERY WORKERS 277
Guidelines for the Nursery Leader 280
A QUESTIONNAIRE FOR CHRISTIAN WORKERS 281
APPENDIX SEVEN: 285
GUIDELINES FOR CALLING A PASTOR 285
APPENDIX EIGHT: A PERSONAL TESTIMONY 289
INDEX OF WORDS AND PHRASES IN INDIGENOUS CHURCHES........... 299
ABOUT THE AUTHOR.. 305

FRUIT THAT REMAINS

In John 15 the Lord Jesus Christ speaks to His disciples concerning fruit bearing. He speaks of bearing ***fruit, more fruit,*** and ***much fruit.*** He says that His Father is glorified when the believer, who is referred to as the "branch," bears ***much fruit.*** The believer is only able to bear much fruit as he abides in the Lord, the Vine, and His Word abides in him. Obviously, the "abiding" necessary to fruit bearing refers to **intimate fellowship and communion with the Lord Jesus Christ.** In spite of this obvious truth many Christians fail to maintain the *abiding relationship* necessary to glorify the Father. Failure in this area destines the servant of God to live and minister in the weakness of the flesh.

In John 12:24 the Lord states, "Except a corn of wheat fall into the ground and die, it abideth alone: but if it die, it bringeth forth much fruit. He that loveth his life shall lose it; and he that hateth his life in this world shall keep it unto life eternal." The ability to be productive and bring forth "much fruit" also requires the church planter to "die daily to self" (Galatians 2:20, I Corinthians 15:31). The missionary church planter may have to "die" to his preferences, likes, rights, comforts, etc. if he is to accomplish the will of God. This is another way of saying that one, "lives for God and not himself" (I Corinthians 5:15).

The Lord's desire for us is not only the fullness of joy that comes as a by-product of the "*abiding relationship*" but the *abundant fruit bearing* that glorifies HIM. In addition to ***much fruit*** He desires "***abiding fruit,*** fruit that He calls "***fruit that remains"*** (John 15:16). If the missionary church planter is to produce ***fruit that remains*** he must live daily abiding in the Lord. The Word of God must also abide in the missionary (vs. 7). The church planter's ministry must be biblical in **purpose**, in **principle** and in **practice**.

The best guarantee we can have that our efforts in church planting will produce *fruit that remains* is to establish *indigenous churches.*

A divinity school graduate wrote:

> "If you want to grow something to last a season, plant flowers;
> If you want to grow something to last a lifetime, plant trees;
> If you want to grow something to last through eternity,
> **plant churches**."

PREFACE

Because the planting of *indigenous* churches is of such great importance to the continuing work of missions I feel it good to provide a practical guide, written from the independent Baptist perspective. There is benefit that can be gained from the materials written by non-Baptists but there is really no reason why we should have to depend on those of a different doctrinal persuasion on this subject. I believe the historical Baptist position in doctrine and practice to be the closest to that of the New Testament teaching, and so, without apology, I seek to set forth the information necessary to the establishment of *indigenous or autonomous,* independent Baptist churches.

I propose to provide the missionary church planter a written point of reference by recording the New Testament principles, methods, and procedures for planting indigenous or autonomous Baptist churches. My prayer is that the materials contained in this book will be a valuable resource for those seeking to prepare themselves and others as church planters.

There are many reasons why *indigenous* churches are not being planted. Very often the church planter is tempted by a course of action that brings some immediate good but that ultimately hinders the establishment of *indigenous* churches. I propose to point out some of the dangers and pitfalls associated with church planting.

The church planting missionary is in a constant spiritual battle. It is a very demanding task. It is probable that every church planter has or will experience the heartache of seeing a congregation he has planted led away by a hireling. People, over whom the missionary has wept, those for which he has interceded before a Holy God, will leave him. He went to them with the good news of the life changing gospel when they were slaves in sin, when their lives were in shambles, their marriages were falling apart and they seemingly had no hope, but this does not keep them from turning on him or going back into the world. Because the missionary loves the people to whom he ministers the wounds caused by those who would turn from him or The WAY, cut deep. In the midst of these trials the missionary could very well lose sight of God's calling and purpose. There are great church planters that have retreated into a comfort zone away from the front lines. They have found a haven in other aspects of the ministry. If even one of these special men can be challenged to renewed commitment to church planting or if just one young church planter can be forewarned, I will feel the effort worthwhile.

I am also motivated to write because I believe it important for the church planting missionary to see the national church leaders for what they can be, fellow-laborers in Christ. Worthy national pastors and other national church leaders should be considered as equals in the Lord and at times more than equals. If a truly *indigenous* church is to be planted it will require nationals of exceptional Christian character, with firm biblical convictions and God given leadership ability. The time and effort invested by the missionary in the lives of the national leaders can contribute greatly to their development. Fortunate is the missionary that recognizes this. There is no reason for the missionary to be intimidated by the emergence of national leaders. I can say that one of my greatest joys as a missionary church planter has been to have "disciples" not only equal me in the ministry, but surpass me as they have become outstanding national leaders (Philippians 4:1).

God's work done God's way will bring God's blessings. Where He is working an *indigenous* New Testament Baptist church can be established.

As missionaries are sent out by local churches to cross cultural boundaries with the gospel, the priority objective or goal should be to plant and establish viable churches that are able to cultivate a natural appearance and form a New Testament, yet culturally relevant growth pattern.

INTRODUCTION

Defining the Indigenous Church:

The word "indigenous" is a biological term. It is used to describe a plant that thrives in a specific location. The ability of the plant to flourish is directly related to the type of soil in which it is rooted and the specific climate of the location. The metaphorical correspondence between the biological and missiological use of the term is easily seen. The goal of missions should be to plant viable New Testament churches that are able to not only exist but to flourish in the various cultural environments of the world. Indigenous churches reflect a practical and functional autonomy.

> **"Indigenous churches are generally understood to be churches that are *self-governing, self-supporting and self-propagating*.**" ("Missiology, An introduction to the Foundations, History, and Strategies of World Missions," edited by Terry, Smith and Anderson, Broadman & Holman Publishers)

> "The New Testament church then was first, **self-propagating**; that is, it had within it sufficient vitality so that it could extend throughout the region and neighboring regions by its own efforts. It produced its own workers and the work was spread abroad by the effort of the Christians themselves. Second, it was **self-governing**; that is it was governed by men who were raised up by the Holy Spirit from among the converts of the locality. Third, it was **self-supporting**; it did not depend on foreign money in order to meet the expenses of the work." ("The Indigenous Church" by Melvin L. Hodges, Gospel Publishing House)

An indigenous church is one that is self-governing. Just as the apostles trained and ordained local leaders (Acts 14:23) to oversee the ministry of the churches they planted, so too modern church planters should train nationals to govern themselves according to the Scripture and the direction of the Holy Spirit. **The indigenous church is also self-propagating.** The churches on the field should be motivated to evangelize the lost, locally, and worldwide. A healthy church will be reproducing itself by continually winning new converts. As the need arises new churches will be planted. **The indigenous church is self-supporting in that the expenses of the local ministry are met by the tithes and offerings of the local church members.**

We have no evidence in the New Testament that the apostles requested funds from the churches in Jerusalem or Antioch to support the ministry or workers of the churches they established. To the contrary we find them raising funds from the churches they established in Macedonia to assist, not the pastors, but the needy saints in Jerusalem. The churches Paul and others established such as in Philippi actually sent funds to support Paul in his missionary ministry (Philippians 4:14-15). The words of Philippians 4:10-19 were written in the context of "a missionary church planter encouraging a church he planted to continue to give to the work of missions." Those who would claim the promise of Philippians 4:19 would do well to remember that Paul was confident that God would supply their needs because they were giving to missions.

Indigenous vs. American

An indigenous church on a foreign field may not necessarily reflect the pattern or model as found in the average middle class American church. The affluence of Christians in the United States allows many benefits that are simply not practical on many fields of the world. The church planter should be cautious about seeking to impose on foreign churches an American form of Christianity. Not everything about foreign culture is wrong. Not everything American is biblically right. The Scripture should be our standard, our measuring rod for determining what cultural changes are needed, if any.

The indigenous church in a country officially *closed to the* gospel may not require a public meeting place. Persecution may force the believers to meet behind closed doors or underground. These churches do not have the same external form as churches in America but neither did the churches found in the "house churches" in Rome in Paul's day (Romans 16: 10-16).

A church in a tribal village may not have more than a thatched roof hut for a meeting place -- no electric lights, no air conditioning, no Sunday school rooms, no piano or organ, etc. A church in a metropolitan area such as New York City or Tokyo may find the cost of owning a multi-acre church facility, as the ones that are so common in many areas of the USA, prohibitive and impractical.

The biblical goal of the church planting missionary should be to plant churches that are able to prosper in the "cultural soil" where they are located. Churches that require a form of "spiritual hot house" or artificial environment to survive are not *indigenous.* Truly *indigenous* churches do not need the continual influence of foreign leadership or infusion of foreign funds.

If the missionary has done his job well he can "commend the national church to the Lord" and move on to plant another church.

Before proceeding from this point it seems prudent to mention that not all missionaries are led of the Lord to develop the same ministry pattern...starting a church, establishing it and then moving on to start and establish another church. Some missionaries, like BIMI missionary, Dr. Rick Martin serving in the Philippines, have been led of the Lord to plant one central church on the field and remain as missionary pastor for many years. Men like Dr. Martin have seen the Lord bless their efforts. Through the ministry of the "central church" many hundreds of daughter churches have been planted. The church planter must find God's will in this matter.

> "The mission of the church is missions and the mission of missions is church planting" Dr. Ray Thompson

Modern missionaries and local churches alike would do well to remember this fact and concentrate their efforts in starting and establishing new local churches patterned after New Testament principles.

A church in a tribal village may not have more than a thatched [illegible] meeting place [illegible] no electric lighting, [illegible] no [illegible]. A church in a [illegible] new [illegible] church [illegible]

The [illegible]

[illegible] nations [illegible]

[illegible] from this point [illegible] that [illegible] starting a church [illegible] on to start another church. Some [illegible] in the Philippines [illegible] been led of the Lord to [illegible] church on the field and remain as [illegible] pastor for many [illegible] have seen the Lord bless their efforts. Through the ministry of the "central church," many hundreds of daughter churches have been planted. The church planter must find God's will in this matter.

[illegible] mission of missions is [illegible]

Modern mission [illegible] local churches [illegible] remember the fact and concentrate [illegible] efforts in [illegible] establishing new local churches patterned after New Testament principles.

CHAPTER ONE

WHY ESTABLISH INDIGENOUS CHURCHES?

A. **It is biblical to plant indigenous churches.** Each of the churches established in the first century existed as an autonomous entity with its own elders, leaders, etc. (Acts 14:21-28). There was no hierarchy, no subsidy, and no looking to others to extend the ministry.

B. **It is Christ's will.** In Matthew 16:18 He *promised* to "build His church." The church is His *possession.* He guarantees by His resurrection that the church shall *prevail* in victory against the gates of Hell.

C. **Indigenous churches should be established because:**

1. Christ has not changed **His *command*** (Acts 1:8; Matthew 28:19-20)
2. The lost are **still *condemned*** (Luke 19:10; Romans 3:23)
3. The Gospel has universal power to ***convert* sinners** (II Corinthians 5:17; Romans 1:16)

D. **The establishment of indigenous churches on the field honors the power of the Holy Ghost and the efficaciousness of the Word of God.** The Holy Spirit is all powerful and capable, through the application of biblical truth of accomplishing in the lives of believers in any and every cultural setting that which He has accomplished in the lives of faithful Christians in the USA. He can transform people of any nationality into dedicated, fruitful believers.

E. **The establishment of indigenous churches is also respectful of the nationals.** We should never consider nationals as inferior or beyond the total transforming power of Christ. There are national Christians that put many American Christians to shame by their commitments to the Lord and the ministry. Many nationals pay a great price to follow the Lord Jesus Christ.

F. **There are very real political and social implications that make it wise to plant indigenous churches.** In many parts of the world, especially in Eastern Europe, Asia, Africa and Latin America, there is the emergence of a critical issue -- new governments are being established at an alarming rate. With the rise to power of these new governments comes the question, "What is the role of the foreign resident (American missionaries, etc) and is their presence recommendable, justifiable, and advantageous to the new government?" You and I would argue, "Most definitely." Ours is a divine mission. At times these new governments are guided by constitutions that provide for a "state religion." Islam or Catholicism is elevated to the role of the officially recognized religion for all the people of that country. At times the new government depends on these state religions to validate their authority and right to rule. This creates a situation that gives the state religion great influence. This influence may result in the secular government limiting the number of foreign religious workers or even result in their expulsion. If the missionary has not established an indigenous church... what fruit will remain when he leaves?

G. **The establishment of truly indigenous churches adds to the number of churches participating in world evangelization.** National churches should be involved in planting churches. Many of the modern day missionaries are from national churches in under-developed countries. Indigenous churches can join the ranks of the "givers" because they are self-supporting and no longer needful of foreign financial aid.

H. **Indigenous churches draw on the unlimited resources of God (Philippians 4:19) as opposed to those which look to man and his limited resources.** Even the best funded missions organizations have limited resources. The members of indigenous churches learn the joy of giving by faith and seeing God provide through them. National Christians, thus, add to their account in Heaven (Phil 4:17).

I. **Indigenous churches are a permanent instrument for evangelism and ministry on the fields of the world.** *The presence of indigenous* churches diminishes the need for foreign involvement through funds and personnel.

CHAPTER TWO

HINDRANCES TO THE PLANTING OF INDIGENOUS CHURCHES

A. **Some Missionaries Do Not Know How To Establish Indigenous Churches**

In spite of the improved curriculums of a number of Bible Colleges and Seminaries there are still many young missionaries who ignore the basics of church planting. They have had little or no exposure to the principles that lead to the planting of *indigenous* churches. The next section is quite lengthy.

B. The Planting of Indigenous Churches Is Not The Primary Objective of Some.

A second reason, beyond the fact that some missionaries ignore how to plant an indigenous church, is that planting indigenous churches is not the primary objective of some missionary ministries. More and more churches are emphasizing "social ministries" (construction projects, digging wells, medical clinics, orphanages, camps, etc.) in place of evangelism, discipleship and the establishment of churches. All of the social ministries should contribute to the establishment of local churches. Para-church and social ministries that are often the primary objective of some missionary ministries should not take precedence over church planting.

While on deputation in 1968 I came across an article in a well-known Virginia newspaper. The article was entitled, "In the Name of God." My interest was stirred. The article was a report on the lives and ministries of three *"missionaries."* Each served in a different part of the world though their ministry objectives were very similar. The three were praised for their great successes. Even from my perspective as a fundamental Baptist there was something very commendable about their life-time accomplishments. The nationals they served benefited, at least socially, from their efforts. One of the missionaries represented the Roman Catholic Church and the other two represented main line Protestant denominations.

They had dedicated themselves to the establishment of schools, medical clinics or hospitals and the "raising" of the average yearly income of the nationals. Most likely they did not "preach the gospel of Jesus Christ with the intent of gaining true Christian converts" because the true gospel does not form a part of the creed or tradition of their sending churches. Biblical church planting was not even considered by them as an objective. They gave themselves to social ministries. The truth of the matter is that, though commendable, their efforts and ministry accomplishments did not and do not fit the New Testament definition of missions. Well might we ask as did our Saviour, *"For what is a man profited, if he gain the whole world, and lose his own soul?"* Matthew 16:26. Is it not interesting that these monumental words are found in the same sixteenth chapter of Matthew where the Lord spoke of building His church?

The Bible believing missionary may very well find it **beneficial to minister to the "total person"** as he seeks to win them to Christ. To do so is to express in a tangible way one's love for the lost. In the process he may establish clinics, schools, orphanages and other socially commendable institutions but he should not lose sight of soul winning and church planting as his primary objectives. How sad to think of people being given physical health in a hospital or educated in a mission school or even having a better standard of living and yet dying without Christ as Saviour and spending all eternity in Hell separated from God. In 2004 more than 6.3 billion people live on planet earth. Most of these folk for which Christ died have no effective gospel witness. Though there are more missionaries serving in more places around the world there are fewer indigenous churches being planted. When indigenous churches are not established the greater portion of the burden for world evangelization continually falls to the foreign missionary.

Because church planting is God's plan, we have to believe it to be the most effective way to fulfill Christ's command and meet the need of those lost in sin in the rural, suburban, and urban areas of the world. **Evangelism and Christian ministry are perpetuated when an *indigenous* church is planted.** Good social ministries can be a natural outgrowth of the local church but the church should come first.

Make no mistake, God is blessing and missionaries are using to great advantage the many peripheral ministries, such as tribal aviation, clinics, forms of mass media, translation work, construction, printing, and other specialized ministries in their church planting efforts. Bible believing missionaries must, however, guard against allowing "good things to replace the best things." Auxiliary ministries should be seen as tools to promote and assist in church planting.

The cause of planting indigenous churches is weakened in part by the notion that "every Christian" is a missionary. The idea that all good work can be called "missionary ministry" tends to minimize what should be our primary objective. My humble opinion is that we better state the truth by saying, **"Every Christian should be a witness for Christ, but in a stricter sense only a few are God called missionaries."** Even national Christians should be involved in missions through the local church through prayer, giving and even going locally. The missionary is one "sent by the local church with the gospel message to un-evangelized areas of the world for the purpose of winning the lost and ultimately organizing the new converts into local congregations."

The apostle Paul stated:

> *"Yea, so have I strived to preach the gospel, not where Christ was named, lest I should build upon another man's foundation;" Romans 15:20*

The "evangelist" of Ephesians 4:11-17 could be the equivalent of the biblical missionary. Once the new church was planted, the "evangelist" was replaced by the more permanent pastors and teachers who would further equip the saints to fulfill the New Testament purposes for every church and believer: evangelism, edification through instruction, fellowship, ministry or service, worship, and missions.

The planting of indigenous churches has been replaced as the priority objective by many good ministries such as jail ministries, rest home ministries, college campus ministries, camping ministries, etc. There is much good done by most of these ministries but could it be that they should be "extension ministries" of an autonomous local church rather than "mission ministries"?

The father of modern missions, William Carey, in 1792 was moved to establish a "Baptist missionary society" because of the lack of missionary action on the part of the churches of his day. In our day sincere people of God with a heart for winning souls and ministering to people not being reached by the local churches have met the need by establishing auxiliary ministries. Unfortunately many church members are content to allow someone else to minister the gospel to those in the local prison, rest homes, or the college campus community. Often Para-church organizations come into existence to fill a ministry vacuum. There is always the danger that these good organizations will sooner or later detract from the local church ministry. Thank God for them but **church planting should be the main objective of missionary activity.**

Very often church planting missionaries are lured away from church planting to dedicate most of their time to peripheral ministries. **Caution!** Once on the field and once you have a church planted you may begin to think it better to invest most of your energies in social ministries. If you have a burden for some particular social ministry ask God to raise up members in the church you are establishing who will share your burden and bear the major portion of the responsibility for it. Finish the work God has for you. With little exception the missionary should not begin or establish a ministry that cannot be continued by the nationals alone.

Allow me to mention one experience we had in Central America. I recognize the Lord has used His word to bring a number of people to Himself in spite of some unethical organizational practices. There was a branch of a well-known international student ministry located in our city. The workers of the organization came to us with their main ministry objective... to reach college students for Christ. They stated they wanted our church to be the beneficiary of their labors. The young people they won would be encouraged to attend our services. Because of the benefits we would receive as a church, they asked that the church support the organization financially on a monthly basis. We had doubts resulting from previous encounters with them so our response was that we would wait for evidence that their activities contributed to the establishment of the local church before the church contributed financially.

Over the next year we had young people from the organization attend the services of the church, though not on a regular basis. As far as I know not one young person involved with them followed the Lord in believer's baptism and became a faithful member of the church. We did notice that the organization had retreats for the young people on Sunday morning at the same hour we had services. There was effort made to draw the young people of the church away from church activities into the organization. The director actually visited lost businessmen that we were seeking to reach for Christ, asking them to give monthly donations to the organization. Members of the church were asked to give their tithe to the organization. Only in eternity will we know what damage was done.

Note: On a recent visit to the field I was made aware that this particular ministry has all but ceased to function. This accents the importance of doing things God's way, the Bible way.

As the church-planting missionary pastor of the new church it was my obligation to train the church leaders in their **responsibility** of guarding the local church ministry. The church leaders learned a hard lesson concerning Para-church organizations from that situation. Whatever detracts from the establishment of the local church is unscriptural.

All extension ministries should find their significance in the fact that they make a positive contribution to the planting or establishment of the autonomous local church. Peripheral ministries should be a by-product of the local church and not the essence of mission's activity.

Solution to the problem

If established churches help their members discover and exercise their ministry gifts there would be more than sufficient numbers of lay workers in the local church for the various extension ministries. This is the whole concept behind the teaching of Ephesians 4:11-18. The saints won and discipled by the "evangelist or missionary" are to be prepared by the pastors and teachers for the work of the ministry so that the body of Christ might be edified. The saints are to do the work of the ministry, not just the pastor, etc. Much damage was done when religious leaders of the past defined Christians as *laity and clergy.* The local church should minister to the needs of the people living in their local influence area through its members. Beyond the local area of ministry influence of the church we find the biblical realm of missions.

Jesus said, *"I will build my church..."* Matthew 16:18

A grave danger for the missionary church planter is that he will become so involved in a worthy extension ministry that he will lose sight of the number one goal, planting churches.

THE MISSIONARY CREED:

"There is a living God. He has spoken in His Word. He means what He says. He always keeps His promise." Hudson Taylor

C. Missionaries Can Grow Accustomed To The Role of "Master Over The Ministry."

1. The missionary may have funds to dole out which allows him to hire and fire.

2. The missionary may use the nationals to make himself *successful* in the eyes of the churches in America. Two good policies:

   a. Use the ministry to *build the people,* not the *people to build the ministry.* Do not become guilty of merely ***using*** people.

   b. Strive to make those about you a success and you will be a success.

      If the missionary makes all the ministry decisions he will fail to teach the nationals how to make wise and godly decisions. People learn to make decisions by making decisions just as they learn to serve by "serving."

      National Christians will make mistakes just as we have. The missionary that "makes all the ministry decisions" is, by his actions, saying to the nationals, "I do not trust you." The national sensing this lack of trust will not trust the missionary. If the missionary is to ever "commend the nationals to the Lord, on whom they have believed" he must train them properly. He must trust them.

   c. The missionary may be more proficient in all aspects of the ministry but if he expects to train the nationals he must allow them the opportunity to gain hands-on experience.

It is better for the church planter to train five preachers to preach than to preach five times.

D. The Over Emphasis of Evangelism May Actually Hinder the Planting of Indigenous Churches

Strangely enough "an over emphasis of evangelism" may be one of the reasons more indigenous churches are not planted. Before jumping to any hasty conclusions about my lack of soul winner's zeal, allow me to explain. Evangelism is super important but **the local church is God's primary instrument for evangelism and church planting.**

All Christians are to be soul conscious and make every effort to win souls for Christ. Pastors and missionaries alike are to do the work of "evangelists". The Greek words for "evangelist" and "gospel" have the same root, "euaggelión." The "evangelist" *announces* the good news while the "gospel" *is* the good news. It seems that the best definition of the word "evangelist" in Ephesians 4:11 is that of the modern day missionary. The biblical missionary would be a person who has the ministry and heart of the Apostle Paul (Romans 15:20). He strives to preach the gospel where Christ has not been named. The missionary sees the need to get the gospel message of salvation through repentance and faith in the Lord Jesus Christ to those who have no effective gospel witness, preacher, or Bible believing local church.

The first part of the Great Commission is evangelism. For fear of being misunderstood I want to emphasize the importance of evangelism. New churches are started as a result of evangelism. The vitality and relevance of the established church are found in evangelistic out reach.

The break down comes when evangelism is over emphasized to the point of becoming **the only goal of the missionary**. This over emphasis of evangelism and neglect of discipleship and church planting may be due in part to the fact that missionaries are rewarded for "reporting great numbers of conversions" as a result of their evangelist efforts. Some supporting churches contribute to this imbalance in missionary ministry by giving greater support to the missionary who dedicates himself primarily or exclusively to evangelism. Each of us desires to see as many folk saved as possible through our ministry. **"CHRIST CAME TO SEEK AND SAVE THAT WHICH WAS LOST"** (Luke 19:10)... that is **EVANGELISM PURE AND SIMPLE**. However, the missionary that fulfills Christ's total command, will of necessity, divide his time and energy **between evangelism and the making of disciples** (Matthew 28:19-20).

Looking into the Scripture as our guide we see the Apostle Paul exhorting Timothy to "do the work of an evangelist"... be a soul winner... but he also charged him "to make full proof of his ministry" (I Timothy 4:5). Timothy could best accomplish that aspect of the ministry, as can we, by teaching and training those won, by balancing his ministry through establishing the local church. **He was to commit to faithful men the things that he had heard of Paul (II Timothy 2:2).** The "faithful men" would be the teaching leaders of the newly formed congregation. When the ministry is biblically balanced the missionary evangelist may move on to new fields where Christ has not been named because he has planted a church that will perpetually do the work of evangelism and discipleship. This order and process cannot be over-emphasized nor can it be improved upon.

I knew a "missionary evangelist" that reported hundreds and even thousands of conversions as a result of his evangelistic efforts. When questioned about follow-up work among these new believers in Christ he said, "I am working with a national pastor and his church. They do the follow-up. There are too many lost yet to be reached for me to take the time to disciple the people I win. God has just called me to reach them with the gospel." He hinted that the question was an indication that we were not burdened for souls. What he failed to share with his supporting churches was that neither the pastor nor the church, with which he left these new converts, was doctrinally sound. Further inquiry resulted in him stating, "Well at least they are saved, and that is what really matters." It is very difficult to know if a person is saved or not when they do not become part of a biblically sound local church and grow in the Lord. Though one is truly saved through repentance and simple child-like trust in the Lord Jesus Christ it is nearly impossible for a person to become a true disciple or follower of the Lord apart from committed involvement in the local church. Our conviction should be, what really matters is the total will of the Lord Jesus

Christ. If the Lord only wanted us to evangelize the lost He would have stated such.

When the need for "glowing reports" is the driving force in a missionary's life he can be tempted to even unscrupulous methods. On one occasion a missionary asked those in the crowd before him how many wanted a Bible (in reality a New Testament). They were instructed to raise their hand. Nearly everyone in the group raised a hand. Later he told the pastors visiting from the States that everyone in the crowd had raised their hands to show that they were accepting Christ as Saviour. He led the pastors to believe everyone in the village had been saved. Unbeknown to him one of the Stateside pastors understood enough of the language to see through the masquerade. The same pastor was also unimpressed with the missionary's statement that they were the first white people the nationals in the village had ever seen. Oddly enough many of the villagers knew the missionary by name. He was a white man wasn't he? That pastor returned to the States and proceeded to lead his church in discontinuing the support of all his missionaries, including the faithful ones planting indigenous churches. It is sad when merchandise is made of the lost to the benefit of a "so called missionary."

These abuses are some of the most extreme and certainly not typical of most missionaries. It is, however, easy for even good missionaries to lose sight of the need for a biblically balanced ministry, one that emphasizes evangelism **and** church planting.

Supporting churches have the biblical authority to hold their missionaries responsible in the matter of planting indigenous churches. To what end evangelism if it is not for planting a local church? If we are to see indigenous churches planted we must maintain a balance between evangelism and discipleship. We do well to obey the Lord's total command.

> *"Go ye therefore, and teach all nations, baptizing them in the name of the Father, and of the Son, and of the Holy Ghost: Teaching them to observe all things whatsoever I have commanded you: and, lo I am with you alway, even unto the end of the world."* Matthew 28:19-20

Before moving on, I wish to express my skepticism concerning practices of both missionaries and people from good churches in America who visit the foreign field on short term (one to two weeks) missions' trips. Great care should be exercised when reporting on the activities and results of these trips to not give false or misleading information. Churches often give the impression that evangelism is **all important** by encouraging their members in questionable practices.

When a teen group, that knows very little if anything about Latin culture, speaks no Spanish (beyond taco bell, burrito, enchilada, no hablo, no intiende [which is telling the Spanish speaking person they don't understand Spanish], etc.), visits a Latin American country and reports that they personally led several individuals to the Lord by simply pointing to a gospel tract, they are deceiving themselves. Nationals may be attracted to special evangelistic meetings by the presence of groups from the US, gospel seeds may be sown in hearts and ultimately nationals may come to Christ but the importance of "hearing the gospel in the native language one speaks," is evidenced by the fact that the Lord gave the gift of languages (tongues) to the disciples on the day of Pentecost (Acts 2).

Mission trip group leaders would do well to educate the team members in certain aspects of foreign culture. For example, many Roman Catholic people of Latin America, as a part of their beliefs, accept Jesus into their heart every day. They also receive him each time they participate in the mass. Pointing to a statement in a gospel tract concerning "receiving Christ into the heart" could very well bring a positive response... a response not necessarily of understanding. One that does not speak the language cannot know with any certainty that the person witnessed to understands the gospel message that has been given. Hispanics are very gracious people and will agree to about anything, in one's presence. I have had them promise to attend church and then never show up. I learned that their culture is such that they want you to "feel good" about them, when in their presence. You can "feel bad" that they didn't keep their promise when they are not present.

There have also been reports, through the years, given by visiting church groups from the USA that several churches have been **established** during their one-week visit to the field. Again it is truly amazing that folk who do not know the language or the culture are able to do in one week or ten days what a veteran missionary on a foreign field or even a church planting pastor in the USA is not able to do in less than two to six years. The honest report would be to say that the group had participated in the **starting** of one or more new mission churches. To state that one or more new churches were **established** in such a short time is misleading at best. A truly indigenous New Testament church is self-governing, self-supporting and self-propagating. These necessary characteristics are not produced over night or in a week. These misunderstandings may be a matter of semantics. Great is the need to choose our words carefully.

There are new church organizational services held in the States and on the foreign field that leave much to be desired biblically and practically. To "organize" a new church without any knowledge of the doctrinal beliefs of the charter members is an invitation to trouble. A missionary church planter who organized his new church following the pattern of a well-known church-planting organization said that all went well for the first weeks. As time went on he realized that he had a false foundation on which to build, precisely because the door of the church was swung open wide for all present, with no consideration given to their background, doctrine, personal testimony, etc. A new church, anywhere, should be composed of a nucleus (even if only two or three) of born again, biblically baptized, followers of the teachings of the Lord Jesus Christ, who have like faith, practice and purpose. The seeds of a new church can be planted in a brief period of time but the growth of a new church takes time. Hit and miss forms of evangelism and church planting leave a lot to be desired. National Christians are not blind or dumb. They will pick up on these questionable practices and either imitate them or will be turned off by them.

"Evangelism is not complete until the evangelized become evangelists." Dr. Don Sisk, President Emeritus of BIMI

E. Unwise Use of Large Amounts of Mission Money Has Been A Detriment To The Planting of Indigenous Churches

Has the writer lost his good senses? I assure you that is not the case. Though it is recommendable that a missionary family have sufficient support to meet their needs, having access to large amounts of money can hinder the missionary church planter in his ministry, especially if he is unwise in financial decisions. The blessings of God on the churches of America have allowed them to give generously to the work of missions around the world. For this we are thankful. There are times when churches in America give without praying.

When one has an abundance of money, even as an individual or as a family, it is easy to make unwise decisions about how it should be used. How many of us have made unwise financial decisions in times of abundance simply because we did not have to "pray for God to provide." We did not have to trust Him.

Missions minded churches need the wisdom of God to avoid doing so much for national churches that they cripple them. The simple fact is that **the unwise distribution of mission's funds can result in a sort of missionary welfare system on the field.** National churches often learn to look to the missionary to meet the needs to which they should look to God to supply. They learn to depend on churches in America for the funds to build their temples and support their pastors.

One veteran missionary recently stated that the missionary should become neither:

> "lord and master nor an ATM for the national churches." Larry Sexton, Missionary to Mexico and Honduras

Often when the national pastor grows accustomed to being paid by a mission agency, the missionary or churches in the USA he is not motivated to build the lives of the people in the mission church he pastors. He does not have to look to them for his income. He does not feel bound or responsible to them. He may be motivated to only do that which pleases the provider of his income. When churches in America, mission agencies or missionaries pay the national pastor's salary ***indefinitely*** they hinder the ministry of planting indigenous churches. They also rob the national Christians of the opportunity to obey God's Word by faith and receive His promised provision. Experience has taught that some national pastors are able to be whatever the missionary or mission agency expects. If a salary hangs in the balance they are able to conform to whatever doctrine or situation. The Lord Jesus Christ called these men "hirelings."

The abundance of mission's funds that exist in America should be distributed and administered with great wisdom. **There are ways to assist nationals without crippling them or converting them into welfare cases.**

Note: The Wyldewood Baptist Church of Oshkosh, Wisconsin under the leadership of Dr. Randy King was able to begin to support many nationals. The church sends funds through several missionaries and mission agencies to help worthy nationals. These funds are to be dispersed to national church planters only through local missionaries. Those of the Omega Ministry, a ministry supervised by the Wyldewood Baptist Church, are concerned that the precious God-given funds are not wasted or invested unwisely. Accountability from real live people who live *among* the nationals - not simple proof represented only by *photographs or brief visits to the field,* are necessary.

Some suggested guidelines for assisting national ministers:

1. National workers should be supported only at the recommendation of local missionaries who are "on the ground" and who can verify that the need is genuine. Exceptions might include countries in which no Western missionary can legally reside such as Burma, India, and Iraq.

2. **National workers should be supported on a limited basis.** The tithe of ten to twenty members should make a

salary in most countries. The goal should be for all national churches to become indigenous.

3. Those who desire to support national workers should channel the funds through missionaries who can monitor the ministry and prevent it from becoming a life-long situation.

4. **Some of the many "nationals only" mission societies in the USA do not provide adequate accountability.** Churches should be very careful when sending mission funds through these types of agencies. It should be remembered that a picture or quick visit to the field by an evangelist does not always give a true clear account. It is always safer to work with established mission agencies and established missionaries that provide true accountability.

5. **Independent Baptist Churches should only support national workers who are independent Baptists and that are doctrinally sound.** Do not be influenced by singing groups or by someone with broken English. Ask, "What do they believe, and what do they teach? Do they teach their people to tithe and give?"

6. **Make sure you or churches like yours are the sole sponsors.** Ask questions about their affiliation with other than Baptist groups. Ask questions. Check with missionaries you know on the field about the group. Ask them to investigate for you. Most of the missionaries we associate with are glad for worthy national workers to receive some temporary assistance.

Hopefully, this information will be helpful to churches in America but also to the missionary church planters. As a church planter you should know that any support given from foreign sources to a national worker, even if in the beginning of a new ministry or for a limited time, can set a precedent that will be difficult to overcome. National workers so easily become accustomed to foreign aid. Endless support of national ministries does great damage to the New

Testament objective of planting indigenous churches and destines them to never become self-supporting.

CHAPTER THREE

IMPORTANT CONSIDERATIONS:

A. **The missionary should know his place and how to relate to the nationals.**

B. The missionary presence and influence should be "temporary" at best. Civil strife, health considerations and even death can end a missionary's time on the field.

C. The "permanent factors" which the missionary should make the center of his church planting activities and the lives of the nationals are:

a. The Lord Jesus Christ

b. The Holy Spirit

c. The eternal Word of God.

I never make that statement without remembering Brother Lester Roloff. His motto was:

"Make much of Jesus and He will make much of you."

It is so important for the missionary to build lives around the Lord Jesus Christ and God's Holy Word.

D. The missionary should avoid building with permanent props.

1. The missionary should not make himself the center of the ministry or indispensable if he expects the new church to continue when he is gone.

2. The missionary should avoid any action that accustoms the nationals to dependence upon foreign or outside financial help. As needs arise do not say, "Let's wait and see what the churches in America will do before we do anything."

Teach your people to pray to God for His provision. He may want to bless them in some special way so that they can meet the need. This is what the churches and brethren in America do.

3. The missionary should never occupy long-term a position that could be filled by a qualified national. The church should help the nationals become qualified. He should "work himself out of a job" by training his replacement.

Note: Melvin F. Hodges in his classic book on planting indigenous churches compares some church planting activities to those of the construction crew that builds a structure using **permanent** scaffolds and props. It would be unspeakable for a builder to build in such a way that he had to leave the unsightly scaffolds and props in place. The church should not require propping up by the infusion of the missionary's continual leadership, funds, or even energies.

C. The missionary should avoid seeking to "Americanize" the national church in the matter of:

1. Music. Scripturally, every instrument, even those rejected by many churches in America, can serve to honor and worship the Lord. I do not personally care for the type of music that seems to be typically Jewish, but they have handed it down from generation to generation. A church planted in Israel, probably, would incorporate some of that style into their meetings. To reject it because it is not American could be a grave mistake. The missionary should teach biblical guidelines for church music.

Paul in Ephesians 5:19 sets down the guidelines for Christ-honoring spiritually edifying music.

2. In the schedule and order of services. The missionary is not in violation of some biblical principle if he has a Sunday service that begins at 7:00 A.M. In a tropical climate it is wise to have the service early in order to

avoid the heat of the noon day sun. Of course this would not be necessary if every church in the world had central air conditioning. Do not allow this to become an excuse for laziness and meet only once a week. Neither should you work yourself to death trying to have services every day. Any day or hour can be used for services. The disciples met daily (Acts 2:46). There is the need, however, to be consistent and accustom the people to set days and times for worship. Sunday is recognized as the day when the disciples met for the purposes described in Acts 2:42. The services should offer the opportunity for worship, evangelistic preaching, instruction, fellowship, service, and the celebration of the ordinances of the church.

3. Dress and other standards. Modesty is the biblical standard, not American style. Seek the road of least offense to the lost and to the saved. ***"Give none offence..."*** (I Corinthians 10:32). Magnify your office as Christ's ambassador (Romans 11:13). Set high standards of godliness that will honor Christ.

If we will be honest... many do not like to examine their standards in music, dress, form of worship, or other personal preferences in the light of the Bible. Some say the Bible does not deal with the modern issues we face. This is sort of like "hiding our head in the sand". The Bible does give principles by which we can discern good from evil. We do well to ask ourselves some tough questions and better yet to teach our people to ask themselves these questions. Very often these matters are dismissed as "insignificant." Consider these questions.

1. Does my preference really glorify Christ? Or does it rather glorify the flesh, my body? Does it serve to exalt Christ in the eyes of others? ***"Whether therefore ye eat, or drink, or whatsoever ye do, <u>do all to the glory of God.</u>"*** I Corinthians 10:31

2. In the matter of dress: Am I really concerned about modesty? Webster defines *modesty* as: decency, propriety, and in females... the word is used as synonymous with chastity, or purity of manners. He says, "Unaffected modesty is the sweetest charm of female excellence, the richest gem in the diadem of their honor." We do well to ask, "Are those of the opposite sex caused to lust by my appearance? Am I more concerned about personal comfort, fashion, style or personal preference than I am about whether my appearance might be a stumbling stone before some weak brother or sister? Women might ask, "Do I recognize the fact that men are tempted more so than women by what they see?" Sadly enough many Christian women seem to be oblivious to the struggle that even godly men have with the forms of female attire that, even in the slightest way, reveal the female anatomy. Are we "our brothers' keepers?" It is extremely important to consider the propriety of one's dress in the light of local culture. Is there not a correlation between the decline in morality and contemporary trends? Do we, Christ's ambassadors, see ourselves and our Bible message as agents of change or are we content to conform to the frame of the world?

> *"I beseech you therefore, brethren, by the mercies of God, that ye present your bodies a living sacrifice, holy, acceptable unto God, which is your reasonable service. And be not conformed to this world: but be ye transformed by the renewing of your mind, that ye may prove what is the good, and acceptable, and perfect will of God... Be kindly affectioned one to another with brotherly love, in honour preferring one another..." Romans 12:1-2, 10*

3. Does our music of preference honor the LORD because it is Scriptural, because it lifts up the spirit, or does it simply appeal to the flesh? Does it lend to worship? Does it minister to others or is it a form of entertainment and merely a "show"? Is there melody? Is it spiritual or sensual? Are the musicians Spirit-filled or filled with themselves? Are they local church members?

4. Is our ministry orderly or is there confusion? God the Father is not the author of confusion, nor is the Holy Spirit. Having numerous Bible versions in use in the ministry of the church is

confusing. Things that are not alike are not the same thing. God has preserved His Word for English speaking people in the King James Bible. Our just Judge will judge us by His Word (John 12:48). It would be unjust on His part to judge us by the Word if we did not have the true Word of God.

5. Do we really understand the principle behind taking the course of least offense? Fewer people, both saved and lost, are offended by higher standards.

6. Are we simply taking the road of least resistance because we do not want to confront new believers with the issues?

7. Does our preference somehow identify us with the world or rebellion? Very often the markings on the bodies of indigenous people are connected to evil spirits and the devil.

8. Do we use "grace" as an excuse for license, carelessness, or concupiscence?

9. Are we really able to win more people to Christ and establish stronger churches by holding our position on certain issues? Is it more probable that the Holy Spirit is grieved with us and thus unable to pour out His power and blessing?

10. Is it simply my preference? Does my position cause division? Do I dismiss those who hold a different standard as legalists or liberal, depending on the case?

11. Do we reason, "It will not keep a person out of heaven so it must not be important?" Unbelief is the one thing that will keep one out of heaven but there are many things that need changing in our lives once we are saved. God states His purpose in Romans 8:29... that we be conformed to the image if His Son, the Lord Jesus Christ.

12. Am I willing to "die to self" for the good of the ministry?

13. Are my real goals to "please Christ" and not quench or grieve the Holy Spirit of God?

The church planter will have to teach his people to deal with all of these tough questions in an honest and Scriptural manner.

D. Some situations may lend themselves to "bi-vocational national pastors.

Allowing the pastor of a small church in a very small town or village to be bi-vocational may be the best way for him to provide for his family. Though Paul teaches that a pastor/elder is worthy of financial assistance we are not told that these leaders of the church were necessarily "full-time" in the ministry (I Timothy 5:17-18). The problem of insufficient funds to support the pastor fulltime may come from:

1. A pastor that lives above the means of his congregation.

2. A congregation ill-accustomed by the missionary, mission agency or other outside entities to having someone else pay or subsidize the salary of the pastor.

3. Unnatural financial expectations placed upon a small congregation. Some small town or village churches may never be large enough to support a pastor fulltime. Allowing the pastor the freedom to subsidize his income through secular work may mean the difference between preserving him for the ministry and losing him.

<u>Note:</u> Some very well meaning individuals and organizations, as well as mission minded churches in the USA have imagined that almost any national pastor, if given a full salary, will be able to grow a large congregation. The belief is that the national pastor who is able to spend all of his time and energy winning souls and caring for the flock will have phenomenal growth in his church. Some even imagine "super churches" being built because the national pastor is provided a full salary.

It should be recognized that some pastors, national or otherwise will never have a large congregation. There are national pastors that do not have the educational preparation, the personal work ethic, the personality, the anointing of the Holy Spirit, or other traits that are characteristic of those used of God to build super-sized churches. The ministry area may not lend itself to this type of growth either.

We as missionaries do the national pastor and national church an injustice when we insist that every national church support the pastor fulltime. If the missionary provides a full salary for the national pastor/worker with the expectation that the new church will assume the load when the missionary moves on to plant another church it may lead to disaster.

E. The missionary church planter may be tempted to raise the funds in America that will allow him to have a number of nationals on his payroll.

He may send them out as an extension of his ministry to start churches, souls may be saved and a work done, but he will find it difficult to ***indigenize*** the work. It is tempting to be able to report, "I have X number of churches or pastors." I have often wondered if we really have an accurate count of the number of souls saved on a particular field when they are reported by the national pastor who has somehow made direct contact with churches in America, by the missionary, and by one or more American evangelists that have that field as a favorite mission's project. All report the same results as *their* results. This goes back to the statements concerning unwise financial decisions made by American churches and the missionary.

It can also be unwise for the missionary to give full scholarships to the students in the Bible Institute. The students come to expect the missionary to pay all the bills. Scholarship funds can be given through the local church on the field. In this way the students learn to look to the local church on the field and not to the missionary.

It seems prudent to suggest at this time that there is an alternative to having a central Bible institute that serves a number of churches. Many local churches now have a Bible institute in their facility as a part of their ministry. There are a number of advantages in this.

- The church facility is given greater use. A separate facility is not required.
- The students can remain in their homes, in their jobs and in their local church.
- The elders of the churches do the teaching. They are the mentors of the students.
- There is no need for lodging or meals.
- Their church planting activities are from and under the supervision of their local church.

Though God is blessing these types of institutes, He is also using the traditional form in various places.

It should be remembered that anything the missionary does that causes the nationals to look to him to bear the greater portion of the financial load of the ministry or make him the center of the church planting activities, instead of the local church, will hinder the indigenization of the churches.

CHAPTER FOUR

HOW TO BEGIN A NEW CHURCH ON THE FIELD

A. On Fruitful Fields White unto Harvest...

Jesus said:

> "... *Lift up your eyes and look on the fields; for they are white already to harvest.*" John 4:35.

It should be recognized that there are fields that are "riper than others" in the sense that some fields yield more fruit more readily. Latin America, some parts of Africa, Asia, and the islands of the Pacific such as the Philippines are examples of areas where in recent decades there have been very many visible results in the form of conversions and new churches established. On these fields that we refer to as "fruitful" it is not always as necessary to develop relationships in order to be able to give the gospel. There are very many being saved that may not even know the soul winner's name. In contrast there are fields that are open to the missionary but for practical purposes closed to the gospel. We will deal with planting indigenous churches on the fruitful fields first.

Planting Indigenous Churches Begins With Evangelism

To say that someone has to do soul winning if a new church is going to be planted is no new revelation. To be able to evangelize the lost souls of a particular area should be one of the prime motives for planting a new church. The church planter should be a soul winner but he should also realize that training soul winners will get him started right as he plants a **self-propagating *indigenous* church. Start right, to finish right.**

After leaving Nicaragua in 1969 and leading up to 1973 Patsy and I had been serving in the Bible Institute "IBERO" and in church planting efforts alongside of The Bruce Bell Family and at least three additional families (The John Woods, The Paul Marshes and the

Roland Garlicks and single missionary, Kathy Underwood) in Matamoros, Tamaulipas, Mexico, in Guatemala City and also in San Salvador, El Salvador. In early 1973 the Lord led us to move to San Miguel, El Salvador to plant another church. Because of the tremendous heat in the area, San Miguel was known as the "antesala del infierno" or "the waiting room of hell." This could be one reason there were no other missionaries living there. Darrell and Shirley Dean and children did join us about three years later. It was such a blessing to have them working with us.

This was a step of faith for us as we would be pretty much alone in our efforts. In the following paragraphs I wish to share some of what God did to establish the "Tabernáculo Bautista de San Miguel" and some of its daughter churches.

New churches should be started by established churches in the area if at all possible. Some fields require what I call *pioneer church planting* because there are no established churches in the area. There may also be times when it is best to "start alone" and do pioneer church planting even though there is an established church close. The sponsoring church, though Baptist by name, may not be the kind of church you plan to plant (not indigenous, separatist, etc.). It is easier to train people right from the beginning than to have to retrain them because of the influence of carnal Christians. Certainly where there is an established church of like faith and practice it is advantageous to get the members of that church involved, if possible.

Note: In some cases we have started new churches with a handful of people already saved, etc. It can be a blessing to have saved folk with whom to start but experience has taught us that within a few months after starting we usually have a whole new congregation. The believers with whom we started were usually unsatisfied with some or all of the established churches in the area and wanted to help start a new church so they could have "one like they thought it should be." It was usually not long until they were dissatisfied with us too. Thank God for those who help you get started but be careful that they are a "help and not a hindrance".

When they decide to leave they will, no doubt, seek to take others with them. The sooner you deal with problem people the less damage they can do. The fewer people you will lose when they leave. Seemingly there is an overabundance of nationals and missionaries who are more than willing to allow someone else to do the work of winning souls and making disciples so that they can come in and have a ready-made congregation.

In my estimation, missionaries and mission agencies that look for established churches or ministries "to purchase" in place of planting and establishing them, are a problem that we can live without. Prepare yourself and your new church for the day when, after you are gone, these opportunists will offer to give a loan to pay off property debts or to pay the pastor a larger salary... if the church will only associate with them. This type of offer can look mighty attractive to a humble church or pastor that is struggling financially... struggling, maybe, but indigenous. Many times we have seen indigenous churches converted into "welfare churches" by the unethical and un-Christian practices of Christians with deep pockets.

You may feel that the preceding comments are a little harsh but as a church planting missionary I have seen firsthand the sad results when national churches and pastors are bought.

You should seek to get the *sponsoring church* involved:

1. Through prayer. If at all possible have them pray with the new converts as the church is getting started. Praying people can teach others to pray.

2. Through their financial resources. They will be blessed as they help meet some of the initial needs. Challenge the new converts to give as well.

3. Through human resources; evangelistic teams, counselors, teachers, musicians, etc. They can be a great help in the beginning of the ministry when there are no local folk qualified to fill these roles.

4. Through material resources; literature, furniture, sound systems, musical instruments, etc. Some of these resources may be on loan or some might be given as a donation to the new church.

The Tabernáculo Bautista de San Miguel was sponsored on a limited basis as a mission of the Iglesia Bautista Miramonte in San Salvador as well as by our sending church in America. Because I served as co-founding missionary pastor of the Miramonte Baptist Church for the first three years of its existence this was a natural sequence of events.

<u>Note:</u> There are many additional details concerning church planting to be found in the book, "The Basics of Church Planting" authored by yours truly. I recommend to all church planters that they obtain a copy for reference. Because the general truths having to do with church planting are available in the book I will only give an overview and seek to touch on the specifics that have to do with the **establishment of "indigenous churches".**

> *"And when they had preached the gospel in that city, and had taught many, they returned again to Lystra and to Iconium, and Antioch, confirming the souls of the disciples, and exhorting them to continue in the faith... And when they had ordained them elders in every church, and had prayed with fasting, they commended them to the Lord, on whom they had believed." Acts 14:21-23.*

Setting an example for us, the apostles "preached the Gospel" in Derbe (Acts 14:21). This **evangelistic preaching** was directed at winning folk to Christ. The Holy Spirit inspired Luke to write these verses so that we would know where to begin with our church planting ministries. What the Scripture says should direct us. Where it is silent it should be an admonishment to us to avoid placing emphasis where Scripture doesn't.

Different areas may require different tactics

The individual church planter should be a soul winner. He may have a temporary team of people from the sponsoring church available to help him. He may have the assistance of a number of Bible Institute, college, or seminary students. He may be able to count on the soul winning efforts of fellow missionaries and national pastors from the area. The soul winning may be done in the context of the distribution of copies of the Gospel of John and Romans, gospel tracts, brochures made up to introduce the church planter and his message, or of a door-to-door canvassing or survey. The soul winner may go door-to-door announcing an evangelist campaign being held in the locale of the new church. Every person in the target area, every person you meet, is a prospect for salvation until proven otherwise.

In San Miguel we received the assistance of six students from the "IBERO" Bible Institute in San Salvador. It was necessary to house, feed, and continue the daily Bible Institute courses of these students during the six weeks that they teamed with us. They were greatly used of the Lord as soul winners. Just their presence stirred much interest on the part of the local community. The students were trained to lead folk to Christ in their home but to also bring them to the special meetings where they could make public their decision to trust Christ. Several people followed the Lord in believer's baptism in the very beginning. **To the Lord Jesus Christ be the glory** and honor but in the few shorts weeks we saw about 25-30 people come to Christ, The members of the "team" as we called it, used their training to lead people to follow through and ultimately identify with the Lord in the new local indigenous church.

It was a great advantage to have a team of trained soul winners available for the beginning but there were additional benefits. The team members could help with the congregational singing, do counseling during the invitation, as well as teach classes for the little children. The day would come when they would have to leave us. Like the missionary, they were "temporary". Knowing this, we allowed them to help us begin teaching (making disciples) the new converts and even help train soul winners.

Getting back to "getting started" I want to say again that <u>evangelism is the first key to planting a church</u>, especially an indigenous church. The ground work you do in the beginning will lay the foundation for the church *to be self-propagating.*

Pastor Roberto Nieto of the present day Tabernáculo Bautista de San Miguel continues to use these steps as they seek to plant new churches. Roberto was saved as a teenager way back in 1974 through the ministry of the Tabernáculo (originally the Iglesia Bautista Central de San Miguel). In about 1980 he felt the Lord directing him to plant a new church in one of the needy areas of San Miguel. At that time the population of San Miguel was about 100,000. With the Lord's help Roberto started and established the Iglesia Bautista Pan-Americana. He started by doing evangelism.

At present time the Tabernáculo is involved in planting four new churches. They have trained leaders, most of which are lay people, and are able to work on a larger scale, where you may be limited in your church planting ministry until you have trained lay people and leaders. In each case the lay members of the church, many of which are also students in the Bible Institute in the Tabernáculo, travel in the church van or in their own vehicles one or two days a week to the targeted towns. After a thorough investigation of the area they chose a day of the week for their soul winning activities according to the local conditions... the day they are most likely to find people at home. In some places they had better response if they went on Tuesday. In another town Saturday or even Sunday afternoon was proven better.

One of the four new churches is being planted and established in San Vicente. About three years ago an earthquake devastated the town. Shortly thereafter I was able to be there for one of the trips and see firsthand the destruction but also the great opportunity for the planting of a new indigenous church. Roberto and his people made several trips to San Vicente to distribute food and clothing purchased with funds sent from churches in the USA. Evangelist Sonny Holland of Zachary, Louisiana (our pastor in Fort Pierce, Florida when we were teenagers) helped with that effort.

The social aspects of the ministry were used to their advantage in San Vicente to win souls. As they were able to lead several towns' people to Christ they became burdened to plant a church. ***They continued to do evangelism for at least six months before seeking to hold a service.*** One does not have to follow this exact time schedule, but I mention it because it has given good results in Central America. They did begin discipleship classes with the individuals that had accepted the Lord. As time went on they began to seek with the help of the converts a house where they could get together for a combined meeting. I mentioned early in the book the wisdom in waiting until there are converts to seek a place to meet. It allows them to have a part in the praying, seeking, and in the ultimate decision concerning where to meet. Since the plan was to plant an *indigenous* church the local converts should be an integral part from the beginning. Including the new converts in the decision making process causes them to feel responsible.

As missionaries you and your wife may be the lone members of the evangelistic team. **You can increase the size of your team by wining folk and then immediately begin to train them to be soul winners.** You can train the men, your wife the ladies. If you want a larger evangelistic team yet, train the soul winners to also train soul winners. The missionary church planter should be a soul winner but more than this he should be a teacher of soul winners (II Timothy 2:2).

> *"And the things that thou hast heard of me among many witnesses, the same commit thou to faithful men, who shall be able to teach others."* II Timothy 2:2

Those you have trained to be soul winners will contribute to your success as a planter of *indigenous* churches. At some point you will have to divide your time between evangelism and the making of disciples, preaching and teaching. If you have trained others you will have someone doing evangelism even though you have had to cut back on your soul winning time. In addition, your people will be able to win folk to the Lord that you might never be able to reach. We ***start with soul winning*** but right away ***we switch to***

teaching. From the very beginning you need to share your burden and passion for souls. As you do so, you will with the Lord's help, be able to lead them to the ***sense of responsibility they should have for their own people.*** This ultimately leads the new church to be ***self-propagating.***

Roberto Nieto, Tony Rivera, Israel Argueta, Victor Quito, Omar Claros, and the other pastors, and churches of San Miguel are living examples of what God can do in and through national believers. The Tabernáculo has grown to over 700 in attendance. The Bible Institute continues to provide fundamental instruction in God's Word for young and old alike. Two years before writing this book I spoke to 86 men and women who were attending classes in the Bible Institute. Some of these were young married couples, two medical doctors, one lawyer and several business owners. Two additional churches in San Miguel have Bible Institutes and through cooperation with the Tabernáculo and/or on their own have planted new churches. All of the six original churches are planting new churches.

The teaching ministries of these indigenous churches provide the foundation on which the future church-planting ministry rests. They have trained soul winners. They have folk who can train others to train soul winners. They have those trained in making disciples. They also have those trained to train others to make disciples. If at any given point the pastors have to be away from the pulpit they have several biblically qualified men who are trained in directing the service, leading the music and preaching God's Holy Word. They know how to carry on the ministry of the church.

A. As a missionary church planter you must recognize that the new church begins with EVANGELISM but you must TRANSITION to the TEACHING ministry as the nucleus begins to form.

Training others is time consuming. It requires much preparation. It is absolutely necessary if an indigenous church with strong national leadership is to be established. Remember the Lord Jesus

Christ selected twelve men to train to carry on the ministry after He was gone.

He concentrated His efforts in these men. If He had poured Himself into only one - Judas - His mission would have ended with Judas. He worked with the eleven as well. **It is a mistake to deposit all your hopes for the ministry into just one man.**

San Miguel vs. San Salvador

San Miguel offered a wide open opportunity for door-to-door evangelism. This was in contrast to the area where the Miramonte Baptist Church (Iglesia Bautista Miramonte) was planted. The team (team member assignments allow each to dedicate their energies to a particular area of ministry... one to direct evangelism, one to supervise the discipleship program, one to oversee the logistics, etc.) of missionaries that God had brought together in the Miramonte subdivision had the strategy of reaching the middle and upper class folk of the area for Christ. The Iglesia Bautista Miramonte was the first church in all of Central America which targeted these folk. The church now has a 1400 seat auditorium in the heart of San Salvador, a Christian day school, a Bible Institute, a social helps ministry and has sponsored the planting of an additional 30 plus daughter churches. **TO GOD BE THE GLORY!**

As we went door-to-door in the Miramonte and neighboring subdivisions we found that it was to the maid or the housekeeper that we were talking. Many of them accepted Christ and became a part of the new church. It was also through some of them that we were ultimately able to speak with the owners of the houses. The children were also used of the Lord to open doors for us. We found that the well to do and educated (medical doctors, dentists, university professors, government officials, etc.) had to be approached differently. It was necessary to win their confidence before they would listen to our message.

It seems some missionaries are intimidated by the wealthy and well educated. God can and does give "holy boldness" to be able to minister to these folk. He died for them too. I will admit that with age comes a needed amount of fearlessness. A good thought to remember is that the well to do and educated have some of the vital resources to reach their own country for Christ. "The gospel is like water in that it flows more readily downhill," is a comment made by Bruce Bell many years ago. In essence he meant that it is more likely for the gospel to flow from the middle and upper class churches to all sectors of society than it is for the gospel to flow upward from a church of very poor individuals to those of the middle and upper class. The ground at the cross of Christ is level, but we must admit that lost people have many prejudices. A congregation made up of consecrated middle and upper class believers has great potential to be a truly indigenous church. The folk we saw saved in the Miramonte would not have had it any other way.

Don't write off the middle and upper class people.

We found it necessary to develop friendships (*Relationships*, Do you remember that word?) and give them the opportunity to interact with us before we could share the gospel with them. An invitation to share a meal in one's home could be a great tool. Don't participate in "sin" but be careful about isolating yourself from the people you desire to reach for Christ. God graciously gave fruit.

B. EVANGELISM ON FIELDS OPEN TO THE MISSIONARIES BUT, FOR ALL PRACTICAL PURPOSES CLOSED TO THE GOSPEL.

Evangelism is also the first step to planting a church on the difficult fields of the world. The approach taken to evangelism will be determined by the condition of people's hearts on the field. Most of us are familiar with the fact that neither William Carey nor Adoriam Judson saw many visible results from their evangelistic efforts for many years.

There are many forms of evangelism. Some forms of evangelism can be classified as "aggressive forms." Aggressive evangelism is characterized by a point blank; matter of fact presentation of the gospel to every person the soul winner meets, whether on the street, in a park, while traveling in some sort of public transportation, or when going door to door. Since the soul winner may have never met the lost person before, he knows little or nothing of the circumstances the individual is living. The Lord has certainly blessed these aggressive soul winning efforts in some parts of the world. It is wonderful to reflect on the number of souls that have been saved listening to and believing the "Roman's Road of Salvation" or the "Four Spiritual Laws." The good results obtained through these efforts are a testimony to the working of God in hearts through the gospel seeds sown by some other witnesses, to the power of the Holy Spirit to convict and draw the lost to the Lord Jesus Christ and to the willingness of many lost people to accept God's Word, even if they have never met the soul winner before. May we allow the Lord work in each of our hearts, as Christians, the compassion and the zeal for lost souls that will cause us to be far more aggressive in our soul winning efforts.

On some fields it is more difficult to win an audience with the inhabitants. The northeastern parts of the USA, parts of Europe, Australia and other countries fall into this category. Though some cringe at the term "life style evangelism" it must be recognized that some lost people are not going to be won by a one-time aggressive presentation of the gospel. Before someone accuses me of being liberal or a neo-evangelical I wish to clarify my position by saying, **"Soul winning should be every Christian's life style."** We should live to witness for the Lord.

One pastor calls this "showcase evangelism." In a recent message from the Book of James he pointed out that we "demonstrate our faith" by honoring the Lord in times of trial and difficulty, by our ***"reaction to trials."*** We show our faith by the ***"restraint of our tongue... the way we talk;*** by ***"respect for other people"... poor and wealthy alike;*** and by ***"realizing that life is a vapor"...***by being conscious of the sanctity and brevity of life in eternity. It is a matter of the Christian living the Christian life before his lost neighbors and earning the right to share his faith verbally with them. This is biblical. The apostle James said:

"Yea, a man may say, Thou hast faith, and I have works: shew me thy faith without works, and I will shew thee my faith by my works." James 2:18

The sad truth is that some Christians have excused themselves from being soul winners by misinterpreting the meaning of life-style evangelism. It is not a matter of preferring one form of evangelism over another but using ***every means*** available to win the lost. It is not for one to say, "Well I am just not made for aggressive soul winning. I will just let my life be my witness." Such individuals have missed the whole point. Others have a difficult time being a soul winner because they have no Christ-honoring testimony. For true the gospel is the power of God unto salvation (Romans 1:16) but also true is the fact that we are to be the "salt of the earth--hopefully salt that has not lost its savor."

There are occasions when the lost may need a demonstration of biblical Christianity in action before they will listen to it being spoken. Our life style or the way **we live** will be a confirmation to them that what we are saying with our **lips** is really true. The missionary church planter serving on the fields we call "difficult fields" may find this, not only the best approach, but it may be the only fruitful approach.

The missionary who expects to win several people to the Lord every week on these "difficult fields" may become disillusioned. Many ministers of the gospel do not have the patience to live out this type of ministry. Those few who do, will do well to establish an *indigenous* church, one that will bare testimony for Christ perpetually, even after he is gone. He may not easily find a replacement

The northeastern States of the USA are considered by some to be a difficult field. A close friend of mine who is doing church planting in Maine has found it to be a fruitful field but one definitely requiring God's power, guidance and wisdom in evangelism. This is of course true on every field but possibly more obvious on some fields. Dr. Todd Bell daily spends designated time in **prayer** for the lost in his community. **He goes about his normal every day life** but seeks to be a witness for Christ throughout the day. He combines aggressive soul winning with other tactics. He does aggressive door-to-door soul winning, inviting folk to the services of his new church. He has discovered that contacts which will not attend the services of his church will accept an invitation to a meal in his home.

He and his family have used this approach very effectively. The dinner guests are able to observe first hand a biblically Christian family. The guests see the husband/wife, parent/children, and even children to children relationships. In addition to a great southern style meal, a portion of the "Bread of Life" is offered. The missionary gives a brief explanation of: **a.** why they moved to the area; **b.** why they are starting a church and; **c.** what their message is. These three points are covered in the "get acquainted" meetings held by the church planter under different circumstances. The setting is different. The objective is the same. The missionary may not have the desired results right away with all their dinner guests but they at least begin ***to develop a*** neighborly ***relationship*** with them.

Some keys to building relationships

Our Lord and Saviour Jesus Christ was known as "a friend of sinners."

> *"The Son of man is come eating and drinking; and ye say, Behold a gluttonous man, and a winebibber,* ***a friend of publicans and sinner!*** *But wisdom is justified of all her children."* Luke 7:34

He was able to be in their homes and even enjoy meals with them. These associations allowed Him to win them unto Himself. Yes, He was criticized but He was able to **associate with sinners without compromise.** From the Lord we learn these keys:

1. The Lord practiced **"immediate acceptance"** of the individual. He accepted people for who they were, where they were and not on the basis of where He wanted them to be. He no doubt saw what they could become, what He wanted them to become, but He did not expect them to be all of that before He could accept them.

We often expect lost people to act like saved people and carnal Christians to act like spiritual Christians before we can befriend them or develop any type of ***relationship*** with them.

a. We do well to remember our own sinfulness with gratitude for Christ's love that caused Him to love us and seek us *"while we were yet sinners."*

b. We should see the potential that each person has in the Lord just as the Lord must have seen in us some Christ-honoring potential.

c. Christ died for them as He did for all lost people and He has accepted the new believer, even if carnal.

d. The LORD sets an example by accepting us unconditionally on the basis of the finished work of the Lord Jesus Christ. Most of us have been moved by the illustration of the young military serviceman who called to inform his Mother that he was bringing a buddy home with him, a buddy that had lost an eye, an arm, and a leg and that would need a permanent place to live. His Mother was willing for the buddy to stay for a short period of time but commented, "The boy would be a real drag and problem for them." The young soldier hung up the phone when he sensed his Mother's rejection of the crippled friend. A few days later they were notified of their son's suicidal death. When they were able to view his body they realized that it was he who had lost the eye, the arm, and a leg. ***Conditional acceptance*** had destroyed their son.

e. There can be risks involved in this type of association but the Holy Spirit who indwells us is able to guard us. If we keep our objective, to win lost souls on their way to Hell to Christ, we will keep ourselves pure... so we can help them.

Note: A neighbor family in Mexico once invited us to go to their house for lunch on Sunday. Their comment was that all the neighbors would be present. I explained to them that we went to church until about 1:00 p.m. on Sunday but that we would be glad to go if arriving late was not a problem. Mario assured us that we were welcome at any hour. When we arrived several of our neighbors were indeed present. Some of them were smoking, most were drinking beer. We were offered a bottle of beer. We declined with the simple explanation that we did not drink. There was no need to say, "We are Christians, drinking is sinful, we don't touch the wicked stuff." We enjoyed the great authentic Mexican tacos and a soft drink.

When we were ready to leave Mario said, "We invited some of the other neighbors that say they are Christians like you but they declined our invitation because they didn't want to associate with us or our habits. Thank you so much for coming." Actually he said, "Muchísimas gracias por haber venido" but I guess you might not understand Spanish. We associated with them without participating in the sinful activities that are typical of lost people. We accepted them as they were. To the Lord's glory, Mario and Alicia Fuentes accepted the Lord as Saviour before we left Mexico.

2. We should be attracted to those to whom we desire to minister the gospel. We are on the field to help them. Our thoughts should be to meet their needs not ours.

3. Our desire to win them to Christ and to edify them in the Lord should bring a *commitment* to the development of a relationship. We should covenant with the Lord to be a determined friend to those who need Him as Saviour. The inspired writer of Proverbs 17:17 says, **"A friend loves at all times, and a brother is born for adversity."** The missionary church planter has been entrusted by God with great opportunities and responsibilities.

4. Relationships such as friendships are nurtured by *openness.* When we are sincere we can be candid. Be real.

5. We must see others as *equals* in God's eyes if we are to develop relationships. The missionary must guard against comparing the *foreign culture* to his culture. He must not be *condemning* or *condescending.* There is no place for the church

planter to manifest an attitude of "superiority." The church planter must place **greater priority on his responsibilities than on his rights.** If we each received *"that to which we are entitled" we* would be in Hell.

6. Loyalty. Determine to be loyal. Believe the best and when there is a question about something involving your friend, go to him or her first.

Note: A missionary, in response to what he thought was a lack of gratitude on the part of some national young people, screamed at them, "I have never, not even in Nicaragua, seen such low down ungrateful people." He had not heard their expression of "Gracias." He did reveal his heart. He was not there to help them but for some other unknown reason. Little wonder he left the field without any remaining fruit.

> *"A man that hath friends must show himself friendly: and there is a friend that sticketh closer than a brother."* Proverbs 18:24

The Word of God tells us that Jesus demonstrated who HE was and the truth of HIS words. He earned the right to speak to the woman at the well.

In John 4:1-42 we are told how He was able to win the Samaritan woman. Jesus set an example for us in that:

a. He went to where she was.

b. He overcame the cultural and racial barriers that could have hindered His presentation of the truth. He knew no prejudices.

c. He understood He was in her territory. He was in a sense the foreigner in her land.

d. He identified with her by asking for water. He showed Himself to be human.

e. He was not condescending or condemning. His words and life were pure. It was her own heart that convicted her.

f. He accepted her as she was. It is necessary to accept people "where they are, not where we want them to be."

g. She was awakened to her need. She came to desire what He offered. He was able to make it desirable as should we make salvation desirable to the lost to which we minister.

There are times when presenting the plan of salvation will be easy compared to earning the opportunity to do so. No matter the field, no matter the methods used, evangelism must be done if a church, an *indigenous* church, is to be established.

The missionary church planter serving on the semi-closed or difficult fields will be obligated to reflect the image of the Lord. God and Christianity must be a reality in his everyday life if he is to ever have the opportunity to share the spoken gospel.

Developing "*relationships*" is the key.

Dr. Ron Bragg shared with us that after four years in Africa, without having won any converts, he had become discouraged to the point of leaving the field. Having come to the end of himself, he frantically searched through his finances in an effort to find enough money to purchase airline tickets to the USA for his family. In his words, "He had had all he could take." In the midst of this hour of desperation he heard a knock at the door. When he opened the door he was face to face with four African men. The four men had been sizing him up for some time and had come to the conclusion that they needed to be saved. They asked him to show them how to be saved that very night. He said they had a "crying good time" that night as they rejoice over the salvation of the four men. They also rejoiced in the Lord who sent just what they needed when they needed it. Stay by the stuff. How sad to find in eternity that one had left the field just a few days before the harvest.

There are two more points that I wish to touch on before leaving the topic of evangelism on the difficult field. First of all the missionary serving on a difficult field must remember that he may be the one doing the "sowing" so that others can reap. I am reminded that **someone sowed for many years**, maybe even fifty to one hundred years, before we arrived in El Salvador. During those years of sowing there were not many converts. In spite of persecution there were enough to plant several gospel preaching churches, not many, but some. Those who did accept the Lord as Saviour were persecuted by the Catholics. They had their houses stoned. They were not allowed to buy daily necessities at the corner store. They were called names, spit upon and even had stones thrown at them. These brave souls endured for the sake of the gospel. **They laid the foundation for the reaping of a great harvest of souls that was to come.** Since 1970 as much as one-half of the population of El Salvador has identified with the gospel. Your ministry may be to sow the seed. It may be your lot to prepare the way for the reapers. The possibility also exists that the major harvest is past on your field.

A missionary to Japan once shared with me the sad truth that we may have missed, right after World War II, the greatest opportunity to evangelize Japan. General Douglas McArthur asked for 2500 missionaries to be sent to Japan soon after the war. Only a few dozen missionaries went. The hearts of the Japanese that were open then have since grown cold, satisfied with the gods of materialism and self-indulgence. There are new converts each year in Japan but the ministry is very difficult. The main time for reaping may have passed. **You may only do some *gleaning*.** The Lord is gracious to give **"handfuls on purpose."** You should however form the "gleanings" into a local *indigenous church.*

The second point is simply that you may have to win the next generation. In many countries 50% of the population is under the age of twenty-five. Reach the children and young people. You may reach their parents in the process. Children and young people do not bring with them the spiritual baggage that makes it next to impossible to reach some adults for Christ. Don't neglect anyone but be practical. Reach the reachable. Forgive me for constantly referring to El Salvador but a great portion of the present pastors of the independent Baptist Churches were won when they were but teenagers. They have grown up in the ministry. They know the importance of the indigenous church because of having lived through twelve years of civil war.

> *"Let no man despise thy youth; but be thou an example of believers in word, in conversation, in charity, in spirit, in faith, in purity..."* I Timothy 4:12

Just remember that the Lord's calling in your life is for a purpose. He placed you where you are to be His witness. Be faithful. Indigenous churches have come into existence in some of the most unlikely places.

Though we are about to move to the second key to planting indigenous churches it is worth mentioning that we have used simple Bible studies based on the various lessons that we normally teach to new converts to lead some folk to Christ. Even on very difficult fields this can be productive. Some lost people that do not want to hear you preach, desire to learn English. Some missionaries teach English as a second language using the Bible as reader or textbook. A simple discipleship course could also be used for this purpose. I always begin discipleship with a review of the plan of salvation and follow with the lessons on eternal security and having the assurance of salvation. Several times we have seen God work conviction in the heart of a lost person using these simple studies of HIS Word.

We are to be "as wise as serpents, yet harmless as doves."

CHAPTER FIVE

DISCIPLESHIP

The Second Key to Planting an Indigenous Church is discipleship

The next step after leading someone to Christ is to "make them His disciple" through, ***"teaching them to observe all things whatsoever I have commanded you..."*** Matthew 28:20. In the New Testament we have recorded, through *divine* ***inspiration,*** the ***revelation*** of the truths that Jesus has commanded. He has given the Holy Spirit to ***illuminate*** the heart and mind of the believer and thus help with the instruction. In John 16:13 Jesus says:

> *"Howbeit when he, the Spirit of truth, is come, he will guide you into all truth: for he shall not speak of himself; but whatsoever he shall hear, that shall he speak: and he will shew you things to come."*

We need the ministry of the Holy Spirit to be effective in evangelism (John 16:7-11), **but we especially need His help with the making of disciples.** Only the Holy Spirit can work in the heart of the new convert comprehension and life changing conviction concerning the Word of God.

Have you come to the realization that making disciples is an imperative? Evangelism, yes! Discipleship? Due to our fear that the "Great Commission" may be dulled, we give to the word "go" the emphasis of an "imperative." In the original language the word translated "go" in Matthew 28"19 is a "participle." The word is "going." Make no mistake. **We are commanded by Christ to take the gospel to the whole world.** The Great Commission is not just a suggestion or recommendation. It is His will. This literal translation gives place to the idea that all Christians, "as they are ***going*** about their daily lives should seek to bear witness of the gospel. This clearly places the **responsibility of being a witness** on the shoulders of every Christian. This also makes every Christian responsible to live in such a way that his or her life honors Christ.

The failure of many Christians to do so makes evangelism more difficult. A church planter cannot afford to be negligent in this area.

Interesting enough the lone grammatical imperative in Matthew 28:19-20 is the "***making of disciples.***" If we emphasize the "go" but not the "teaching" then we have a twisted concept of our responsibilities. Somehow we feel that only those sent (going as missionaries) are responsible to win souls and make disciples. The truth is that all Christians are to seek the lost as they go -- as they go to school, to the work place, to the super market, to the mall, to the park, to all the places we normally go in the course of our daily lives. Every Christian is to also be involved in "making new disciples."

First, the missionary church planter should be constantly working to *"develop relationships,"* relationships that will open the door to communicate the gospel, an open door to do evangelism.

Secondly, the church planter should strive to make the converts in the new church "*responsible* Christians" through disciple-ship.

RESPONSIBILITY DEFINED:

According to the Merriam Webster Collegiate Dictionary ***"responsibility"*** is the quality or state of being responsible. It involves: **a.** moral, legal, or mental accountability **b.** reliability, trustworthiness **c.** something for which one is responsible, a burden. A responsible person is one liable to be called on to answer; one who is accountable for one's conduct and obligations; one who is trustworthy and able to choose for oneself between right and wrong; and one in subjection to authority, or control by a designated authority. I suggest that the missionary church planter must teach his converts to be "responsible" if he is to establish an ***indigenous church***. If a national church is to be *indigenous it must have* a nucleus of members that will be ***responsible*** for the church and its ministry.

As I read this definition I was impressed with the following words: *accountability, reliable, trustworthy, burden, able to choose for oneself between right and wrong, authority, and control.* As the church planter "makes disciples" he will seek to instill in the new convert, through the teaching of the Bible, his responsibility to the Lord, His Word, to the Holy Spirit. He will teach him to be in subjection to God. He will seek to make the new convert accountable for the fulfillment of God's will in his life. He will teach him to be ***responsible*** for the truth, for right and wrong, for his choices, etc.

The sooner the church planter begins to disciple the new convert the sooner the establishment of the *indigenous* church begins. It is imperative that arrangements be made to begin discipleship classes with the new convert, or new member, for that matter, as soon as possible. Those won to the Lord in the privacy of their home or someplace other than the church meeting place should be led to make their acceptance of Christ as Saviour, public. Hopefully the new church will grow in number and the day will come when the missionary or pastor will be able to assign a mentor (a maker of disciples) to the new convert when they make their public profession during the invitation. If a convert does not attend the church services, except for reason of extenuating circumstances, it could be evidence that there is a lack of sincerity. There will be folk that may require additional visits and encouragement before they will feel comfortable with their new "relationship." In some special cases the missionary may offer to begin the discipleship classes even if the new convert has not attended the church services.

Initially the missionary and his wife may be the only people trained to make disciples. The discipleship load can become very heavy if they do not work toward training others to assist them. Because a man of God should never be alone with someone of the opposite sex that is not his wife or daughter, extreme caution should be taken when counseling or teaching discipleship classes. If the new convert is a female it is wise to have one's wife present or better yet allow her to disciple the individual. No exceptions, brother. You too Sister. The appearance of evil is all that is needed to shipwreck one's life and ministry. Ladies should teach ladies, not men. The ideal situation would be that the husband be taught first so that he can teach his wife and children (I Corinthians 14:35). Unfortunately we do not always have the "ideal" when planting a new church.

The missionary's wife can be a great blessing to him and the ministry, but wise is the man that guards his wife from excessive demands. As a missionary husband/father, be very *considerate of your wife*. Remember she is also the mother of your children. Protect her from unreasonable demands on her time and energy. Let her decide what is reasonable. I have found it a good policy to never expect my wife to do more than is expected from the average dedicated Christian lady member of the church. Because she loves the Lord and souls I have every confidence that she will be involved... as much as God wants her involved. The, "Bless God she is a missionary too and she needs to be right there beside me every day and every night, going just like I do attitude," is not what honors God. Your, "I love you darling," will sound more like tinkling cymbals and sounding brass (I Corinthians 13:1) if that is your attitude.

You ask, "What does this have to do with planting *indigenous* churches?" I am glad you asked. There are many small things that contribute to success in church-planting. The small things can also derail the church-planting ministry. The biblical *relationship you have with your wife* can be one of your greatest assets. The wrong type of relationship can also be a real hindrance as you seek to lead the national couples of your new church into the biblical husband/wife relationship. The strength of a new church is often relative to the strength of the married couples. Strong families can make for a strong church.

Some years ago the Lord gave to me and the pastor of the Tabernáculo Bautista de San Miguel the opportunity to speak at a couples retreat for national pastors and their wives. Almost as soon as the local leader picked us up at the airport he let us know that we needed to *preach really hard* and direct to the wives of the younger pastors. It was his opinion that these wives were holding their husbands back. He wanted us to straighten them out. "Tell them to get their hearts right with the Lord, to get behind their husbands," he said. It has always been an effort in futility for any preacher to tell me or Roberto what to preach. We had to get our directions from the One who called us to preach, the Lord Jesus Christ.

The Lord directed us to preach, *"Husbands love your wives."* The conference leader wanted us to preach, "Wives obey your husbands." After each of our messages the man would spend several minutes putting his spin on the message in an attempt to make our words say what he wanted. After several messages, in frustration, he said, "We are going to give the ladies a chance to testify." I honestly do not know what he expected but after several long minutes of prodding not one of the ladies stood up. He kept on, "Now is your chance ladies." Finally, the leader's wife stood and said, "I did not want to say anything but he just kept on insisting. I do not feel my husband loves me. If a member needs a curtain rod hung or if a couple needs a visit in the middle of the night, he goes without hesitation. I can't get him to do around the house any of the things he gladly does for others. He must love everyone else more than he loves me." The leader wanted to hide. The truth had come out. This preacher's wife of fifty years was saying in essence, "Men, love your wives the way God intends for you to love them and they will follow, honor and help you." She had been faithful to follow her husband, but seemingly, she felt unloved or appreciated. New converts so much need to **see** an Ephesians 5:21-28, husband/wife relationship in practice.

Speaking of wives... In the words of my dear missionary friend, the late Dr. J.T. Lyons, "It is not good for a single man to go to the field." He told me in no uncertain terms that I should marry a faithful wife before going to the field. He said I would face too many temptations if not married. At the same time allow me to say to the young missionary church planter, "Make sure your wife knows it is God's will for her to go to the field." Make sure she shares your passion for His will. If there are doubts, settle them before applying to be missionaries. God certainly uses single men but they generally face greater temptations and difficulties.

Now back to *discipleship.* Though a new member that comes from another church may question why he or she has to take the discipleship classes, especially since they have been saved for many years, it is a good policy to require them to do so. I recommend it if for no other reason than to prepare them for the day when they can possibly disciple others. The studies may be a review for them but it will bring parity. The new convert and longtime Christian will be on the same page doctrinally. Though our *love* for one another will certainly give evidence that we are His children, it is *doctrine* that is the touch stone for Christian unity and fellowship (Ephesians 4:13). The hope is that each new disciple will become in time a maker of disciples -- using of course, Bible study materials common to all.

Some missionary church planters say, "I prefer to just have the people come to the Sunday School Bible study or preaching services. They can get all they need from listening to my messages." I agree that if anyone needs to pack their preaching with teaching it is the church planter. So often though while preaching, the preacher will say, "This is what the Bible teaches, but, we do not have time to turn to the passages." In the discipleship class there is not only time to look in detail at the Bible, but the new convert can also express his or her doubts, lack of understanding and even fears. The preacher should never single out one or more individuals and their problems in his preaching from the pulpit. In a one-on-one setting a person is far more likely to open up his/her heart. In discipleship class the individual is the center of attention. Remember **the idea is to make a disciple, not just cover the materials.**

Imagine how wonderful it would be to have a nucleus of believers that not only know *what* they believe but *why* they believe it because you have taken the time to teach them. Hebrews 5:11-14 is a vivid reminder of the consequences of believers not having a solid doctrinal foundation on which to build their lives.

> *"Of whom we have many things to say, and hard to be uttered, seeing ye are dull of hearing. For when for the time ye ought to be teachers, ye have need that one teach you again which be the first principles of*

the oracles of God; and are become such as have need of milk, and not of strong meat." Hebrews 5:11-12

All Christians need a well-placed doctrinal foundation on which to build their lives. The fact is that believers are not able to build a life of faithfulness and *responsibility* that contributes to the strength of local church if their foundation is weak. There will be problems even in churches that have a strong discipleship program. There will no doubt be carnal Christians too. But, the church is far more likely to be *indigenous* if it is made up of people who have a good understanding of the truths known as "the first principles of the oracles (words) of God." The writer of Hebrews 6:1-2 mentions some of the key doctrines that would serve as "building blocks" in the foundation: "Repentance from dead works, faith toward God, doctrine of baptisms, laying on of hands (local church authority), the resurrection of the dead, and of eternal judgment."

Discipleship Considerations:

1. **Choose the training materials wisely.** There are good materials available, but you may have to search for them. Consider producing your own materials only as a last resort. Producing your own materials will be very time consuming.

    a. They should be doctrinally sound.

    b. They should use the Bible version you use in the language on your field. The KJV in English ministries.

    c. They should be on the level of the student (consider age, educational background, etc.)

    d. They should cover the necessary doctrines beginning with salvation, security of the believer, the certainty of salvation, the Person of God, the Father, the Son, the Holy Spirit, prayer, baptism, the Lord's Supper, the church, giving, worship, service, missions, separation, abiding in Him, how to know the will of God, standards, church discipline, family devotions, Christian character, soul winning, the fullness of the Holy Spirit, things to come, how to study the Bible, etc. --- just to name a few.

2. Train several key people to disciple others. From this group will surface future leaders. Their relationship with Him and you can be used of God to work in their hearts the responsibility required for leadership roles in the new church. He will cause the truths they have studied to be more than just Bible doctrines to be learned, they will see them as convictions to be lived. There is great importance in training several individuals. A grave mistake made by many missionary church planters is to pour themselves into one man, with the expectation that he will be "the leader" of the new church. The apostle Paul, *"ordained elders in every church"* (Acts 14:23).

3. Make no exceptions. Discretion should be exercised in assigning a teacher to a new convert. Be careful of being a "respecter of persons."

4. Always remember that "making disciples" is:

    a. His **command** (Matthew 28:19-20)

    b. **Necessary** to prepare new members for membership in the local church.

    c. A test of the **sincerity of the believer**. The student should be assigned verses to memorize, passages to read, lessons to be reviewed. A good policy is to require a demonstrable understanding and acceptance of the truth of a lesson before proceeding to the next lesson. If a new member does not understand or accept a certain truth, time should be spent helping them. If they refuse to accept as biblical the truths discussed, consideration should be given to discontinuing their discipleship classes. There is no need to spend time with one who has a closed heart and mind to God's Word. Pray for them. Be a friend to them.

Note: We once had a fellow disagree with the plain teaching of the Bible concerning abstinence from strong drink. He could not be a member of the church if he insisted on holding that position. He was shocked to hear that he would not be able to continue with the discipleship classes. Compassionately, he was told he was welcome to attend all the services of the church, but he could not become a member. Some may feel that our position was too strong. I personally am not interested in playing church games.

5. As the discipleship ministry develops assign someone to be supervisor over the discipleship ministry of the church.

By allowing a maturing man this responsibility you will help him prepare for other leadership roles. Make sure he knows what is expected of him, his responsibilities. You may want to assign a lady to oversee the discipling of the ladies. Though they should be accountable to the missionary or pastor allow them to exercise some personal initiative. Allow them room to grow in grace.

6. When training someone to make disciples it may be necessary to train them "how to teach" as well as "what to teach." Blessed is the church planter that has teachers as a part of his new ministry. Ask the Lord to help you recognize the ministry gifts each individual possesses.

7. Use the discipleship classes to develop an attitude of accountability in the new convert. Make them accountable to the teacher. They should be accountable for the materials studied, for the application of those truths to their daily life, for weekly memory verses, for their daily devotions, for their daily prayer time, for their personal testimony before the lost, etc. The teacher should also be accountable, to the supervisor, who in turn is accountable to the pastor.

8. Make sure the discipleship class does not become a "gossip session."

9. Encourage the students to purchase a good study Bible (Thompson, Ryrie, Scofield, etc.), a Bible dictionary, a concordance, a notebook for filing notes, questions, definitions, a prayer list, answers to prayer, personal victories, etc. You may offer any or all of these as a reward for completion of the discipleship course but *do not give the new convert everything.* Nationals can come to expect the missionary to pay for everything. They should be taught *financial responsibility* from the very beginning. They will treasure what has cost them something. The Lord knew what He was saying when He said, *"For where your treasure is, there will your heart be also."* Matthew 6:21

10. **Teach the student to seek, through independent personal Bible study, answers to questions they may have.** The leaders of an indigenous church need to be dependent on the Holy Spirit and the Word, not the missionary. They need to develop Bible based convictions.

11. Train your people in such a way that they come to see the discipleship training as a natural pre-requisite for any and all leadership roles. All who serve in an official role (usher, counselor, teacher, song leader, nursery worker, etc.) should complete the discipleship course of study.

12. **Meet on a regular basis with the supervisors.** Help them prepare as supervisors. Allow them to meet regularly with those doing the teaching. It is good training for them if you will *remain in the back ground* when they do meet with those they supervise. It should be standard policy to never embarrass the people accountable to you by scolding them or correcting them publicly. Your goal is to have a church that is ***self-governing.*** One must be considerate of those the Lord has entrusted to him.

13. **Have a set time each week.** The church planter/pastor, and later the supervisor, should see that the classes take place at a time convenient to the teacher as well as the student. Some folk find it convenient to arrive an hour before the church services or stay an hour after services to receive their

discipleship studies. Others prefer to receive the classes at home or even in the office at noontime.

14. **It is also important to have a place without distractions.** A noisy machine shop or house where there are three or four screaming babies is not adequate. The student must be able to concentrate.

15. **Train your teachers to be formal and professional in their demeanor.** They are Christ's ambassadors. Just as the missionary should magnify his office so too each believer should honor the post the Lord has given to them.

16. **Do not allow the student to stray from the topic of the lesson.** Do not allow them to run ahead to some future topic. Stay with the lesson plan.

17. **The teacher should understand that it is no crime to ignore certain truths.** Teach them to admit it when they do not know an answer. Teach them to tell the student that they will try to have an answer for them by the next session. If at all possible lead the student in finding the answer. We all need reminding, from time to time, that there are some things God has not revealed (Deuteronomy 29:29). None of us have all the answers.

The discipleship ministry is an important key to the development of an indigenous church. Do not wait until the last few months before furlough to start training your people to assume leadership roles. Do not wait until the last year before furlough to share with them that you are leaving. **From the very beginning they should know your goal is to plant a church that can stand on its own in the Lord, under their leadership.**

A typical discipleship class could go as follows:

1. Be punctual, be prepared, begin on time.

2. Take a moment to greet the student.

3. Begin with prayer. Lead the student to pray to the Holy Spirit for understanding.

4. State the objective of the day's lesson, i.e. Today we are going to begin the study of the doctrine of the local church, its origin, its order, its ordinances, its officials, its obligations and opportunities.

5. Have the Bible open. Make sure the student finds the passages used as proof texts. Be careful to not embarrass a student that may not be able to read.

6. If the student has books with an outline allow him/her to make notes or fill in the blank spaces using the information found in the verses being studied.

Lead him/her to find the answers but do not just give the answers to him/her.

It is imperative that the new believers learn to find Bible truth for themselves. It is not enough for them to believe something because the teacher says so.

7. Cover the assigned materials if possible but do not push ahead at the expense of the students' comprehension. It is better to proceed at the students own pace.

8. Finish the class on time. Be sure the student understands the assignment (memory verses, daily Bible reading, daily devotional time, etc.).

9. Encourage the student to attend the church services, invite friends and family, etc.

10. After the session is concluded, go your way.

At the same time that you are doing evangelism, making disciples and training folk to be soul winners and makers of disciples you will be having the regular activities of the church. The biblical messages that you preach in these services should confirm in the hearts of the new converts the truths that they are studying in their discipleship classes.

CHAPTER SIX

THE ORGANIZATIONAL SERVICE OF THE NEW CHURCH

You should have in your mind a targeted date for the organizational service of the church. There are differences of opinion in this but I personally believe it requisite to have a nucleus of biblically baptized believers of like doctrine and purpose, to officially organize a new congregation. The Bible does not stipulate the number required but it is reasonable to believe that there should be more than one or two. The churches that we have planted have been organized with as few as fifteen and as many as thirty-four adult members. By God's grace and to His glory, these churches are still in existence to this day.

Of great importance is that the members, no matter the number, understand the significance of the organization of the congregation into a local church. Those that have become disciples through study of His Word should have a fairly good comprehension of the *why* and *what for* of the organizational service.

The Purposes of the New Church

They will understand the need to covenant together as a group of believers to ***serve the Lord*** through ***worship***, to ***celebrate His ordinances***, to preach and teach His Word for ***the edification of the church body***, to encourage one another through ***fellowship*** and to ***reach*** out to ***the lost*** in their community and around the world.

The organizational service is similar to the "tip of the iceberg." We are told that only 10% of the iceberg protrudes above the surface of the water. The larger portion of ice remains hidden below. Though very important the organizational service is only a small indication of what God has been doing in lives. The realization of an organizational service indicates that God has honored the soul winner's faithfulness, the dedication of the teachers who have labored to make disciples and the prayers and participation of all involved, going all the way back to the sponsoring church.

The organizational service affords the opportunity to declare to all present the ***responsibilities and privileges of the charter members***, to document their commitment to the Lord and one another. The church planter should emphasize to all who sign the Church Covenant the seriousness of their participation. **Before the organizational service**, it should be decided who qualifies biblically to sign as charter members. Their names can be printed in the register of the church, leaving space to affix their signature during the service. This will help avoid the confusion that could arise if a general invitation is given to **all** present that want to be charter members of the new church. Lost people or members of other non-Baptist churches may feel they want to be charter members. Provision can be made for charter members to be accepted for a period of time, possibly a month, after the organizational service.

The Pastor of the New Church

Very probably the missionary will be named as the temporary or provisional pastor of the new congregation. This is appropriate but should not be done simply, "as a matter of fact." The church planter should prepare the leaders of the church by explaining to them beforehand the teaching of the Apostle Paul found in I Timothy 3 concerning the qualifications of the pastor. He should also explain his reason for being "temporary." You know the answer to that question. He is a church planter seeking to establish an *indigenous* church. He intends to move on when his work is complete. **For every new event in the life of the members of the new church there should be a presentation of its biblical basis.** The new converts must know that decisions are based on Scripture, not the whim of the missionary.

Involve the Nationals in the Ministry

Before and after the church is organized you should have people who have finished the discipleship classes. From those who have successfully completed the discipleship course you should be able to select some to assist in various aspects of the church ministry. Discuss with the leaders the various assignments. *Teach* accountability *by practice*. Teach by practice the wisdom found in a multitude of counselors. Counsel yourself with them. They know their people. They are schooled in the local culture. Do not insist on having your way when the majority of mature members have doubts. Learn to *respect* the wisdom of *the nationals.* Respect them and they will most likely respect you. You may find that *the nationals have insight* that you have not yet gained. When biblically correct, graciously stand your ground. Teach them to do the same but when dealing with personalities and opinions exercise caution.

Set Biblical Standards

The graduates of the discipleship course will understand that serving in the church is more than a ***privilege,*** that it is also a ***responsibility***. Some of the new members may have a distorted view of what is required for one to have a leadership role in the church ministry. From the very beginning of the ministry you will have to set biblical guidelines. Help them understand the reason for the guidelines. Show them that the guidelines have to do with the members and not the casual attender or the lost visitors that may attend.

The leaders should understand that most anyone and everyone is welcome in the services of the church. Visitors should never be shamed because of their dress, socio-economic status, etc. "Bienvenidos Todos" should be the invitation over the church entrance. Note: "Bienvenidos Todos" is Spanish for "All Are Welcome." One missionary sort of let his words slur and said "Bienvenidos Toros," which is "Welcome Bulls."

(We had to tell some Mormon missionaries they were not welcome if they insisted on gathering the names and addresses of our people so they could visit them. They would only be allowed to come and listen to the Word of God.)

The leaders should understand that a different, higher standard exists for those who are saved and especially for those who participate publicly in the ministry. More can be expected from believers and even more from leaders. Generally speaking people do not rise to the highest standard without help. As sinners we tend to fall short. The higher the doctrinal knowledge, holiness, personal separation, sanctification, spirituality, maturity and faithfulness standard is set, the higher the leaders are likely to rise. Setting a low standard only means they will achieve less. One preacher said, "Aim for the sky. If you fail to reach your goal you will at least be higher than if you aim low."

The missionary church planter and his gospel message are God's agents for change... change which reflects the elements of godliness and the image of Christ.

> *"For whom he did foreknow, he also did predestinate to be conformed to the image of his Son..."* Romans 8:29

> *"For the perfecting of the saints, for the work of the ministry, for the edifying of the body of Christ: till we all come in the unity of the faith, and of the knowledge of the Son of God, unto a perfect man, unto the measure of the stature of the fullness of Christ..."* Ephesians 4:12-13

Work to Make Them the People's Standards

You will do well to communicate to your people how you came to set the guidelines. This is best accomplished by showing them the guidelines as they are found in God's Word. Be biblical... not American, etc. Be careful about imposing on nationals middle class American Christianity and culture. Teach Bible principles. Show them how God blesses high standards. **Do your best to make them their standards.** If you fail in this they will change the guidelines as soon as you are gone.

Note: If you spend your time building a kingdom for yourself, for your mission agency or the Bible College you attended you may fail in establishing an indigenous church. The nationals on the field will probably never feel the loyalty to you, to your mission board or to your Bible College that you think they should. They can be totally loyal to the Lord Jesus Christ. Many of them probably will be, if you build the ministry around Him.

Nationals Will Not Be *Responsible* For a Church If They Do Not Consider It Theirs

You may wonder why I have not mentioned building a church building. I will at an opportune time but suffice for now, to say, **building a building is not building a church**. If the church planter, with God's help will build the lives of the members of the church they will build the needed building. In one Latin American country there are numbers of "church buildings" built by a fundamental Baptist missionary that sit empty or are being used by churches of other than Baptist beliefs. It usually is a mistake to build a church building for 10-15 new converts. National churches do not grow automatically because they have their own building, any more than churches in America grow because they have a building.

Do not do for the nationals what they can do for themselves with God's help.

Review

If the missionary does everything, pays all the bills, makes all the decisions, preaches all the messages, teaches all the lessons, makes all the visits, counts the offerings, hires and fires, directs the services, baptizes all the candidates, serves the Lord's Supper alone, he will not establish an indigenous church. It will be forever his church. The nationals will not own it as theirs. ***The nationals will not be responsible for what is not theirs.*** **Teach them God's plan, to seek God's will and provision. Allow God to work in them.**

An **organized congregation** is not an established church. The organizational service does give some much needed structure to the new congregation. It is a defining of what the church believes, who belongs as members and thus it means a commitment by the members to the Lord and to the church. It means accountability. Biblically, the church has authority delegated to it by the Lord Jesus Christ (Matthew 18:15-20) -- He who has all authority (Matthew 28:18). The church does not have authority over anyone that does not submit to it... or is not, in other words, a member.

Note: Some argue against having a church roll or membership. There is evidence that the early churches had lists of members. In Romans 16:1 the Apostle "commends Phebe to the believers at Roman" but of more interest to us is the fact that he associates her with the *"church which is at Cenchrea."* His statement, "...Phebe our sister, which is a servant of the church which is at Cenchrea," could be interpreted as meaning she was an active member of the congregation in that locale. Should need arise in her life, it would be the church at Cenchrea that had the authority to discipline her and seek her restoration. I suppose this is one of the reasons why many Christians prefer to float from church to church and not submit themselves to one particular congregation. Since they are "not members" they feel no obligation to attend faithfully, tithe, or submit themselves to the authority of one particular local church.

For the missionary church planter to be able to teach the nationals in every aspect of church ministry it is necessary to have an "organized congregation." For example: If the church planter is to teach biblical church discipline there must be a congregation. It is not the place of one person, such as the pastor (Galatians 6:1; I Corinthians 5:1-13), a missionary or even a mission agency to discipline an erring believer. It is the responsibility of the local congregation. **The organized church serves as a platform on which to build.**

"It is not the type of peril that was faced by the early apostles that derails many servants of God in our generation but the peril of making too much of personal prominence, preferences, pleasures and comforts."

Allow me to insert a reminder that can revolutionize our lives and ministry. We are in a spiritual battle. The closer one is to the front lines the more his thoughts are concentrated on one thing, the enemy. The front line is a place where fellow soldiers are knit together. In the heat of the battle they share several key objectives. They are to attack the enemy and gain victory at all costs. They seek to stay alive and avoid being a casualty. They help one another, protect one another, and even at times die for one another. Men, I know, testify to the love they developed for their comrades in arms. The front line is no place for envy, jealousy, or discussions over minor issues.

Only in the "rear area" away from the battle does one find soldiers (missionaries) complaining about the hard cot, cold chow, poor mail or laundry service, kitchen patrol or guard duty. Arguments and conflicts are common and even brawls over petty issues happen. It would seem more Christians need to get in the battle. A world is dying.

CHAPTER SEVEN

PRODUCING THE THREE KEY ELEMENTS OF INDIGENEITY

We have mentioned the need for ***evangelism*** both by the church planter and his people. We have given some insight concerning ***discipleship training.*** The congregation has been formally organized. It is time to be specific about the three elements necessary for a church to be ***indigenous or autonomous.*** The three characteristics already mentioned are: ***self-governing, self-supporting, and self-propagating.*** By this time, if you have won converts and made several disciples, taking into consideration the information provided in the previous chapters, you should be well on your way to establishing an indigenous work. I cannot emphasize enough the importance of starting right. I will say, however, that God is very gracious in that He blesses us in spite of ourselves -- most of the time. You should already have a fair comprehension of "do's and don'ts." As you can see, from the beginning, it is hard for me to mention certain aspects of planting indigenous churches without wanting to fully develop the thought. There is consolation in the fact that repetition improves learning.

A. SELF-GOVERNING

I prefer to place ***self-governing*** at the head of the list because a church that does not govern itself will not be motivated to be self-supporting or self-propagating. To be self-governing the church must have strong local leadership and the absence of foreign interference and dominance. The key is for the church planter to train the national members to be ***responsible*** for the government of the church. The church planter must go about his task ever conscious that his words, attitudes, and actions will either be used of God to produce responsible national leaders or they will be counter-productive. The church planter must constantly ask himself, "Will this decision, this word, or this action strengthen or weaken the national leaders?"

Some years ago I was staying in the home of a prominent national church leader. As is often the case with folk, he had arranged for me to stay in his home because he wanted to "discuss" a situation in the church with me. His conversation began with, "Brother Green aren't you the founding missionary church planter of our church? Don't you have a college degree in Bible? Don't you have far more experience than the men who are pastors of the churches here? Since you do, can't you remove so-and-so from the pastorate and put someone else in his place?" He was stroking my ego but I saw where he was headed. He didn't care for the way the present pastor was doing things. According to his thinking I should be able to remove the pastor and install a new one better to his liking. I probably could have done what he asked, but not without violating my own indigenous church-planting principles.

I explained to him that it was not his church or mine. It was the Lord's. The pastor was not my servant or his but the Lord's (Romans 4:1-7). It was for the Lord to decide whether the pastor was to stay or go. I encouraged him to pray about the situation. He needed to pray for the Lord to work in the pastor so he would do the right things the right way. He was also to pray that the Lord, not the missionary, would make any changes that were needed.

I suggested that if I removed the pastor he might be happy but there would certainly be others that would not be happy with my action. This would cause me to lose respect in the eyes of the church, alienate some dear friends, including the pastor and could very well result in a church split. The Lord could solve the problem without my interference. He agreed to pray and trust the Lord.

It is good to report the Lord did work in the situation. Within two years the pastor resigned and a new man was called by the church. The member was thrilled to see God work in answer to his prayers. He had been encouraged to respect the autonomy of the local church. He was taught to respect God's man, even if he disagreed with him. He was also given instruction that would help him toward becoming a wiser national leader.

It was very evident that, originally, he was influenced by the local culture. He was thinking as a "carnal Christian." The situation afforded the opportunity to help him, instruct him, and point him to the Lord Jesus Christ. Be careful about giving credence to the words of seemingly well-meaning individuals. Of course it later came to light that there were some shortcomings in his life that needed to be corrected. Isn't that so often the case?

Another word of caution; be very careful about *judging* God's servants whether missionaries, national pastors, etc. They fall or stand according to His judgment, not yours or mine.

> *"Who art thou that judgest another man's servant? To his own master he standeth or falleth. Yea, he shall be holden up; for God is able to make him stand."* Romans 14:4

Get in the battle and be thankful for those guarding your flanks. Back-to-back, side-by-side, defend the nationals who are your fellow servants.

Earlier in the book I mentioned the privilege I had to speak to the students in the Bible Institute in San Miguel. At the end of the session one of the students suggested that I might schedule to speak again the next night. My response seemed innocent enough to most, but the pastor of the church, the main authority over the Bible Institute recognized my response as one that respected his authority. I simply replied to the student, "I would love to do so but we need to discuss the possibility with Pastor Nieto first." As the founding missionary and father in the Lord of many of the students, I could have replied, with disregard for the pastor, "Sure it would be great to have another session tomorrow night." That week the pastor shared with me how important it seemed to him that I respected his authority. My response had promoted his authority in the eyes of the students. In an *indigenous national church* the missionary church planter is no longer "the authority." Once a church has been established and turned over to national leadership, a good policy is for the missionary to be involved only at the request of the national leaders. How can a national church be self-governing if the church planter continues to over-ride and over-rule the national leadership?

Because the national leaders must be *responsible* for every aspect of the church ministry they should be ***maturing*** in the Lord. In the same way the missionary must have a vital *relationship* with the Saviour, so too the national leaders. We can very well say that the national leaders needs to be experiencing biblical development in all of their relationships as a Christian, as a husband/wife, as a parent, as a professional, as a student, etc. **The church planter sets an example, provides the biblical instruction, and propitious environment conducive to this development.**

By the way, do not slight the older men that God gives to you. The leaders of the early church were the "elders," -- those mature in years. Young men and women can learn much from the elderly. If God allows, we will all be old someday. An elderly man named Valentín Reyes was a special help and blessing to me when we worked to establish the Tabernáculo Bautista in San Miguel, El Salvador. He had been saved many years before we met. His life was characterized by much biblical wisdom and fortunately God brought him into our lives and ministry.

Spirit-filled Leaders

The church planter must pattern the "Spirit-filled" life for the nationals. They must be encouraged to walk in the Spirit. Spirit-filled national leaders will have the fruit of the Spirit produced in their lives by the Spirit who controls them (Ephesians 5:18; Galatians 5:22-23). Missionary church-planter friend, is this fruit being produced in you?

> *"But the fruit of the Spirit is love, joy, peace, longsuffering, gentleness, goodness, faith, meek-ness, temperance…"* Galatians 5:22-23
>
> *You and I will have a very difficult time leading our people to practice what we ourselves are not practicing. Some Christians **work** at these qualities but it should be remembered that machines **work,** living organisms **produce fruit.** A mechanical form of spirituality will not*

endure. This fruit will only be produced by submission to the control of the Holy Ghost.

"And they that are Christ's have crucified the flesh with the affections and the lusts. If we live in the Spirit, let us also walk in the Spirit." Galatians 5:24-25

The new church will need leaders who meet biblical qualifications.

The Lord inspired Paul for a definite reason to set down the qualifications of a pastor/elder/bishop. The missionary church planter who does not meet these requirements will have difficulty planting an indigenous church. We do well to review I Timothy 3:1-7 on a regular basis. We need reminding very often of the life that we are to pattern for the national leaders.

"This is a true saying, If a man desire the office of a bishop, he desireth a good work. A bishop then must be blameless, the husband of one wife, vigilant, sober, of good behaviour, given to hospitality, apt to teach; Not given to wine, no striker, not greedy of filthy lucre; but patient, not a brawler, not covetous; One that ruleth well his own house, having his children in subjection with all gravity; (For if a man know not how to rule his own house, how shall he take care of the church of God?) Not a novice, lest being lifted up with pride he fall into the condemnation of the devil. Moreover he must have a good report of them which are without; lest he fall into reproach and the snare of the devil." I Timothy 3:1-7

Pastors, Elders, Bishops & Deacons: Qualifications

I Timothy 3:1-13, Acts 6:1-7

A. Blameless (I Timothy 3:2) means "nothing to take hold upon" – that is, there must be nothing in his life that Satan or the unsaved can take hold of to criticize or attack the church. No man on earth today is sinless, but we must strive to be above reproach.

B. Husband of one wife (vs. 2). The office of "pastor" or of "deacon" is not given to a woman. This expression also means that a pastor and/or deacon must not be divorced and/or remarried. A man's ability to manage his marriage and home indicates that he probably has the ability to oversee a local church. Dedicated Christians who have been divorced and/or remarried may serve in other offices in the local church, but they are disqualified from being pastors or deacons.

C. Vigilant (vs. 2) means temperate or sober. This is the ability to keep one's head in all situations. It is to be able to exercise sensible judgment in all things.

D. Sober (vs.2) means he does not cheapen the ministry by foolish behavior. He is a serious person and earnest about his work. He should have a sense of humor, however.

E. Of good behavior. This can be understood as orderly or organized.

F. Given to hospitality (vs. 2). "Loving the stranger." Open and friendly.

G. Apt to teach (vs. 2). The pastor and deacon as leaders of the church should be able to teach. For one to be a good teacher, he must first be a good student.

H. Not given to wine (vs. 3). The pastor and deacons must not give themselves to the use of alcoholic beverages. Wine was used for medicinal purposes in Christ's day. Some medicines today contain alcohol but there is a definite difference between social and medicinal purposes.

I. No striker (vs. 3). "Not contentious", not looking for a fight (verbal or otherwise).

J. Not greedy of filthy lucre (vs.3). The man that sees the ministry as a means to make money is disqualified.

K. Patient (vs.3). Gentle, willing to listen, able to take criticism without reacting.

L. Not a brawler (vs.3) a peacemaker, not one that stirs up trouble. One that can disagree without being disagreeable. Short tempers lead to short ministries.

M. Not covetous (vs.3) of money, fame, etc.

N. A godly family (vss. 4-5). Not necessary to be married or have children, but if so, he is to have a consistent testimony at church and at home.

O. Not a novice (vs.6) literally means, "One newly planted" as in reference to a new Christian.

P. A good testimony outside the church (vs.7). He should have a good reputation with the saved and unsaved with which he does business. Good character.

The Deacons

The deacons (Greek word meaning "servant") were first elected in Acts chapter six. In the church today, deacons should assist and relieve the pastor of certain tasks so that he may, concentrate on the ministry of the Word, prayer, and spiritual oversight. Though the deacons are not assigned the same authority as the pastor, they should meet basically the same qualifications.

A. Acts 6:3 states they were to be chosen from the congregation, men of honest report, and full of the Holy Ghost and wisdom. Such men were effective witnesses for the Lord. (I Timothy 3:8-13

B. Grave (vs.8). Worthy of respect. He is to use the office to serve, not just fill it.

C. Not double-tongued (vs.8) not a gossip. Not a liar.

D. Not given to much wine (vs. 8).

E. Not greedy of filthy lucre (vs. 8). Deacons handle church funds and should be above reproach. A spiritual attitude toward money is necessary.

F. Doctrinally sound (vs. 9). The word "mystery" means truth once hidden but now revealed by God. Deacons must understand Christian doctrine and obey it with a good conscience. Decisions must be based on the Word of God, not personal preference, or opinion. A deacon should know and understand the spirit and letter of the church's by-laws, but it is more important that he know and live the Word of God.

G. Tested and proven (vs. 10). An untested Christian man is an unprepared Christian.

H. Godly home (vss. 11-12). The deacon's wife must also be qualified, or she will disqualify her husband.

I. A willingness to **work** (vs. 13), **not rule.**

No one in the church is perfect, but a man and his wife should meet these basic qualifications if they are going to serve as officers in the church. Each of us should strive to qualify in every point. Because a man is the "husband of one wife," and he should be, does not mean that he meets all the remaining qualifications. There are ordained men of God that are contentious, mean-spirited, impatient, covetous, silly (as opposed to sober), careless, gluttons, unorganized, etc. who should either allow the Lord to correct these faults or else remove themselves from the ministry.

Those who cannot qualify should not look at that as reason to drop out or do nothing in the service of the Lord. Some will not be able to meet these qualifications but will certainly be able to serve in some other area. Older Christians should seek to set an example before the young and challenge them to give their lives as young people to the Lord for unrestricted service. Challenge the young people to "seek God first" in their lives before planning their lives from start to finish.

As you go about modeling what a church leader should be, the Lord will raise up qualified men and women for leadership roles. You will want to work with these especially, with the intent of helping them develop the responsibility and qualifications of church leaders.

It is also very important to help *disqualified* individuals understand the importance of their attitude toward their situation. As a church planter you will discover that there are fewer and fewer people whose lives have not been affected by bad decisions. You may wonder if there is anyone in the community who can qualify as a church leader. Throughout the world there are selfish believers, disqualified from certain areas of ministry service by bad decisions they made early in their lives. Many seemingly do not care what damage they cause to the church by insisting they have their way. They want to pastor, teach, or serve as a deacon in spite of the fact that they fail to meet biblical requirements. Though God graciously forgives each of us our past sins through the precious blood of the Lord Jesus Christ, He does not void all that happened in our lives before we were saved. Divorcee's spouses are still their spouses as their children are still their children. Disqualified believers do well to accept the limitations they have brought into their lives. They can honor the Lord by setting an example for the younger generation. Their acceptance of limited service can say, "Keep yourself wholly (and holy) for the Lord. Avoid making decisions that may hinder you from serving Him without limitations." Accepting the limitations with a proper attitude can be a form of Spirit-filled service in itself. One needs God's special grace and wisdom to help folk work through these difficult situations.

Brethren, the blessing of having Spirit-filled men and women will only come to you through agonizing prayer, fasting, and the working of an all gracious God. This will be one of the most difficult battles to be fought. But oh, how wonderful to know that it is His battle (I Chronicles 20:15). He promised to build His church. He knows the new congregation needs godly, Spirit-filled leaders. Church planting is not for the faint hearted or fearful. ***"Have faith in God,"*** as Dr. Lee Roberson said so often.

"...thus saith the LORD unto you, Be not afraid nor dismayed by reason of this great multitude; for the battle is not yours, but God's." II Chronicles 20:15

It is amazing the number of things that fall into place when people are Spirit-filled. **Live this, teach this, and expect this.** What is true in your life can be true in the lives of your disciples. Pour into them your passion for God, for His will, His Word, your love for lost souls, for the church, for the ministry; your thrill at being saved and seeing God someday. Be all you can be for God so you can lead them to be all they can be for Him. The major portion of the work of preparing leaders falls to God but you as a church planter can do your part by teaching them the theology and practice of church leadership.

The church planter can train national leaders through formal and informal means.

Spend informal time with your prospective leaders. Visit in their homes. Stop by their places of business. You will need to exercise wisdom in this but when you have the opportunity pray with them, give them a spiritual/Scriptural nugget upon which to meditate. Informal visits may allow you to show them how Christ should be the center of their lives, in the home, at work, at play, in their community. If the situation is such that you can do so, go to work with them, go to their children's ball game, etc. These times will help you better understand them, their culture, their needs, fears, desires, etc.

Dr. John Wilkerson, Pastor of the First Baptist Church of Hammond, Indiana has said, "A pastor should smell like sheep." How does that happen? He spends time in close association with his sheep – his congregation.

There was a man in one of the churches we planted that delivered "cream" from the local dairy. He had to report to the dairy at 4:00 a.m. every day to purchase the cream. He then made his rounds with two or three of the old type milk cans in his beat up old pickup truck. Everyone in town knew him by his nickname, "Chico

Crema," which is Chico Cream. By the way he was also named Francisco. As we bounced along on the bumpy dirt roads, he would blow the horn of his truck and call out "crema!" What a great opportunity to talk about how important it was for him to have a good testimony for Christ. I could see potential temptations as many of the customers were women dressed only in their night clothes. Not many people were up at that time of the morning but when the opportunity arose he introduced me, telling them I was his pastor. My being with him just that one morning gave us a special bond in the Lord. He and his wife are dear friends to this day. There were potential dangers but I also saw great potential in him. They are faithful in church and many friends have come to know the Lord because of his testimony. He is a leader in a quiet sort of way.

The time you spend with your people away from the church or the pulpit will give them the opportunity to observe you in an everyday setting. The prospective leaders need to see how you act and react when faced with the same problems or everyday situations they face. They need to know that you know you are human too. They need to know how Christ fits into the everyday scheme of things. You can show them, "knowing Christ does make a difference."

For what areas of church government do the nationals need to be *responsible?*

The nationals need to be responsible for sound doctrine, ministry (evangelism, instruction), order, ordinances, discipline, finances, the church property, church officers, church spirit, etc. In Acts 2:41-47 the Lord, through Luke, gives to us some helpful insight into the structure and activities of the New Testament church.

> *"Then they that gladly received his word* (salvation) *were baptized* (church ordinance)*: and the same day there were added unto them* (church membership) *about three thousand souls. And they continued steadfastly in the apostles doctrine* (doctrine was taught) *and fellowship* (gathered together for worship), *and in breaking of bread* (the Lord's Supper), *and in prayers."*

The church planter must teach sound doctrine. The nationals who are going to be responsible for governing the church must know what the Bible teaches. They should know what they believe and why they believe it. They will be the defenders of the faith. The church planter can pattern his ministry after that of the apostle Paul.

> *"And how I kept back nothing that was profitable unto you, but have shown you, and have taught you publicly, and from house to house, testifying both to the Jews and also to the Greeks, repentance toward God, and faith toward our Lord Jesus Christ."* Acts 20:20-21

Do you see from whence come my recommendations concerning ***"showing*** our Christianity, ***teaching*** in a ***public*** and also ***house to house*** setting***?"*** There can be no improvement on the biblical way of doing things.

> *"But none of these things move me, neither count I my life dear unto myself, so that I might finish my course with joy, and the ministry, which I have received of the Lord Jesus, to testify the gospel of the grace of God…*
>
> *For I have not shunned to declare unto you all the counsel of God. Take heed therefore unto yourselves, and to all the flock, over the which the Holy Ghost hath made you overseers, to feed the church of God, which He hath purchased with His own blood.*
>
> *Therefore watch and remember that by the space of three years I ceased not to warn every one night and day with tears. And now, brethren, I commend you to God, and to the word of His grace, which is able to build you up, and to give you an inheritance among all them which are sanctified."* Acts 20:24, 27-28, 31-32

The truth is Paul taught **doctrine** (the whole counsel of God) from house to house and publicly and night and day. He knew the leaders of the churches would have to guard the doctrine he had taught to them, so he taught them well. An *indigenous* church must have leaders that know Bible truth***. In reality all else that you teach to the leaders, concerning the ministry of the church, the ordinances, order, church discipline, and so forth, is Bible doctrine.*** There are only a few specifics to which the Scriptures do not speak directly. The church planter will need God's wisdom as he prepares the leaders for every eventuality.

The leaders will need to guard the ***total ministry of the church.*** If they understand the biblical significance of each area of the church ministry it will be easier for them to stay the course. They will have to hold the standards in the matter of membership, the selection of officers, materials taught, individual participation in public services, church activities, etc. They will only know what you have taught them from God's Holy Word.

At some point in the process of training the national leaders, guidelines should be taught relating to "associations." By this I mean that they should be made aware of the dangers that exist in the matter of associating the church with various denominational groups. They should be taught Baptist history and heritage. They should be taught the difference between having personal fellowship with individuals of other churches or denominations and aligning themselves with other churches for ministry activities. When independent Baptist churches join hands with churches of a different doctrinal persuasion for ministry purposes (services, evangelistic efforts, etc.) they are in danger of losing their identity. These *ecumenical* associations can cause much confusion in the minds of new converts. National leaders must be trained to not only guard the doctrine of the church but the identity as well. Teach your converts to practice the truth with a loving spirit but teach them the importance of avoiding association with the National and World Counsel of Churches.

Most likely there will be invitations to associate with certain groups for financial reasons. There will also be invitations to join in association with other churches to form national organizations. The nationals should be taught to guard the ***autonomy*** of the local church. Fellowship with churches of like faith and practice can be very beneficial for the congregation but affiliation that goes beyond *biblical fellowship* can be detrimental.

Pastors who aspire to grandeur may encourage the local church *to join* some national or international organization. The benefits will be touted, but a local church should avoid any and all associations that would sacrifice their autonomy. Some pastors feel the need to hold offices beyond the high office of pastor. Some may seek significance as the head of a multi-church organization. Better to stand alone in the Lord than to compromise.

The missionary church planter is a leader of leaders if he has worked to train and develop leaders. Some missionary evangelists are only interested in drawing a crowd. Preaching to a crowd is great but the missionary who plants *indigenous* churches and develops nationals as leaders can have his *crowd* and see the beginning of a great *movement...* a movement to Christ's glory which results in many indigenous churches being planted.

Note: One missionary planting one small church will not get the job done. I do not mean to diminish the value of small churches, simply seek to point out that **the planting of many churches, both small and large, is what is needed.** It takes a church planter between five and six years to establish an autonomous church. At this rate, it would take the missionary fifty years to establish ten churches, but if a missionary will practice II Tim. 2:2, and train national church planters, the process will be multiplied.

There is also need for formal training through the local church Bible Institute.

A local church Bible Institute can be established to meet the need for more extensive training in the Word and the ministry. The students should mostly be the members of the church. This will keep your people close. So often students go away to school and never return. Provision can be made for students of other good churches in the area, but do not neglect those of the sponsoring church. The Institute should take into consideration singles, and married students, the young and the mature (older). The classes should be scheduled at night or at a time convenient to the largest number of members. The Institute should not necessarily replace the Bible Study time on Sunday but should build upon the foundation provided by the discipleship materials and Sunday school lessons. It should provide the in-depth training in the Word of God necessary for leadership roles in the church. Emphasize courses on Old and New Testament Survey, Evangelism, Theology or Bible Doctrines, Hermeneutics, Pedagogy, Homiletics, Eschatology, and studies on individual books of the Bible, et cetera.

Adapt. Establish the Institute to meet the need.

In Chajuraña, a tribal village in the jungles of Venezuela, missionary Clint Vernoy had his Institute classes scheduled as modular courses one week in length, several times a year. This allowed the students from other villages to attend without leaving their families for more than one week at the time. Since they hunt, fish and scavenge for plants for food in the jungle, it was vital that they not be away for longer periods of time. Set the school up to meet the need. An unfriendly government forced the Vernoys to leave. The nationals are on their own now. The indigenous principles taught by the Vernoys were vital to prepare them for this situation.

You like the idea of having a Bible Institute and being able to teach? Hope you like the next idea, because it will help you establish an *indigenous church*. You should work toward having the nationals teach when possible. This will cause them to see the Institute as their church ministry. I have taken what we might call a sophomore student, which made an "A" in elementary doctrines class and helped him prepare to teach the entering freshman class. Of course his testimony, teaching ability and communication skills were taken into consideration too. What would be wrong with taking a school teacher and working with her/him so she/he can teach the course on "pedagogy?" What better person to teach people how to teach than a godly school teacher, who has been saved, completed the discipleship course and is a maturing faithful member of the new church? You ask, "Don't you wait until they have earned their Bible Institute diploma to allow them to teach?" No señor! The church planter needs the help ASAP.

I nearly blew all of my emotional, spiritual and physical fuses in 1976 because I was pastoring the new church we were starting, teaching all first year and second year courses but one in the Bible Institute, and trying to develop a village aviation ministry with the plane. I was working about 20 hours a day. Dumb! Oh, I was busy--too busy. I learned my lesson. Hope you learn from my mistake. Make your people responsible by teaching them and by letting those to whom God has given the ministry gift of teaching exercise their gift as soon as is practical.

Nothing will cause a national member to be ***responsibl***e like the satisfaction they have of knowing they are a part of something, like knowing the church and Bible Institute are theirs. We are laboring to establish a **self-governing indigenous** church by training the people in the Word (theology) but also by putting them to work (practice). We are making the nationals *responsible* by making them a part of what is going on, by making what is going on a part of them.

Note: Some insight can be gained by what happened in one national church with regard to their Bible Institute. A missionary appeared on the scene. He realized the church had a flourishing Bible Institute and he decided to get in on the action. He approached the pastor and leaders with an offer to build a campus for the Institute if they would associate with him. Sounds like an ecclesiastical opportunist to me. He would raise the funds in the USA to buy the needed property and construct the classrooms. He of course wanted to do some of the teaching. Much to his surprise the church leaders responded with a resounding "No thank you!" He did not understand their rejection of his offer.

They explained to him that the Institute was a local church Institute. The Church's facilities were more than adequate. They did not want to disconnect it from the Church, even in location. They also explained that the Church and Institute had been started by an independent Baptist missionary many years before and they had made out just fine remaining independent. Their response made the founding missionary's day. ***Glory to God and the Lamb forever!!!***

Teach your people but remember it is far more important to train your people to teach.

If the missionary church planter trains the member well and allows the Holy Ghost to work in them as only He can, the new church will most likely be self-governing.

[illegible] teach your people but remember it is far more important to train your people to teach.

If [illegible] missionary church planter trains [illegible] and allows the Holy Ghost to work in them [illegible] church will most likely be self governing.

CHAPTER EIGHT

B. SELF-SUPPORTING

If the missionary church planter has taught his people well they will want to trust the Lord for his provision allowing them to be self-supporting. As long as the missionary governs the church he will find the people hesitant to support it. This is why I began by stating that the national church should be self-governing. Human nature dictates such.

Start on the right foot financially. By paying for everything yourself you will confirm in the minds of the nationals what many think -- that all Americans are wealthy. The financial precedent you set from the get-go will stay with you. Teach your people to give. Teach them to be obedient to God's Word in the matter of tithing. Teach them to trust God. Teach them financial responsibility. Teach them to save.

> *"I have shown you all things, how that so laboring ye ought to support the weak, and to remember the words of the Lord Jesus, how he said, It is more blessed to give than to receive."* Acts 20:35

Don't you believe the words spoken by the Lord Jesus Christ? Is there not a blessing for your people if they give? Paul questioned the Christians at Corinth.

> *"Have I committed an offense in abasing myself that ye might be exalted, because I have preached to you the gospel of God freely? I robbed other churches, taking wages of them, to do you service."* I Corinthians 11:7-8

Paul seemingly is saying that it would have been far better for the Corinthians to have paid their fair share. The nationals on your field are advantaged because you are supported as a missionary by churches in other lands. They do not have to supply your wages. There-fore they certainly can do something.

When one looks at the costly cathedrals in heathen lands it should be a reminder that the nationals paid for these. The missionary responds, "Yes, but it took many years." I reply, "Will our haste permanently cripple the national church we seek to establish?" I repeat, "The church planter should not accuse (or excuse) the nationals of being ***too poor***." I can only say that if you do for them what they can do and should do for themselves with God's help you will rob them of the blessing of knowing how He can provide. You rob them of their self-respect. You may convert them into welfare cases. You will find most likely that your efforts come to naught when you exit the field. Great things were happening while you were on the field but when you withdrew the infusion of foreign funds, the ministry began to dry up.

The Keys

The Keys to planting a self-supporting indigenous church are:

1. Make the nationals responsible for the finances from the beginning. Teach them to pray and look to God. Discuss the needs with them. Get them involved.

2. Do not begin by paying the rent and all the bills unless you are starting without any local believers and it is a very temporary situation of a few months.

3. Do not hand out money as loans or gifts. You are not an ATM... or are you? Give through the church. You may tithe to your sending church. You will be asked for money but should decline to make loans. A sure way to lose friends or church members is to lend them money. Benevolence should be a ministry of the local church not the missionary. A missionary may be more easily deceived. The nationals can assist in screening those who are truly worthy of church assistance. This practice will cause the people, in time, to be drawn to the church and not to you.

4. Gauge your giving through the new church so as not to accustom the people to having your money with which to develop the

ministry. Neither do you want to cripple the church by having to pull it away from them when you leave to start another new church. The tithe alone given by some missionaries might equal a month's salary for some nationals.

5. Guard against an extravagant lifestyle. A word of caution: There are nationals who will be critical of the missionary and his family no matter how frugal he is with his funds. For example, the missionary for the security of his family may need to live in a "guarded community." Missionaries (foreigners) are often the target of thieves, kidnappers, extortionists, etc. Take the necessary precautions but there is no need to be extravagant or live in luxury.

6. Be patient. Wait upon the Lord.

7. Build the lives of the believers. In time they will build the buildings.

8. Do not approach every need with: "Let's wait and see what the churches in America first" or "I do believe I can raise x-amount of money in the USA."

9. Work toward the national pastor being *bi-vocational* if need be. Develop lay leaders as pastors. In some areas it would be far better to have three or four laymen that can work together in shepherding the flock. The church at Antioch had no less than five elders or pastors (Acts 13:1).

10. Do not build the ministry by American standards. The ministry may not require as large or as fine a building as you think. Far better to have a packed out modest building constructed with local funds than to have a half-empty fancy building built with foreign money. All the fancy buildings will one day be destroyed. Be practical. The only things we are going to take out of this world are the souls of men, women, boys, and girls we have won to Christ. Consider having two services each time if needed to accommodate the overflow crowds.

11. Avoid making "yourself" the center of the ministry by having deep pockets.

12. Train local people to supervise and direct the finances of the ministry. Train men to receive the offering in each service. Show them the importance of accountability to one another as well as to the congregation. Make sure that at least three people are involved in counting the offering. The three should sign a receipt for the amount collected in each service. The receipt should be given to the pastor or financial secretary of the church. The bank deposits should agree with the amount on these receipts. Show them how this protects them as well as the church. It is best to pay all bills using checks. Wisdom teaches that each check should require at least two signatures. Teach them to keep good accounting records and to give regular financial reports to the congregation.

13. Do not support a national pastor yourself. Teach the biblical principles concerning the church's' responsibility giving "double honor" to the teaching elder. The church should provide financial assistance to the pastor/pastors as able. If you help, do it discretely through the church on the field.

14. Any foreign assistance given to national workers or churches should be temporary. It too should be done anonymously through a local church. Have a set date when it will be discontinued.

15. It is not wise and may violate mission policy if the missionary holds in his name, as personal property, the title deeds to church or ministry property. It is unethical for missionaries to raise funds for mission's projects such as churches, camps, vehicles (cars, trucks, boats, and aircraft), equipment (printers, musical instruments, etc.) and even personal housing and then gain personally from the sale of them. Some missionaries hold the deeds to church properties under the pretext of "guarding the property in event the congregation turns from sound doctrine." This should not be. ***Teach*** the people, ***train*** the people, and

trust the people. Many times nationals will not give to projects if they know the missionary or other individual holds the title deeds in his name. As soon as the local church on the field can be incorporated with national church leaders as the corporate officers the missionary should transfer the deeds to the church.

16. A good rule of thumb is to never invest in anything from which you are not willing to walk away. The "things" of the ministry and life are only given to us so that we can "steward" them for the LORD. Do your work as a church planter following Scripture and depend on the Lord to care for what is beyond your control.

17. The funds that are raised from the various sources belong to God. We are only stewards. Much care should be exercised to avoid projecting to all nationals the dishonesty practiced by a few. There are exceptions to every rule but generally speaking this type of action will promote the establishment of strong indigenous churches, churches that are self-supporting.

Expose your people to the members of other indigenous churches on your field. It will help them to see *indigeneity* in action. They will, hopefully, realize that if fellow countrymen are able to practice New Testament giving, they should be able to do so too. Do not bring them to the USA for this purpose. It is often a grave mistake to bring nationals from under-developed countries to the USA. Do not use the nationals for personal gain. Those who have done so have found it counter-productive.

You may find it tempting to ignore these principles, thinking that your ministry will be the exception. Don't be deceived. You will always find people ready to take a handout. You will probably find these will come to resent you in time. Sooner or later enough will not be enough. You must decide from the outset of your church-planting ministry what type of churches you wish to plant. God is able to raise up self-supporting churches anywhere.

According to some, El Salvador is supposedly an under-developed country. There is much poverty nationwide. The citizens came through twelve years of what is referred to as a civil war. In spite of all of these problems the Lord has blessed. In spite of the generally poor economy God has allowed many Salvadorian independent Baptist churches to build facilities to house their ministries. Several have received some foreign assistance but most have depended principally upon the funds from the local members to construct their edifices. I have seen the sense of pride they feel knowing they have built with Salvadorian funds which God provided. I have also sensed the disdain they project toward the nationals who have built almost exclusively using foreign funds. As the ministry there has matured there are believers who are donating land for projects that include new churches, Bible camps, and one family even donated land for the purpose of building modest homes for Christians in need. They have found God faithful to His promises.

As the believers of Macedonia, they have given in spite of ***persecutions*** and great ***poverty.*** They have given within their own ***power*** by placing their resources in the offerings, but they have given beyond their own power by believing God's ***promises*** and bringing His resources into the picture (II Corinthians 8:1-5). If you are not familiar with Grace Giving or the Principle of Faith Promise please read first this passage and then the book (Faith Promise, Grace Giving for Missionary Stewardship) written by Dr. John Halsey, former Far North Director of Baptist International Missions, Inc. (BIMI). This book is available through BIMI, P.O. Box 9215, Chattanooga, TN 37412.

You and I cannot possibly meet all or even most of the financial needs that exist on the foreign field but we know one who can. Teach your people to look to the "God who can.

> *"Yea they spake against God; they said, Can God furnish a table in the wilderness?"* Psalm 78:19

Dr. Harold Sightler used to preach the message, "Can God?" taken from this text. His answer, as should be ours, **"YES! GOD can!"**

> *"But my God shall supply all your need according to his riches in glory by Christ Jesus."* Philippians 4:19

> *"Bring ye all the tithes into the storehouse, that there may be meat in mine house, and prove me now herewith, saith the LORD of hosts, if I will not open you the windows of heaven, and pour out you a blessing, that there shall not be room enough to receive it."* Malachi 3:10

It is a tremendous blessing to see national churches enabled by the blessings of God, in response to their faith in Him, support not only the local ministry, their pastor or pastors, domestic missions works, and even foreign missions. There are Salvadorian missionaries now serving in ten foreign countries.

God is able to raise up indigenous churches that are self-supporting and definitely not selfish -- they are sending the gospel to others.

CHAPTER NINE

C. SELF-PROPAGATING

The third key characteristic of an *indigenous* church is that it is self-propagating. In plain language, we mean that the indigenous church will be multiplying itself locally through evangelism, in the neighboring states or provinces through the planting of new churches and world-wide through its missions program. Any local church that ceases to propagate itself will stagnate and ultimately wither away.

A very sad condition exists in many churches in the world. Churches have internalized their ministry to the point that 90% of all activity and effort is directed at the local church membership. The music program takes center stage, literally. Great effort is put forth to produce "a feel-good time." The lack of true worship of the LORD and Scriptural holiness has left many of these churches spiritually anemic and unable to have any convicting influence in the lives of the lost in the local community. Only on a rare occasion do any lost people darken the doors of the church. Understandably many have no new converts in a year's time.

- Baptisteries are used for storage of the Christmas play scenes.
- Church splits are numerous.
- Dozens of "preachers" sit idle on the padded pews waiting for the pastor to go on vacation, move to another church, or just die. These preachers would not hear to the suggestion that they go plant a church in one of the thousands of towns nationwide or worldwide that do not have a fundamental, Bible preaching, soul winning, New Testament congregation.
- "Fellowship" and eating seemingly are more important than reaching the lost or planting new churches.

God help us as missionaries to plant churches with a burning zeal to evangelize the world, and to plant churches worldwide.

God's instrument for evangelism worldwide is the local indigenous church. When a vigorous *indigenous* church has been established, God's plan for propagating the gospel has been implemented. I will not repeat with detail the information already given concerning this third characteristic. However the new church is started through evangelism, the propagation of the gospel. Emphasis has been placed on the need to train soul winners. Neither the missionary nor the soul-winning members of the new church should become negligent in seeking the lost. As has been said by many, "The church should be a spiritual delivery room where new born babes in Christ are birthed." Nothing will bring life to a family like the birth of a new "babe."

The missionary church planter can guarantee the continual propagation of the gospel by:

1. **Encouraging** new and old converts alike to share their faith every opportunity they have. New converts are usually thrilled at what Christ has done in and for them. Do not stifle them by insisting that they have a complete course in soul winning before sharing with others what Christ has done for them. Irreparable damage can be done to a new convert if he is told he should leave soul winning to others. The simplest form of witnessing is to share what Christ has done in one's own heart.

2. **Recognize** the successes of all soul winners. Do not rob them of their reward in heaven by going overboard with praise, but a little recognition does go a long way. Let them know they are appreciated.

3. **Provide** the gospel tracts or other literature they may require.

4. **Take believers** with you as you go soul winning. Go with them as they go but on these occasions allow them to do the

witnessing. Your knowledge can benefit them and your zeal may be renewed by theirs.

5. Have at least one service a week dedicated almost exclusively to evangelist messages. Encourage the believers to bring their lost friends to that service especially. I give the gospel each time I preach even if it is a message directed to the needs of Christians because I never know who in the service may need the Lord as Saviour.

6. Those chosen to be leaders (ushers, teachers, choir members, officers, supervisors of the discipleship ministry, etc.) in the new church should be soul winners. Leaders who **never make any effort to witness** for the Lord are not filled with the Holy Spirit. Christ said, in paraphrase, that the primary evidence of the fullness of the Holy Spirit is that those filled will be witnesses for Him, in Jerusalem, in all Judea, in Samaria and unto the uttermost parts of the earth. If the leaders of the church practice this very important truth, the church will be ***self-propagating***. Teach the people about the four areas to be evangelized. I personally do not think one is qualified to be a leader in a church, on any field, if they are not a soul winner. They do not have to win someone every week or even every month but all leaders should be making a personal effort to reach the lost.

7. Have soul winning conferences, evangelist campaigns and other special activities that promote evangelism.

8. Encourage the members to "look on the fields that are white unto harvest." Encourage them to evangelize their neighborhood.

9. Encourage them to visit their town of origin with the gospel. It is natural for folk to be concerned for their hometown. Assist in these efforts but be careful of giving the idea that you as the missionary have to be involved in everything that happens. You do not have to be in control of every

evangelistic effort. **Train nationals. Turn them loose.** If souls are saved in a certain town plans can be made with the leaders of the church to investigate the need and potential for a new church.

10. **Lead the church to sponsor the planting of new churches.** Previous chapters contain many details concerning the planting of new churches and how the members can be used of the Lord in propagating the gospel message. A church does not, and probably should not, wait five to ten years to begin its own sponsorship of a new church. The missionary pastor/church planter would do well to lead the church into sponsoring a new church under his direction. He can use the occasion to train the national leaders in church planting.

11. Above all else... Churches that have ***Spirit-filled members*** will be zealous in the matter of winning souls and planting new churches.

Lest there be misunderstanding concerning my position, I want to say that there are several approaches to planting churches on the foreign field. God uses different people in different ways. Regardless of our approach we should all be working toward the establishment of *indigenous* churches.

There is the missionary church planter who starts several churches and each time moves on.

Most missionary church planters go to an area, start a church, and in three to five years, after it is established, turn it over to a national leadership. They then move on to start another new church in a needy area. This is the pattern the apostle Paul used in his ministry. For true, God is blessing the efforts of some of these wonderful missionaries. Some are establishing truly *indigenous* churches that perpetuate evangelism and church ministries. This is the main approach to church planting.

There are missionary church planters who establish a central church which becomes the sponsoring church for the planting of satellite or daughter churches. These missionaries may remain as missionary pastor of the central church for extended periods of time, even for as much as ten to fifteen years, or more. Not every situation lends itself to this approach and not every missionary will be prepared for this type of ministry. It is definitely detrimental to indigenous church-planting efforts for a missionary to pastor a small congregation of 30-40 people indefinitely.

A missionary might very well lead, indefinitely, a flourishing church with several hundred or even thousands in attendance if by doing so he is able to better train the national leadership and lead in the planting of many daughter churches.

Very small congregations become accustomed to the missionary pastor because of the resources he brings to them. If a missionary pastors a church for an extremely long period of time it makes it difficult for the nationals to accept a national as their pastor.

Because of the influence of the chapel ministry of the great Highland Park Baptist Church of Chattanooga, Tennessee under the leadership of Dr. Lee Roberson and Dr. J.R. Faulkner, I had planned to plant and establish a "central church" in Central America. I imagined the central church being mature numerically, spiritually, and economically. My desire was to have a Bible institute in the central church for training the national workers that would be needed. The aviation ministry was to be a part of this ministry. Our first attempt at this approach, the ministry in Estelí, Nicaragua did not develop at all, but later, churches we were involved with did develop somewhat along these lines. We never had the intention of building one large church. Instead our purpose was to build a central church that would allow the establishment of a number of strategically located satellite or daughter churches. What we started, very able national pastors with God's blessings have strengthened and built.

The **central church concept is great.** There are missionaries and nationals who are using the plan effectively with God's blessings. Generally speaking, the larger the central church and Bible Institute, the more demands are made on the missionary's resources, especially his time and energy. Some have continued to serve as missionary pastor of the central church with great success. The quest for church *indigeneity* compels the missionary pastor to train national assistants who join him on staff. One or more of these assistants should be candidates to become his successor. Many workers can be prepared through the ministry of the central church and Bible institute, workers who in turn go out and start new churches and even new Bible Institutes. A major consideration in this type missionary ministry would be to insure there is **a successor prepared** to follow the missionary leader.

> "Without a successor there is no continuing success." (Unknown author.)

When a missionary church planter is able to share his soul-winning, church-planting passion with the nationals with which he is working and he also leads them to live in the fullness of the Holy Spirit, there will be a fire burning in their hearts that will drive them to reach their own people and the world for the Lord. This shared passion is the spark that is needed to begin a great church-planting movement. As missionaries we need to envision, yea work toward such a movement on the field to which God has assigned us. One missionary planting one church will not meet the need unless that church plants more churches.

> "Attempt great things for God, expect great things from God." William Carey (Missionary to India)

However God leads in the matter of a church-planting approach, be sure to establish an *indigenous* church that is ***self-propagating.***

CHAPTER TEN

THE CONCLUSION

Before a church planter can consider "commending" a new congregation to the Lord under national leadership many things must transpire. Much agonizing prayer will have been made; souls will have been won to Christ. Many or most of these will have completed discipleship training. Members will have matured in the Lord and will have begun to live and serve in the fullness of the Holy Spirit. An organized biblical church ministry (worship, instruction, celebration of the biblical ordinances, ministry, discipline, etc.) will have become a reality. National leaders will have been trained and will be leading. The church may or may not own the property and facilities that house the ministry but an adequate place for the ministry will have been acquired. A church-based Bible institute might be in place. A missions program will have been established, just to name a few of the things necessary for the missionary to leave.

Planting an *indigenous* church can be a daunting task. It is a task for men and women of unwavering faith in God.

The time comes in the life of most church planters when they must leave. There is no hard and fast rule saying when a church planter should leave. Blessed is the man who can prepare the church and himself and plan well, because circumstances allow him to ***schedule*** his departure. Sensitivity to the Holy Spirit will allow one to know when it is time. There will also be signs given by the nationals. To leave too soon is like abandoning an infant child but to stay too long is akin to never weaning that child.

If the work has been done well, leaving may be as simple as just packing and moving. In some situations it may mean simply allowing the national leaders that you have trained to continue without your presence. Other situations may require the church planter to guide the nationals through the process of finding and calling a permanent pastor or replacement for the church-planter pastor. If you will allow the Holy Spirit to guide you He will make the path clear. Though saying "Adios" can be difficult, the transition can be a time of blessing, especially if a truly ***indigenous church*** has been established. Some may not realize that "Adios" does not just mean good-bye or so-long. It is the composition of the "A" which means "to" and "dios" which means "god." When we say it we are, in a sense, commending those to whom we say it, to God. That is what the church planter does when he leaves an ***indigenous church.***

> *"And when they had ordained them elders in every church, and had prayed with fasting, they commended them to the Lord, on whom they believed."* Acts 14:23

Let's plant... indigenous churches!

"You may learn the mechanics and methods necessary to planting a church from a seminar, but only God's Holy Spirit can work in you the heart of a soul winner and church planter."

Appendix One:

Various Church Documents

Please remember that these church documents are only samples. The church planter can modify or change them as he deems necessary to reflect the doctrinal position of his sending church.

A Sample Doctrinal Statement

1. We believe in the Scriptures of the Old and New Testaments as verbally inspired of God and inerrant in the original writing, and that they are of supreme and final authority in faith and life. That the King James version of the Bible is God's preserved Word for English speaking peoples.(II Timothy 3:16,17; II Peter 1:19-21)

2. We believe in one God, eternally existing in three persons: Father, Son, and Holy Spirit. (Exodus 20:2,3; Matthew 28:19; I Corinthians 8:6)

3. We believe in God's direct creation of the universe, without the use of pre-existent material, and apart from any process of evolution whatever, according to the Genesis account. (Genesis 1:1-31; Exodus 20:11; Colossians 1:16,17; Hebrews 11:3)

4. We believe that Jesus Christ was begotten by the Holy Spirit and born of Mary, a virgin, and is true God and true man. (Isaiah 7:14; Luke 1:35; Galatians 4:4)

5. We believe that the Lord Jesus Christ died for our sins according to the Scriptures as a representative and substitutionary sacrifice, and that all who believe in Him are justified on the grounds of His shed blood. (Isaiah 53:4-11; Acts 13:38,39; Romans 3:24,25; 4:5, 5:1,8,9, 6:23; II Corinthians 5:19-21)

6. We believe in the resurrection of the crucified body of our Lord, in His ascension into heaven, and in His present life there as High

Priest and Advocate. (Matthew 28:1-7; Acts 1:8-11; I Corinthians 15:4-9; Hebrews 4:14-16)

7. We believe that the Holy Spirit baptizes, seals, and indwells every believer at the moment of salvation and that the Holy Spirit empowers every believer for holy living. We believe that the Holy Spirit today bestows service gifts upon believers and that the sign gifts were restricted to the apostolic period. (Ephesians 1:13, 4:11-12, 5:18; Romans 8:9, 12:6-8; I Corinthians 12:13; Hebrews 2:3,4; I Corinthians 13:8-13; Ephesians 2:20)

8. We believe that man was created in the image of God, that he sinned and thereby incurred not only physical death but also that spiritual death which is separation from God, that all human beings are born with a sinful nature and are sinners in thought, word and deed. (Genesis 1:26,27, 3:1-6; Romans 5:12, 19, 3:10-13; Titus 1:15,16)

9. We believe that all that receive by faith the Lord Jesus Christ are born again of the Holy Spirit and thereby become children of God. (John 1:12,13, 3:3-16; Acts 16:31; Ephesians 2:8,9)

10. We believe in the "Eternal Security" of the believer, that it is impossible for one born into the family of God ever to be lost. (John 6:39,49, 10:28,29; Romans 8:35-39; Jude 1)

11. We believe in "that blessed hope": the personal, premillennial, pretribulational, and imminent return of our Lord and Savior Jesus Christ, when the Church will be "gathered together unto Him." (John 14:1-3; I Thessalonians 4:13-18; I Corinthians 15:51-58; II Thessalonians 2:1-13)

12. We believe in the literal fulfillment of the prophecies and promises of the Scriptures, which foretell and assure the future regeneration and restoration of Israel as a nation. (Genesis 13:14-17; Jeremiah 16:14,15, 30:6-11; Romans 11)

13. We believe in the bodily resurrection of the just and the unjust, the everlasting blessedness of the saved, and the everlasting

punishment of the lost. (Matthew 25:31-46; Luke 16:19-31; I Thessalonians 4:13-18; Revelation 21:1-8)

14. We believe that a local New Testament Baptist Church is an organized body of believers immersed upon a credible confession of faith in Jesus Christ, having two offices (pastors and deacon), congregational in polity, autonomous in nature, and banded together for work, worship, the observance of the ordinances and the worldwide proclamation of the gospel. We further believe in the church, which is Christ's body, the spiritual organism consisting of all born-again believers of the New Testament dispensation. (Matthew 28:18-20; Acts 2:41,42; I Corinthians 12:13; Ephesians 1:22,23; I Timothy 3; I Peter 5:1-3)

15. We believe that the Scriptural ordinances of the church are Baptism and the Lord's Supper and are to be administered by the local church; that Baptism, by immersion, should be administered to believers only as a symbol of their belief in the death, burial and resurrection of our Lord and Savior Jesus Christ and as a testimony to the world of that belief and of their death, burial and resurrection with Him; and that the Lord's Supper should be partaken of by baptized believers to show forth His death, "till He come." (Matthew 28:18-20; Acts 2:41-47, 8:26-39; I Corinthians 11:23-28; Colossians 2:12)

A Sample Constitution

The ____Name______________ BAPTIST CHURCH of ____Name of the location____________

PREAMBLE

We, the members of the ______________BAPTIST CHURCH, in orderly manner do hereby establish the following principles by which we mutually agree to be governed in the affairs of our church.

ARTICLE I – NAME

The name of this organization as incorporated under the laws of ____________ shall be ____________ BAPTIST CHURCH OF ______________________.

ARTICLE II – PURPOSE

The purpose of this local church shall be to:

(1) To carry out the great commission of Christ, as given in Matthew 28:19-20.

(2) The administration of the ordinances of the New Testament, baptism and the Lord's Supper.

(3) To edify the saints of God through the preaching and teaching of the Word of God as set forth in the Articles of Faith of this church.

(4) Means of Promoting the Purposes: In order to fulfill these purposes, this church shall engage in activities and conduct ministries which may include, but are not limited to, worship services, evangelistic services, prayer meetings, youth activities, radio and television programs, a day school, a Sunday school, a bus ministry, missionary activities, nursing homes, a Bible institute, college, and/or seminary.

ARTICLE III – ARTICLES OF FAITH

1) THE SCRIPTURES - We believe that the Bible is the Word of God; that it was written by men who were moved by the Holy Spirit so that their writings, in the original, were supernaturally and verbally inspired and free from error, as no other writings have ever been or ever will be. They are the complete and final revelation of the will of God to man, and so are the supreme authority in all matters of faith and conduct.

2) THE TRUE GOD - We believe in one God, eternally existing in three persons, Father, Son, and Holy Spirit.

a) God the Father – We believe in God the Father, perfect in holiness, boundless in love, infinite in wisdom, measureless in power. We believe that He concerns Himself mercifully in the affairs of men, that He hears and answers prayers, and that He saves from sin and death all that come to Him through Jesus Christ, His Son.

b) God the Son – We believe in Jesus Christ, God the Son, pre-existent with the Father begotten by the Holy Spirit and born of the Virgin Mary; sinless in His nature and life, infallible in His teaching, making atonement for the sins of the world by His substitutionary death on the cross. We believe in His bodily resurrection, His ascension into Heaven, His perpetual intercession for His people and His glorious second advent according to promise. We believe that the promise of His second coming includes: first, *"The Blessed Hope"* of the believer, namely, the personal, premillennial and pre-tribulation return of our Lord and Saviour, Jesus Christ, to rapture His church according to I Thess. 4:13-18; Second, His return with His saints to set up His millennial reign.

c) God the Holy Spirit – We believe in the deity and personality of the Holy Spirit. We believe that He came from God to convince and convict the world of sin, of righteousness and of judgment: and to regenerate, sanctify, indwell, and comfort and empower those who believe in Jesus Christ.

3) MAN – We believe that man was created in the image of God; that he sinned and thereby incurred not only physical death, but also that spiritual death which is separation from God. We believe that all human beings are born with a sinful nature and in the case of those who reach moral responsibility, become sinners in thought and deed by choice.

4) SATAN – We believe in the reality and personality of Satan.

5) SALVATION – We believe that the Lord Jesus Christ died for our sins according to the Scriptures, as a representative and

substitutionary sacrifice, and that all who by faith receive Him as their personal Saviour, are justified on the grounds of His blood shed on Calvary and His resurrection from the dead and are born again of the Holy Spirit and thereby become the children of God.

6) THE CHURCH – We believe in the visible local church, which is a company of believers in Jesus Christ, baptized on a credible confession of faith, and associated for worship, work, and fellowship. We believe that to these visible churches was committed for perpetual observance, two ordinances; the baptism of believers by immersion and the Lord's Supper. We believe that God has laid upon these churches the task of preaching the Gospel to every creature, and the edification of the individual members of the Body of Christ.

7) LAST THINGS – We believe in the bodily resurrection of all the dead, the saved to eternal life and blessedness in Heaven and the unsaved to eternal, conscious suffering and woe in Hell (John 5:29).

8) ASSURANCE – We believe in the eternal security of the believer (John 10:27-29)

9) CHURCH AND STATE - We believe that every human being has direct relations with God, and is responsible to God alone in all matters of all faith; that each church is independent and autonomous, and must be free from any interference by an ecclesiastical or political authority; that, therefore, the church and state must be kept separate as having different functions, each fulfilling its duties free from the dictation or patronage of the other.

10) CHRISTIAN LIVING – We believe that every saved person should manifest the Christ-life in a consistent walk in the Holy Spirit, fully and constantly yielding his members to the indwelling Christ, so that he may always be by life and word showing forth the praises of him who has called him out of darkness into His marvelous light. We believe in a separated life for all believers

as set forth in II Cor. 6:14-7:1, including separation from mixed (saved with unsaved) marriages and worldly alliances, pleasures, methods of work, worldly societies, etc.

NOTE: You may add Scripture if you feel this is necessary.

ARTICLE IV – CHURCH COVENANT

Most covenants are good...depending on how you plan to use them and what you plan to include on discipline.

ARTICLE V – MEMBERSHIP

SECTION 1. RECEPTION OF MEMBERS

(A) By Baptism, upon profession of their faith in Jesus Christ as Saviour and Lord and by accepting the Articles of Faith and the Church Covenant, upon baptism, are received into the membership.

(B) By letter, from another Baptist church of like faith and practice.

(C) By statement, have already professed Jesus as Saviour and having been scripturally baptized (immersed), by another church of like faith and practice.

(D) By restoration, Excluded members may be restored to membership on confession of their error and giving evidence of repentance.

SECTION 2. PROCEDURE FOR MEMBERSHIP

Every candidate for admission to the church shall relate his or her Christian experience to the membership of the church for a vote.

SECTION 3. DISMISSAL FROM MEMBERSHIP

(A) Death

(B) Transfer a member leaving this church for good and proper reasons may be granted, by vote of the church, a letter of transfer to unite with another Baptist church of like faith and practice.

(C) Discipline: Discipline is that procedure including Christian teaching, training, admonition, and rebuke both private and public, with the view to helping the individual grow in grace, mature in the individual faith, break off from worldliness, and live wholly for the Lord. At such time that a member shall refuse to receive such help it will be necessary for the church to exclude him from membership.

Section 1. Differences between individuals or sins not generally known, the wronged party shall follow Matthew 18:15-17. A person bringing a matter into the public or before the church before following this scripture shall be subject to rebuke.

Section 2. Matters of formal accusation shall be:

1. Public sins or sins known by the church or the general public.
2. Holding and persistently propagating false doctrine.
3. Any failure to abide by the church covenant; such as failure to attend the three weekly services without reasonable excuse, failure to contribute to the church, failure to be reconciled to another member, etc.

Section 3. Charges must be made in writing, signed, and presented to the church clerk. The church clerk shall give at least one week's notice in writing, with charges stated, to the accused member to appear at a designated meeting for a hearing. If the accused member fails to appear the church may proceed. The accused may call to his aid another church member to speak for him.

Section 4. A member formally accused is automatically released from any office or position, cannot speak at business meetings except at the hearing, and is deprived of his right of vote.

Section 5. At the close of the hearing, the congregation shall vote, by ballot to determine if the accused is guilty. If the accused is found guilty he must be excluded even if he repents. Statement of exclusion, including reasons and admonitions, shall be presented to the excluded by mail. After time has elapsed and his repentance is proven to be genuine he may again apply for membership.

Section 6. An excluded member can be received back into membership only after repentance and public confession of the sin(s) and following the constitutional procedure for being admitted.

NOTE: This is the most complete section on discipline that I have found.

SECTION 4. DUTIES OF MEMBERS –

You might consider this if necessary

ARTICLE VI – ORGANIZATION

SECTION A.

The government of this church is vested in the membership.

SECTION B.

The officers of this church shall be pastors and deacons.

SECTION C.

PASTOR

(1) The duties of the pastor shall be the spiritual oversight of the church.

(2) The qualifications of the pastor are those given in I Timothy 3:1-7; Titus 1:5-9 and Acts 6:4.

(3) The pastor shall have the ex-officio representation in all organizations and committees. The pastor shall act as the Moderator in all meetings of the church unless the church is without a pastor, at which time the deacons will elect a Chairman that shall preside.

(4) The pastor shall be called for an indefinite term, which shall terminate upon thirty days written notice by either the pastor or the church.

(5) In the event the church is without a pastor the deacons shall act as a Pulpit Committee.

SECTION D.

DEACONS

(1) The duties of the deacons are to be servants to the pastor and the church.

(2) The qualifications of the deacons are those found in Acts 6:1-7 and I Timothy 3:8-13

(3) The term of office for a deacon shall be three years at which time they may be re-elected if qualified.

(4) The following officers shall be elected from among the deacons:

a) Church clerk

b) Church treasurer

c) Financial secretary

d) Head usher

ARTICLE VII – MEETINGS AND ELECTIONS

SECTION A.

The church shall hold a business meeting once a year or when deemed necessary.

SECTION B.

The annual meeting shall be held the third Wednesday of January.

SECTION C.

Special meetings may be called by the pastor, the deacons (when the church is without a pastor) or at the written request of ten voting members. Notice of the special meeting must be given from the pulpit for two consecutive meeting days.

SECTION D.

Those members ___ years old and over may vote. Any member who has been absent for ___ consecutive Sundays is not eligible to vote.

SECTION E.

Quorum ___% of the voting membership shall constitute a quorum at any meeting. A ____% majority of the voting members voting at a meeting shall be necessary to carry action except in the case of calling or dismissing a pastor, buying, selling, or encumbering property, then ___% of the voting members shall constitute a quorum with ___% majority vote.

SECTION F.

Except where it is contrary to this Constitution, Roberts Rules of Order shall govern the conduct of the business meeting.

ARTICLE VIII – AUXILIARY ORGANIZATIONS

No auxiliary group shall organize without receiving authority from the church.

ARTICLE IX – AMENDMENTS

This Constitution may be amended at any regular business meeting, providing notice has been given of the anticipated amendment at ___ regular services of the church and also that the proposed changes have been conspicuously posted in the church ___ weeks in advance.

ARTICLE X – DISSOLUTION

In the event of dissolution of this organization, proceeds shall be used for a non-profit organization chosen by the membership that meets the requirements of the Internal Revenue Code Section 501 (c) 1943.

A SAMPLE DOCUMENT:

ESTABLISHING THE CHURCH AS A NON-PROFIT RELIGIOUS CORPORATION

Articles of Incorporation Of the ____________(Name) Baptist Church of (city), (state)

ARTICLE I

We the undersigned, a majority of whom are citizens of the United States, have associated and do hereby associate ourselves together for the purpose of forming a religious, non-profit corporation, in accordance with Chapter ____ of the State Statutes, and we do hereby adopt the following Articles of Incorporation:

ARTICLE II

The name of this corporation, which is a congregation of believers, shall be known as (name of the church) and shall be located at (complete address).

The corporation is and shall be charitable in its nature. The objective of the corporation shall be to minister the Gospel of Jesus Christ for all purposes required in or consistent with the Bible, including but not limited to the purpose of:

1. Evangelizing the lost through personal soul-winning, visitation, and preaching of the Word of God;

2. Edifying believers through the systematic teaching of the Bible;

3. Establishing fundamental Baptist churches around the world through an energetic missionary program;

4. Educating our adults and their children in a manner consistent with the requirements of the Holy Scriptures, both in Sunday and weekday schools of Christian education.

ARTICLE III

This church shall be an independent, autonomous Baptist church subject only to Jesus Christ, its Head. It shall have the authority to conduct itself as a Baptist church in accordance with the Word of God as interpreted by the Covenant, Constitution and Articles of Faith adopted by this church.

This church has the right to cooperate and associate with other fundamental Baptist groups on a voluntary basis, but shall not be subject to any control by such groups. This church shall not associate nor cooperate with any person or group who is a part of, or cooperates with liberalism, neo-evangelicalism, the charismatic movement, secret societies, or cults. It has the right to disassociate from any group with which it may have become affiliated.

ARTICLE IV

The government of this church shall be vested in its membership. Membership in this church shall be open to all those who:

1. Profess to be born again through faith in Jesus Christ alone;

2. Have been baptized by immersion following their profession of faith;

3. Are in agreement with the Covenant, Constitution, and Articles of Faith of this church.

Membership shall not be denied to any person on the basis of race, color, sex, or social status.

The presence of twenty-five percent of the voting members shall constitute a quorum. Active members in good standing who are sixteen years of age and older shall be eligible to vote, except in those matters for which the law of this State requires the minimum age to be higher.

The pastor and deacons shall serve as the trustees (directors) of this corporation.

ARTICLE V

This church shall have the right to own, buy or sell tangible properties, both real and personal, in its own name and through properly elected officers, when so authorized by vote or this church.

No part of the earnings of this corporation shall inure to the benefit of, or be distributable to any officers, trustee, or member of this corporation or to any other private person; provided however, that the corporation shall be authorized and empowered to pay reasonable compensation for services rendered and expenses incurred in furtherance of the purposes for the corporation.

Notwithstanding any other provision of these Articles, the corporation shall not carry on any other activities not permitted to be carried on by a corporation exempt from Federal income tax under Section 501 © (3) and 170 © (2) of the Internal Revenue Code of 1954 or corresponding sections of any prior or future Internal Revenue Code or federal, state or local government for exclusive public purpose.

ARTICLE VI

In the event of the dissolution of the church, all of its debts shall be paid in full. None of its remaining assets or holdings shall be divided among the members or other individuals, but shall be irrevocably designated by corporate vote of this church prior to dissolution to non-profit fundamental Baptist organizations which are in agreement with the Articles of Faith adopted by this church and in conformity with the requirements of the United States Internal Revenue Service Cod of 1954 (Section 501 C-3) and the laws of this state.

IN WITNESS WHEREOF, we, the undersigned subscribers, have hereunto set our hands and seal. This _______ day of ________________ 20 ____.

(Signatures) (Residence)

________________________ ________________________

________________________ ________________________

________________________ ________________________

State of ____________________ County of _________________

BEFORE ME, the undersigned authority personally appeared (names of the above signatories) known to me to be the subscribers to the foregoing Articles of Incorporation of (name of the church) and they acknowledge to me that they intend in good faith to carry out the purposes and objects set forth in the foregoing Articles of Incorporation.

WITNESS, my hand and official seal at (address where signing occurs), this ______ day of ________________. 20_____.

____
(Signature of notary public)

APPENDIX TWO:

TEACHING GIVING

"**I have shown you all things,** how that so laboring ye ought to support the weak, and to remember the words of the Lord Jesus, how He said,

I. Teach "giving" according to the Scripture.

The missionary should, in the process of planting or establishing the church, teach methodically and extensively, to the nationals **all** that the Scripture teaches concerning giving. The missionary church planter, the Apostle Paul, states that he taught the Christians of Ephesus to work so that they might be able to "give" and even reminded them of Christ's words concerning giving.

a. Begin with the truth concerning "giving themselves first" to the LORD. (Romans 12:1-2;)

"And this they did, not as we had hoped, but **first gave their own selves to the Lord** and unto us by the will of God." II Corinthians 8:5

The national believers must understand:

1. God wants them not just their possessions. (I Samuel 3:1-8)
2. He purchased them and has every right to all they are and have. (Acts 20:28; I Corinthians 6:19-20)
3. He does not need them or what they have.
4. All Christians need Him, His plan, His will, and His provision for their lives.
5. By "giving" God's way, Christians are blessed. (II Kings 4:1-7)

6. Being surrendered and submissive to God opens the door for God to bless and meet every need.

b. Teach all the Bible says concerning "stewardship." (I Corinthians 4:1-2)

All we are and all we possess belong to God and it is our responsibility and privilege to care for and invest what He has entrusted to us... for His glory.

c. Teach concerning "tithing"

Proverbs 3:9-10; I Chronicles 29:9; Deuteronomy 16:17 (Matthew 5:42); Matthew 6:2; I Corinthians 16:2; II Corinthians 9:7; Genesis 14:20; 28:22; Leviticus 27:30; II Chronicles 31:5; Malachi 3:8-10; Matthew 23:23;)

d. Teach concerning "giving offerings" above the tithe.

Proverbs 11:24; 31:13; Ecclesiastes 5:10-13; Matthew 26:6-13; II Corinthians Chapters 8 and 9;

e. Teach concerning the dangers of "covetousness."

Exodus 20:7; Luke 12:15; Colossians 3:5; I Timothy 6:10.

II. Teach "giving" by example.

The missionary should exemplify all that the Scripture teaches. We should say by our lives, "Do as I do and not just as I say". **Nationals learn more from** "watching" the missionary live out biblical Christianity than they do from hearing the missionary "teach" about Christianity.

a. Give according to Scripture. The national should see that you have truly given yourself to Christ first. That you "daily" give yourself to the Lord.

b. Place all that you are and **have** at **HIS** disposal. Be a good steward.

c. Don't ask the nationals to do what you are not doing.

d. Use discretion in your giving. Your giving should not become a hindrance to the work (indigenous principles).

e. Do not live outlandishly. Be careful about making the nationals feel you rich.

f. Do not become an "ATM" for the church or the members. Don't lend money.

g. Avoid making yourself the "focus or hope" for the needs of the church or the members.

h. Challenge the members to pray for God's provision.

i. Strive to make the "needs of the ministry" the national's. Make it their burden.

j. Don't suggest, "Let's see what the people in America will do for us".

k. Teach them to pray. (Phil. 4:6)

l. Teach them to pray in His will and for His will. When we pray according to His will we can pray with confidence.

m. Teach them to "trust God" by showing them you trust God.

n. Start with small things and move to larger matters of trust.

o. Teach them that "missions giving" is for missionary support, not other projects, vans, buses, etc.

p. Teach them "grace giving: to give by faith.

III. Teach them by personal practice that God's promises are fulfilled and His provision comes as we give. (Phil 4:10-19)

IV. Consider the socio-economical context.

It can be counterproductive to talk of "large sums" in a society where the average tithe might only be $1.50 a week. Hearing of "faith promises" by folk in the USA might be beyond some believer's comprehension.

Start where the people are and challenge them for greater faith and grace offerings.

Note: A missionary has not completed his church-planting task until the church he establishes takes its place as a self-propagating entity. Every local church should be sending and supporting the world-wide missionary effort.

APPENDIX THREE:

A SAMPLE MISSIONS POLICY

An Explanation: Please remember that this Missions Policy is only a "sample." You may very well desire to use the Missions Policy used by your sending church. The new church may choose to not have a Missions Policy. This one is offered only as a sample and can certainly be modified to meet the need of the church you are establishing on the field. It should also be remembered that the local Church has authority granted by the Lord and His Word. The guidelines of the Missions Policy are just that - guidelines. The Congregation has the authority to over-rule any part of the Policy should it be led to do so by the Holy Spirit. A policy of this type serves to insure that decisions are made on the basis of Scripture and the doctrinal position and practice of the Church, and not based on "emotion."

MISSIONS POLICY

I. Definition of Missions

A. General

1. The nature of missions is rooted in the character of God.

2. The work of missions is rooted in the command of God.

a. Matthew 28:19-20

b. II Corinthians 5:18-21

c. Genesis 12:1-3

d. Galatians 3:6-16

3. The objective of missions is to reach the human race that is alienated from God by sin.

a. Romans 6:23

b. Romans 3:23

c. God's loving and righteous response to man's need was to send Jesus Christ to pay sin's penalty by dying on the cross.

d. This gospel is the power of God unto salvation (Romans 1:16).

e. Since sinful man does not know about God's wonderful plan of salvation, He has commissioned His people, the church, to proclaim His Gospel to mankind.

4. Missions is believers proclaiming, sending, and going to people groups culminating in establishing local, independent, autonomous Baptist churches.

a. The message - I Corinthians 1:13-18

b. The messenger - Acts 13:1-2

c. Accountability - Acts 15:31-35

B. Specific

1. In view of what mission is and what missions is to accomplish, we are determined to do our part in obedience to the above Scriptures.

2. We will be involved in the Gospel:

a. Proclaiming

b. Making disciples

c. Establishing churches

II. Priority of Our Church Missions Program

A. Encourage our members to be involved in missions in their own areas of influence.

B. Encourage our members to be open in heart and mind to the real possibility of full-time missionary service.

C. Encourage our members to pray regularly for the missionaries that our church supports.

D. Encourage our members to give faithfully that missionaries might reach their field for Jesus Christ.

E. As a supporting church, faithfully be involved in our missionaries' lives by:

1. Faithful and regular prayer support.

2. Faithful and regular financial support.

3. Being available to encourage, exhort, counsel and assist our missionaries.

F. Evaluate current needs and future needs of our missionaries.

G. Interview, evaluate, and counsel prospective candidates for mission service.

III. Structure of Missions Committee

A. Committee

1. Nominated to a one-year term by Chairman of Missions Committee and Pastor.

2. The Pastor and Leadership Council will nominate the chairman, having the following qualifications, for a three-year term.

a. Not a novice

b. Knowledgeable of missions

c. Effective communicator

d. Leadership abilities

3. The committee will consist of men and women. This number may fluctuate as needs change.

4. Women will not be involved in confrontational matters involving doctrine or discipline of a missionary

B. Membership Criteria

1. Member in regular attendance and good standing of First Baptist Church.

2. Giving evidence of progressive spiritual maturity.

3. Interest and vision concerning missions.

4. Understanding and acceptance of Missions Policy

5. Willingness to make a substantial time investment in missions.

6. Willingness to be faithful to meetings, conferences, and services.

C. Member Responsibility

1. Attend committee meetings

2. Pray regularly for missions

3. Maintain interest in communicating with supported missionaries.

4. Engage in continuous self-education on world missions.

5. Serve as source of mission education to congregation.

D. Meetings to be called by chairman or pastor as needed.

IV. Strategy of Missions Program

A. Priorities of Mission Effort

1. Resistant Areas - People either resistant to the Gospel or un-churched people in their own cultural setting

2. Growth Areas - Areas where the church is growing rapidly and training and discipleship are urgently needed.

3. Foothold Areas - Areas where additional evangelism and discipleship are needed.

4. Home Missions - Areas with emphasis on the un-evangelized and un-churched.

B. Mission Education in the Church

1. Reading of missionary letters regularly in services.
2. Mission bulletin board with letters and items of interest posted.
3. Adopt-a-Missionary program.

C. Missions Conference

1. The Pastor and Missions Committee will plan the annual Mission Conference.

2. Purpose:

a. Focus attention on world missions by exposing church members to a variety of missionaries.

b. Provide opportunity for church-supported missionaries to present a report and have fellowship.

c. Motivate members to become personally involved.

d. Challenge people to surrender to specific missionary work.

3. Conferences format to be determined by the Pastor and Missions Committee.

4. Funding for the Conference will be provided through the church budget, as approved by the congregation.

D. Missions Budget

1. The Chairman of the Missions Committee and Pastor will prepare an amount to be included in the annual budget.

2. When possible, an amount will be included to increase mission support, or to increase our current number of missionaries.

V. Church/ Missions Board Relations

A. Definition of Mission Board: An organization or group as opposed to individuals involved in missionary outreach.

B. Qualifications:

1. In agreement with doctrinal statement of First Baptist Church.

2. Effective administration with a functioning board of directors.

3. Sound fiscal policy with emphasis on as much money as possible going to the missionary.

4. A stated purpose and strategy consistent with biblical principles and mission policy of our church.

5. A biblical attitude characterized by supportive encouragement to the missionary.

6. Willingness to communicate and cooperate with the local church.

7. Require all our missionaries to hold the Church's stated position on doctrine and practice.

C. Relations:

1. The Missions Committee will establish and maintain communications with the Mission Boards.

2. Each year the Missions Committee will contact the Boards to learn of any change in doctrine, purpose, strategy, and to obtain a financial statement.

3. Any changes in the Mission Board will result in a complete review of the agency by the Pastor and Missions Committee with a report given to the Church.

VI. Church/Missionary Relations

A. Mission Recruitment

1. The primary source is our own congregation.

2. The secondary source will be those outside our church body.

3. Missionary recruitment will be a goal of the Christian Education program of our church.

4. Equal emphasis will be placed on all ages.

5. Members considering missionary service will be encouraged to meet with the Pastor and Missions Committee for counsel, encouragement, and direction.

B. Determination of Qualifications

1. Personal Qualifications

a. Missionary candidates who are members of First Baptist Church will be given priority.

b. Members must be active for two years preceding candidacy.

c. Evidence of maturity

1) Emotional stability

2) Occupational stability

3) Family stability

d. Health

1) Have complete physical exam.

2) Perfect health is not the issue. The candidate must be in condition to fulfill the objectives of his ministry.

3) The candidate must have adequate health insurance.

2. Training and Experience

a. Training

1) It is preferable that a candidate and his spouse be graduates of an accredited Bible college with at least a Bible minor.

2) Candidate's course of study should be in his chosen field of ministry.

3) For those with a college degree, excluding Bible, it is recommended that the candidate seek additional Bible training.

b. Experience

1) The candidate should have a proven track record in his area of ministry. Letters of reference will be sent to verify experience.

2) The candidate should be involved in study of language and culture of the country to which he will be going.

3) The candidate must already be commissioned by his local church and approved by a recognized Mission Board or agency.

3. Financial

a. A candidate must give evidence of sound financial planning, such as a budget, a savings plan, a retirement plan, etc.

b. Candidates must show evidence of a biblical approach to family finances.

4. Marital Situation

a. Single persons will be encouraged to pursue their missions effort.

b. Married persons will also be encouraged if:

1) Their mates are in one accord in this endeavor.

2) Their marriage exhibits biblical qualities.

3) They have seriously considered the effect of missionary service on their children.

5. Spiritual Qualifications

a. Genuine evidence of conversion.

b. Qualifications found in I Timothy 3 and Titus 1.

c. Working knowledge of the Scriptures as they relate to life.

d. Consistent lifestyle.

e. Usable as a missionary

1) Salvation - I Peter 2:9; Romans 8:30

2) Holy Life - I Thessalonians 4:7; I Peter 1:5

3) Freedom - Galatians 5:13 (Law vs. License)

4) Confident response to missionary service - Philippians 1:6

5) Confident direction of their life and place of service.

6) Actively involved in evangelism and discipleship in his local church.

6. Doctrinal Qualifications

a. Must be in agreement with our church doctrinal statement.

b. Must clearly state beliefs about:

1) Charismatic movement

2) Divorce and remarriage

3) Abortion

4) Bible translations

5) Legalism

6) Affiliation and separation

7) Church and Para-church organizations

8) Sufficiency of Scriptures as they relate to life

C. Selection Procedure

1. The candidate must submit their request in writing to First Baptist Church.

2. A copy of the mission policy will be given to the candidate.

3. A personal interview will be arranged with the Pastor.

4. Mission Board will be contacted for their recommendation and evaluation.

5. After the recommendation and evaluation are received, the Pastor and Missions Committee chairman will conduct an in-depth interview with the candidate and spouse.

6. The Missions Committee will meet and consider the candidate for support.

7. The recommendation for support from the Missions Committee will then be presented to the church.

D. Responsibility of the Church to the Missionary

1. The church will faithfully provide financial and prayer support to our missionaries.

2. The church will maintain an open line of communication with its missionaries at all times.

3. The church will respond to all special requests of missionaries based on available resources and prayerful consideration.

4. The church will maintain contact and support with our missionaries through the Adopt-a-Missionary program. This will allow the church to become more knowledgeable and familiar with its missionaries. Various families in the church will adopt a missionary of their choosing for the term of one year.

5. Members of the Missions committee will be assigned individual missionaries for prayer support on a yearly basis.

6. First Baptist Church reserves the right of, but is not responsible for, the missionary's support beyond retirement.

a. Each Missionary of First Baptist will be evaluated upon announcement of their retirement, including areas of total retirement income to be received, future financial stability, future ministry (if any) to be participated in.

b. Decisions regarding continued support beyond retirement will be based on Missions Committee recommendation and church vote.

E. Responsibility of the Missionary to the Church

1. Missionary letters will be read to the church and then posted on the mission board. With the advent of e-mail, each missionary is urged to communicate monthly, with a requirement to communicate quarterly, on his or her present ministry. As the church strives to communicate better with its missionaries, we expect the same courtesy.

2. Each missionary is to contact the church when on furlough in order to present their report.

3. If possible, the missionary will attend our Missions Conference while on furlough.

4. It is expected that the missionary channel financial requests through the Pastor and Missions Committee.

5. The missionaries are responsible to advise First Baptist of any changes in status, and if requested, the reasons for the change.

6. Missionaries will be in compliance with Section 1 of the Missions policy in regards to the function and definition of missions of the church.

7. Failure to adhere to one or more of these guidelines will result in reevaluation by the Pastor, Missions Committee Chairman, and Missions Committee.

F. Reevaluation/ Termination

1. Reevaluation of the missionary will begin should any change in their status be received.

2. Reevaluation procedure will be initiated by the Missions Committee for:

a. Change in doctrinal position

b. Change in Board

c. Change in ministry

d. Change in health status

e. Change in personal qualifications

f. Behavioral problems

g. Family problems

h. Missionary's choice

3. Each missionary supported by First Baptist Church will be automatically reviewed yearly to determine effectiveness of ministry. A report of this review is to be given to the church.

4. Missionary reevaluation will not be based on emotional preferences, but rather sound biblical principles and proper applications of good stewardship. The guidelines for such decisions will be based on the Section 1 of the Missions Policy.

Missionary Profile

Name____

Wife ____

Children and ages:

____

____

Address ____

Phone ________________________e-mail ________________

Mission Board:_______________________________________

Sending Church and Pastor ___________________________

1. Please give your salvation testimony (Husband and wife).
2. Please list your ministry training experiences.
3. Please share your perspective of your call to ministry and your call to missions.
4. In what areas are you gifted by the Lord?
5. What personal debts do you carry at this time?
6. List your previous ministry experiences.
7. Give three personal/ministry references. Not family members.
8. To what field and type of ministry are you heading?
9. How much monthly support does your family require?
10. What is your current support level? What Percentage?
11. Please give a brief answer of your beliefs on the following:
    a. Sufficiency of Scripture as it pertains to life.
    b. Charismatic Movement.
    c. Local church authority.
    d. Bible Translations.
    e. Personal and ecclesiastical separation.
    f. Submission to authority.

APPENDIX FOUR:

FAITH PROMISE OR GRACE GIVING TO MISSIONS

In the last pages of the Gospel of Matthew we have the commission given by the Lord Jesus Christ to take the Gospel to the entire world and to establish local churches through the making of disciples or the teaching of believers to "observe all the things He had taught them.

> *"Go ye therefore, and teach all nations, baptizing them in the name of the Father, and of the Son, and of the Holy Ghost: Teaching them to observe all things whatsoever I have commanded you: and, lo, I am with you always, even unto the end of the world. Amen."* Matthew 28:19-20
>
> *In another passage John recorded the words of the Lord Jesus Christ when He said, "...Lift up your eyes, and look on the fields, for they are white already to harvest."* John 4:35

Christ's command is very clear. The need to take the Gospel to the lost is obvious.

The plan for providing funds for missions giving "Faith Promise or Grace Giving" has been proven effective by many local churches. This plan:

- Provides more funds for missions;
- Permits local churches to send and support more missionaries;
- Serves to allow more believers to participate as individuals in the missions program of the church;
- Increases the believer's faith. It requires faith.
- Is dependent on the resources of God.

The Faith Promise or Grace Giving Plan functions like this:

1. Faith Promise cards (See sample) are prepared and given out to the members of the church over a period of a week or two, usually in connection with the Missions Conference.

2. Each member is encouraged and challenged to pray and seek God's will concerning the amount of money they will give, by faith or grace, above their tithes and regular offerings.

3. The members fill in the card with the weekly or monthly amount they believe God would have them give to support missions.

4. The name of the individual is not placed on the card. The Faith Promise offering is just between them and God. This is not a pledge but a promise made by faith to give voluntarily each week or month the amount that God has provided. No one will ask the individual for the amount promised.

5. The church can make a note of the total amount promised and by this way have an idea of how much will be available to support missionaries and other missions projects.

6. Since the Faith Promise offering is not the tithe of the individual it does not take away from the funds that are needed to support the ministry of the church.

7. So that the members can deposit their missions offering on a regular basis, as God provides, there should be provision for the offering to be placed in the offering envelopes.

8. As the individual members pray and trust God to provide, and as He provides the offering should be given. These funds should not be used for other aspects of the church's ministry (i.e. bus ministry, camp ministry, etc.).

The blessings associated with this type of giving are multiple and abundant.

1. God is glorified because He is the One who provides for the needs of the believers and also the funds for the Faith Promise missions offering.

2. The local church enjoys a greater capacity to participate in the fulfillment of the Great Commission.

3. The will be more funds available to support the missionaries.

4. God responds in a positive way when He sees the "faith" of the believers (Matthew 6:33).

5. God honors the faith of the congregation (Hebrews 11:6) and provides for the total ministry of the church.

Why should a person obligate himself or herself to give an offering "Faith Promise?"

Some biblical reasons:

1. It is a way to confirm and demonstrate my love for God. "I speak not by commandment, but by occasion of the forwardness of others, and to prove the sincerity of your love." II Corinthians 8:8

2. It is a personal way to participate in the Great Commission. The Lord repeated in the gospels of Mark, Luke, John, and also in Acts 1:8 that it is His will that the Gospel be taken to the entire world. There are still millions of people that do not have the Gospel. My missions offering will help provide the funds to send more missionaries with the Gospel. *"And how shall they preach, except they be sent?"* Romans 10:15

3. This type of giving "exercises my faith" in God. *"...so faith without works is dead also."* James 2:26

4. So as to "abound in the grace of giving." "Therefore as ye abound in every thing, in faith, and utterance, and knowledge, and in all diligence, and in your love to us, see that ye abound in this grace also." II Corinthians 8:7

5. To follow the biblical examples of those who "gave by faith." The widow of Zerephath of Zidon, by faith, gave to the needs of Elijah (I Kings 17:9-15). We also have the example of the Macedonian believers (II Corinthians 8).

6. As we give by faith we follow the example of the Lord Jesus Christ. "For ye know the grace of our Lord Jesus Christ, that though He was rich, yet for your sakes He became poor, that ye through his poverty might be rich." II Corinthians 8:9

7. Paul, under divine inspiration, counsels us to give by faith. "And herein I give my advice: for this is expedient for you, who have begun before, not only to do, but also to be forward a year ago." II Corinthians 8:10

8. To experience the "promised blessings" of the Lord. "... and to remember the words of the Lord Jesus, how he said, It is more blessed to give than to receive." Acts 20:35 and Luke 6:38

9. To encourage others to give by faith. *"... and your zeal hath provoked very many."* II Corinthians 9:2

10. To "sow abundantly in this life. "But this I say, He that soweth sparingly shall reap also sparingly; and he which soweth bountifully shall reap also bountifully."

11. II Corinthians 9:6

12. To experience the fullness of the love of God. "... *for God loveth a cheerful giver."* II Corinthians 9:7

13. To prove the faithfulness of God and His promises. "...and prove me now herewith, saith the LORD of hosts, if I will not open you the windows of heaven, and pour you out a blessing, that there shall not be room enough to receive it." Malachi 3:10b

14. To glorify God. "Whiles by the experiment of this administration they glorify God for your professed subjection unto the gospel of Christ, and for your liberal distribution unto them, and unto all men." II Corinthians 9:13

15. To deposit more in your heavenly account. "...But lay up for yourselves treasures in heaven..." Matthew 6:20 "Not because I desire a gift: but I desire fruit that may abound to your account." Philippians 4:17

16. To please God. "...the things which were sent from you, an odour of a sweet smell, a sacrifice acceptable, well-pleasing to God." Philippians 4:18

The Cards

The cards used for collecting the "faith promises" of the members of the local church may be obtained from Baptist International Missions, Inc. (BIMI) at P.O. Box 9215, Chattanooga, TN 37412

APPENDIX FIVE:

SAMPLES OF VARIOUS FORMS

A Sample Church Membership Covenant

Having been brought together providentially by our common relationship to Jesus Christ as our Savior, and having a mutual desire to serve Him faithfully as our Lord, we do now both solemnly and joyfully enter into covenant with one another as a body of Biblically baptized believers comprising a New testament local church.

WE PURPOSE THEREFORE to live daily by the strength and guidance of God's Holy Spirit; to search the Scriptures regularly and faithfully for direction in personal, family and church life; to seek the salvation of souls for whom Christ died; to strive heartily for the building up of this Body of Christ in faith, hope and love; to function within the Body according to the gift(s) given to each one for its benefit.

WE FURTHER PURPOSE to put away from us progressively the patterns of thought, word and deed of the old life," putting in its place the patterns of the "Christ-life;" to do all things to the glory of God and in the name of the Lord Jesus; to exercise our Christian liberty in such a way as not to grieve, offend or cause a brother to stumble; and to recognize the Bible as the final Authority in all relationships with one another.

TO THESE ENDS WE PURPOSE to consider the local church an essential part of our lives; to pray for, encourage, and submit to the rightful authority of its leadership; to attend its meetings when not providentially hindered; to support financially its ministry as God enables and directs; to guard its public testimony; and in any way possible to further its goals of reaching the lost and edifying through instruction, exhortation and fellowship the believer.

THIS COVENANT WE MAKE GLADLY, in humble dependence upon the Spirit of God for the power to carry out its provisions.

Sample Letter Calling for an Organization Council

Date of letter

New Testament Baptist Church

Any Street

Any Town in the World

Dear Brethren:

Being a company of immersed believers who have joined ourselves together for the purpose of organizing ourselves into a local independent Baptist church on date of the organizational meeting and desiring to have fellowship with other churches of like faith and order, we request that you send your pastor and two leaders of your church to sit in council on date of the recognition meeting at the name and location where the meeting will be held to consider the propriety of recognizing us as a duly organized Baptist Church.

The council will convene at time.

The following churches and individuals have been invited: _List of the names of the churches and individuals with their addresses.

Enclosed please find copies of our charter, covenant, constitution and articles of faith for your examination prior to the meeting of the recognition council.

Done by order of and on behalf of the church.

Name of the Church______________________

Church secretary or clerk, church address, phone number and email address

Agenda for a Recognition Council

1. Congregational Song:
2. Prayer
3. Reading of the letter calling for a recognition council
4. Motion to convene the recognition council
5. Election of a moderator
6. Election of a clerk
7. Roll call of churches and individuals invited
8. Motion to seat messengers and other visitors
9. History of the new church (pastor or representative of the new church)
10. Reading of the Church Covenant (questions & answers)
11. Reading of the Church Constitution (questions & answers)
12. Reading of the Church's Articles of Faith (questions & answers)
13. Council moves into executive session for discussion
14. Motion to approve the recognition of the new church
15. Right hand of fellowship extended to the new church
16. Motion to adjourn and dissolve the council

Recognition Service Order

1. Congregational Song: Hymn # ___
2. Opening Prayer

3. Report of Council Action by Moderator

4. Scripture Reading: I Timothy 3:1-16

5. Charge to the Church

6. Prayer: Commending the Church to God

7. Congregational Song: Hymn #___

8. Charge to the Church

9. Congregational Song: Hymn #___

10. Message

11. Benediction

(Use visiting pastors or guest speakers for the various responsibilities.)

A Covenant for the Leaders and Workers of the Local Church

Having received Jesus Christ as my Personal Savior and as an active baptized member in good standing of the Name of the Church, I fully recognize the great privilege that it is for me to serve as a leader and worker in the Church ministry. I recognize and accept the responsibility of being, "an example to the believers in word, conduct, love, spirit, faith and purity." I promise to strive, with the help of the Holy Spirit, to fulfill my obligations and responsibilities as a leader and to always abide by this covenant.

1. I subscribe willingly to the doctrinal position, the practice, and program of this church and I promise that I will support it both publically and in private.
2. I promise, as a leader, to be faithful in attendance to the services and activities of the church (Hebrews 10:25)
3. I promise to support the ministry of the church through my prayers, my presence, and my finances.

4. I will be loyal to the members and the leaders of the church, especially the pastor and staff. I will refrain from any form of gossip or criticism. If I have a problem with one or more of them I will go to them directly to seek resolution.
5. I will seek to guard my personal testimony and promise not to use tobacco products, alcoholic beverages, illicit drugs, or substances and avoid worldly activities such as the use of pornography, gambling, dancing, and other questionable practices, etc. I promise to avoid any and all things that could bring reproach upon the name of the church or the Name of our Savior, the Lord Jesus Christ. I will seek to live a godly, Christ-honoring life.
6. I promise to make daily time in personal prayer and Bible study a vital part of my life.
7. I promise to guide my wife and my children in having devotions in our home.
8. I will seek to live a godly life in my home, in the church, at work and wherever I may be.
9. I will seek to be punctual and faithful in the fulfilling of all my responsibilities and will magnify my place and position of service, recognizing that I am a servant of the King of kings and Lord of lords.
10. If for any reason I am not able to fulfill my obligations, I will notify the pastor and or other leaders of the church. I realize it may be necessary for someone else to take my place of service.

Name: ______________________________

Signature: ______________________________

Date: ______________________________

APPENDIX SIX:

ACTUAL STATEMENT OF FAITH (SOF) AND BYLAWS OF A LOCAL BAPTIST CHURCH

What follows is a SOF and Bylaws used by an Independent Fundamental Baptist Church in the State of Georgia, USA, to Biblically guide their church. The preparation of the document was based upon information such as found in this work. Every church should develop their own SOF and Bylaws by carefully using the examples in this work and diligently constructing guidelines for their church.

Please note that the **page numbers** for the "Table of Contents" and "Index of Words and Phrases" at the end of this actual document may not be accurate in this book. The document was prepared by several members of a local Baptist church from several sources that included suggestions from the Christian Law Association whose web address is: http://www.christianlaw.org/cla/index.php. The document was approved by the unanimous vote of the church.

TABLE OF CONTENTS

TABLE OF CONTENTS 171
ARTICLE 1—NAME AND PURPOSE 177
SECTION 1.01—NAME 177
SECTION 1.02—PURPOSE 177
ARTICLE 2—STATEMENT OF FAITH AND COVENANT 177
SECTION 2.01—STATEMENT OF FAITH 177
I. THE HOLY SCRIPTURES: THE BIBLE 177
A. Its Inspiration and Inerrancy: 178
B. Its Supreme Standard: 179
C. Its Preservation: 179
D. It's Proper Original Language Texts: 179
E. Its Interpretation: 180
F. Its Words were "once delivered" to the prophets and apostles: 180
G. Its Faithful English Translation: 180

a. The Superiority Of The King James Bible: 180
b. The Use Of The King James Bible: 180
II. THE TRIUNE GOD: THE GODHEAD 181
III. THE LORD JESUS CHRIST--HIS VIRGIN BIRTH 182
A. THE LORD JESUS CHRIST: HIS PERSON: 182
B. THE LORD JESUS CHRIST: HIS BLOOD: 183
C. THE LORD JESUS CHRIST: HIS BLOOD ATONEMENT: 184
D. THE LORD JESUS CHRIST--HIS BODILY RESURRECTION, BODILY ASCENSION, HIGH PRIESTHOOD, AND BODILY RETURN 185
a. His Bodily Resurrection: 185
b. The Lord's Descent: 185
c. His Bodily Ascension: 185
d. His High Priestly Work: 185
e. His Bodily Return: The Second Coming: 186
IV. GOD THE HOLY SPIRIT 186
A. His Person And Presence: 186
B. His Ministries: 187
C. His Temporary Gifts: 187
D. His Counterfeit: 187
V. THE CREATION OF THE UNIVERSE 188
VI. THE CREATION AND FALL OF MAN 188
VII. THE CHRISTIAN'S TWO NATURES 189
VIII. THE CHRISTIAN'S SERVICE 189
IX. SATAN AND FALLEN AND UNFALLEN ANGELS 190
A. Satan's Creation And Fall: 190
B. Satan's Influences: 190
C. Satan's Judgment: 191
D. Unfallen Angels: 191
E. Man Lower Than The Angels: 191
F. Fallen Angels: 191
X. THE FALL OF MAN 192
XI. THE RIGHTEOUS AND THE WICKED 192
XII. SALVATION ONLY THROUGH CHRIST 192
A. The Basis Of Salvation: 192
B. The Means Of Salvation: 193
C. The Reception Of Salvation: 194
XIII. THE NEW BIRTH 194
A. The Definition Of The New Birth: 194
B. The Results Of The New Birth: 194
XIV. JUSTIFICATION 195
XV. SANCTIFICATION 196
XVI. THE ETERNAL SECURITY OF BELIEVERS 196
XVII. THE ASSURANCE OF THE BELIEVERS 197
XVIII. THE CHURCH 198
A. Definition Of The Church: 198

STATEMENT OF FAITH

ARTICLE 1—NAME AND PURPOSE

SECTION 1.01—NAME

This congregation of believers shall be known as the ________________________ Baptist Church.

SECTION 1.02—PURPOSE

This congregation is organized as a church exclusively for charitable, religious, and educational purposes within the meaning of *Section 501(c)(3)* of the Internal Revenue Code of 1986 (or the corresponding provision of any future United States Revenue Law), including, but not limited to, for such purposes, the establishing and maintaining of religious worship, the building of churches, parsonages, schools, chapels, radio stations, television stations, rescue missions, print shops, daycare centers, and camps; the evangelizing of the unsaved by the proclaiming of the Gospel of the Lord Jesus Christ; the educating of believers in a manner consistent with the requirements of Holy Scripture, both in Sunday and weekday schools of Christian education; and the maintaining of missionary activities in the United States and any foreign country.

ARTICLE 2—STATEMENT OF FAITH AND COVENANT

SECTION 2.01—STATEMENT OF FAITH

The following comprise the Scriptural beliefs of this church and its members.

I. THE HOLY SCRIPTURES: THE BIBLE

A. Its Inspiration and Inerrancy:

We believe in the authority and sufficiency of the Holy Bible, consisting of the sixty-six books of the Old and New Testaments (Genesis through Revelation); that the sixty-six books of the Bible are a completed revelation; that the process of its Divine inspiration has never been, nor will it ever be, duplicated; that the entire Bible was originally written by a process of the plenary, verbal, inspiration of God; that the Bible is infallible and of unlimited inerrancy in the areas of creation, science, geography, chronology, history, and in all other matters of which it speaks **(2 Timothy 3:16-17; 2 Peter 1:21; 1 Thessalonians 2:13; John 17:17)**; that the books known as the *Apocrypha* are not the inspired Word of God in any sense whatever; that, as the Bible uses it, the term "inspiration" (or the process of being "God-breathed") refers to the **original writings**, *not* to the writers **(2 Timothy 3:16-17; 1 Corinthians 2:13)**; and that the writers are spoken of as being "holy men of God' who were "moved" (or "carried" or "borne" along) by the Holy Spirit **(2 Peter 1:21; Acts 1:16)** in such a definite way that their writings were supernaturally, plenarily, and verbally inspired, free from any error, infallible, and inerrant, as no other **writings** have ever been or ever will be inspired **(2 Timothy 3:16-17)**. We believed the inspired Words of the faith were *"once delivered"* **(Jude 1:3)** and the Words were preserved **(Psalm 12:6-7)**. We believe God has supernaturally superintended the preservation of those original autographs in the apographs of Hebrew Masoretic Text and the Greek Traditional Text more commonly known as the Received Text. We are therefore committed to using only the English translation known as the King James Version as the most accurate and faithful translation of those preserved autographs. **(Psalm 19:7-11; 2 Timothy 3:16-17; 2 Peter 1:16-21; Luke 24:13-28; John 16:12-16; Psalm 12:6-7; Isaiah 40:8; Psalm 138:2).** We believe God chose every Word in the original autographs and breathed out those words to be recorded by God's chosen secretaries in the Old Testament prophets and the Apostles of the Lord Jesus Christ. We believe this revelation ceased with the writing of the Revelation of Jesus Christ. Plenary Inspiration:

Plenary inspiration asserts that God inspired the complete text(s) of the Bible, from Genesis to Revelation, including both historical and doctrinal details.

B. Its Supreme Standard:

We believe that all the Scriptures center about the Lord Jesus Christ and His person and work in His first and second coming; that no portion, even of the Old Testament, is properly read or understood, until it leads to Him **(Luke 24:27, 44; John 5:39; Acts 17:2-3; 18:28; 26:22-23; 28:23)**; that all the Bible was designed for our practical instruction **(Mark 12:26, 36; 2 Timothy 3:16-17)**; that the Bible is to be the true center of Christian unity **(John 17:17)**; that it is the supreme standard by which all human conduct, creeds, and opinions shall be tried **(2 Corinthians 5:10; Revelation 20:12)**; and that the subjects of this judgment include all groups and individuals.

C. Its Preservation:

We believe God has promised in both the Old and New Testaments to preserve His Words as given to us in the original Hebrew/Aramaic and Greek texts **(Psalm 12:6-7; 78:1-8; 119:89, 111, 152, 160; Isaiah 30:8; 40:6-8; Ecclesiastes 3:14; Matthew 4-4; 5:17-18; 24:35; 28:20; John 10:35; Colossians 1:17; 1 Peter 1:23-25; 2 John 1:2** and elsewhere**)**; that, by His Providential care, God has kept His Word pure down through the ages as He promised; and we believe what our Baptist forefathers wrote in their London Baptist Confession of 1677 and 1689, which states in part:

> *"The Old Testament in Hebrew, (which was the native language of the people of God of old), and the New Testament Greek (which at the time of the writing of it was most generally known to the nations) BEING IMMEDIATELY INSPIRED BY GOD, and BY HIS SINGULAR CARE AND PROVIDENCE **KEPT PURE IN ALL AGES**, are therefore AUTHENTICAL*

D. It's Proper Original Language Texts:

We believe that the original language Texts which have been Providentially preserved and are the closest to the original autographs of the Bible are the Old Testament Traditional Masoretic Hebrew Text that underlies the King James Bible, and the New Testament Traditional Greek Text that underlies the King James Bible (as found in *The Greek Text Underlying The English Authorized Version of 1611* as published by the Trinitarian Bible Society in 1976).

E. Its Interpretation:

The Scriptures shall be interpreted according to their normal grammatical-historical meaning, and all issues of interpretation and meaning shall be determined by the pastor. The King James Version of the Bible shall be the official and only translation used by the church **(2 Timothy 3:16-17; 2 Peter 1:20-21)**.

F. Its Words were "once delivered" to the prophets and apostles:

> *Jude 1:3 "Beloved, when I gave all diligence to write unto you of the common salvation, it was needful for me to write unto you, and exhort you that ye should earnestly contend for* ***the faith which was once delivered unto the saints.****"*

G. Its Faithful English Translation:

a. The Superiority Of The King James Bible:

We believe that the King James Bible (or Authorized Version) of the English Bible is a true, faithful and accurate translation of these two Providentially preserved Texts, which in our time has no equal among all of the other English Translations; that the translators did such a fine job in their translation task that we can without apology hold up the King James Bible and say "This is the WORD OF GOD in English!"; that, in some verses, we must go back to the underlying original **language Texts for complete clarity; and that we must** compare Scripture with Scripture.

b. The Use Of The King James Bible:

We believe that the King James Bible should be used in all preaching services, in the Sunday School, in all Christian literature and publications, in all memory work, and in all other places; that all the verses in the King James Bible belong in the Old and the New Testaments because they represent words that were in the original Texts; and that, though there might be other renderings from the original languages (e.g. archaic words) which could also be acceptable to us today, for an exhaustive study of any of the words or verses in the Bible, the student should return directly to the Traditional Masoretic Hebrew Text and the Traditional Received Greek Text rather than to any other translation for help.

II. THE TRIUNE GOD: THE GODHEAD

We believe in the Deity, unity, equality, and eternality of the Triune God: God the Father, God the Son, and God the Holy Spirit **(Genesis 1:26; Matthew 28:18-19; John 1:14; 16:7-18; 2 Corinthians 13:14; Hebrews 1:1-3; 1 John 5:1-8)**; that these Three are one God, having precisely the same nature, attributes, and perfections **(Deuteronomy 6:4; Matthew 28:19; Mark 12:29; John 14:10, 26; Acts 5:3-4; 2 Corinthians 13:14; Revelation 1:4-6)**; that They are worthy of precisely the same homage, confidence, and obedience; that this Triune God is the One and only living and true God **(Exodus 20:2-3; 1 Corinthians 8:6)**; that He is everlasting, immutable, of infinite power, wisdom, holiness, justice, goodness, and truth **(Revelation 4:11)**; and that He is the Maker and Preserver of all things, both visible and invisible; subsisting in Three Persons, of one substance, power, and eternity **(Genesis 1:1; John 1:3; Colossians 1:15-16)**.

III. THE LORD JESUS CHRIST--HIS VIRGIN BIRTH

We believe that, as provided and proposed by God and as preannounced in the prophecies of the Scriptures, the eternal Son of God came into this world that He might manifest God to men, fulfill prophecy, and become the Redeemer of a lost world **(Genesis 3:15; Isaiah 7:14)**; that He was begotten of the Holy Spirit in a miraculous manner, born of Mary, a virgin, as no other man was ever born or can be born of woman **(Matthew 1:18-25; Luke 1:35)**; that He received a perfect human body and a sinless human nature; and that He is both the eternal Son of God and God the Son—perfect God and perfect Man **(John 1:14, 18; Hebrews 4:15)**.

A. THE LORD JESUS CHRIST: HIS PERSON:

We believe in the essential, absolute, eternal Deity, and the real and proper, but perfect and sinless, humanity of our Lord Jesus Christ; that Christ is the eternal Son of God, and God the Son, the Second Person of the Trinity, being very and eternal God, of one substance and equal with the Father **(John 1:1-2, 10:30)**; that when the fulness of time was come, He took upon Him man's nature, with all the essential properties thereof, including a perfect human spirit, soul, and body, yet without sin; that He was conceived by the power of the Holy Spirit in the womb of the virgin Mary, of her substance; that the two whole, perfect and distinct natures, the Godhead and Manhood, were inseparably joined together in one Person, without conversion, composition, or confusion; that this Person is very God and very Man, yet one Christ, the only Mediator between God and man **(John 1:14; Philippians 2:5-8; 2 Corinthians 5:17-21)**; that, on the human side, Christ became and remained a perfect man **(Luke 2:40; 2 Corinthians 5:21)**; that He was without sin throughout His life; that He could not sin; that He retained His absolute deity, being at the same time very God and very man; and that His earth-life sometimes functioned within the sphere of that which was human and sometimes within the sphere of that which was divine **(2 Corinthians 5:21; Hebrews 4:15; Matthew 9:4; 14:15-21; Luke 4:30; John 2:7-11; John 11:35).**

We believe that the Lord Jesus Christ in His human nature thus united to the Divine, was sanctified, anointed with the Holy Spirit above measure; that He had within Him all the treasures of wisdom and knowledge; that it pleased the Father that in Him all fulness should dwell; that He was holy, harmless, undefiled, and full of grace and truth; and that He was thoroughly furnished to execute the office of Mediator and Surety and to make intercession for us. **(Matthew 21:18; Luke 4:2; Romans 8:34; John 1:14; 10:30; 1 Timothy 2:5; Hebrews 7:24-25; 1 John 2:1-2)**

B. THE LORD JESUS CHRIST: HIS BLOOD:

We believe that the doctrine of the Blood of the Lord Jesus Christ is of great importance in the Bible; that Christ's Blood has been under attack in centuries past as well as in recent decades by modernist apostates (there are many), that Christ's Blood is not a mere figure of speech or "metonym" to be equal to "death"; that Old Testament sacrifices had two distinct parts: **(1)** the death of the sacrifice; and **(2)** the application of the blood of the sacrifice; that death was not sufficient, but the blood had to be applied properly **(Exodus 12:6-7; Leviticus 16:6, 14, 15)**; that it is the blood that makes "atonement for the soul" **(Leviticus 17:11)**; that Christ's Blood was "shed for the remission of sins" **(Matthew 26:28)**; that Christ's Blood "purchased" the Church **(Acts 20:28)**; that Christ's Blood was from God, as to its source, hence, it is Divine **(Acts 20:28)**; that Christ's Blood provides redemption **(Ephesians 1:7; Colossians 1:14; 1 Peter 1:18-19; Revelation 5:9)**; that Christ's Blood is incorruptible **(1 Peter 1:18-19)**; that Christ's Blood propitiates God the Father; that Christ's Blood justifies us through faith **(Romans 5:1, 9)**; that Christ's Blood brings us near to God **(Ephesians 2:13)**; that Christ's Blood gives us peace **(Colossians 1:20)**; that Christ's Blood provides forgiveness **(Ephesians 1:7; Colossians 1:14; Hebrews 9:22)**; that Christ's Blood provides reconciliation to God **(Colossians 1:20)**; that Christ's Blood purges the conscience **(Hebrews 9:14)**, purifies the heavenly things **(Hebrews 9:22-23)**, cleanses us from all sin **(1 John 1:7)**, and washes us from our sins **(Revelation 1:5; 7:14)**; that some of Christ's Blood was taken by Him to heaven and placed on the heavenly mercy seat thus cleansing the heavenly tabernacle **(Hebrews 9:12-14; 18-24; 10:19-22)**; that Christ's Blood is now in heaven as the "Blood of sprinkling" **(Hebrews 12:22-24)**; that Christ's Blood gives us boldness and access to the holiest in heaven **(Hebrews 10:19)**; that Christ's Blood makes us perfect in every good work to do His will **(Hebrews 13:20-21)**; and that Christ's Blood overcomes Satan **(Revelation 12:11)**.

C. THE LORD JESUS CHRIST: HIS BLOOD ATONEMENT:

We believe that Christ was made like unto us in all things, sin and its consequences only excepted, from which He was clearly void, both in His flesh and in His spirit; that in fulfillment of prophecy He came first to Israel as her Messiah-King, and was rejected of that nation; He, according to the eternal counsels of God, gave His life as a ransom for all **(John 1:11; Acts 2:23; 1 Timothy 2:6)**; that He came to be the Lamb without spot, Who, by the shedding of His incorruptible Blood in the sacrifice of Himself once made, **(1 Peter 1:18-19; Acts 20:28)** takes away the sin of the world **(John 1:29)**; that in Him is no sin **(1 John 3:5)**; that all the rest of us, although born again in Christ by faith, offend in many things; and that if we say we have no sin, we deceive ourselves, and the truth is not in us **(1 John 1:10)**.

We believe that, in infinite love for the lost, Christ voluntarily accepted His Father's will and became the divinely provided sacrificial Lamb whose shed Blood took away the sin of the world **(John 1:29)**; that He bore the holy judgments against sin which the righteousness of God must impose **(Romans 3:25-26)**; that His death was, therefore, substitutionary in the most absolute sense, "the just for the unjust" **(1 Peter 3:18; 2 Corinthians 5:14; Hebrews 10:5-14)**; that by His sacrificial death and the shedding of His Blood He became the Savior of the lost.

D. THE LORD JESUS CHRIST--HIS BODILY RESURRECTION, BODILY ASCENSION, HIGH PRIESTHOOD, AND BODILY RETURN

a. <u>His Bodily Resurrection:</u>

We believe that, according to the Scriptures, Christ arose from the dead in the same body, though glorified, in which He had lived and died **(Matthew 28:6-7; Mark 16:6; Luke 24:2-7; 39-40; John 20:20, 27; Acts 2:27-31; 5:30; 13:34-37; 1 Corinthians 15:4)**; and that His resurrection body is the pattern of that body which ultimately will be given to all believers. **(Philippians 3:20-21.)**.

b. <u>The Lord's Descent:</u>

After His death by the shedding His precious blood, He descended into Paradise and led captivity captive **(Leviticus 17:11; Eph. 4:8-9)**, which consisted of all Old Testament saints saved by faith in the God of the Bible Who gave His only begotten Son as our Saviour **(John 1:18)**.

c. <u>His Bodily Ascension:</u>

We believe that in departing from the earth in His resurrection body, Christ ascended into Heaven **(Mark 16:19; Luke 24:51; John 20:17; Acts 1:9-11)**; that there in heaven He presented His Blood on the Divine Mercy Seat in fulfillment of the Day of Atonement type **(Leviticus 16:14-15, 17; John 20:17; Hebrews 9:7, 12-14, 22, 24; 12:22-24)**; and that He was accepted of His Father and that His acceptance is a final assurance to us that His **redeeming work was** perfectly accomplished **(Hebrews 1:3)**.

d. <u>His High Priestly Work:</u>

We believe that, in Heaven, He now sits at the right hand of God the Father as our Great High Priest and as our Advocate, interceding for His own **(Mark 16:19; 1 Timothy 2:5; Hebrews 1:3; 2:17; 5:9-10; 7:25; 9:25; 12:2; 1 John 2:1)**; that He became Head over all things to the church which is His body; and that, in this ministry He ceases not to intercede and advocate for the saved.

e. His Bodily Return: The Second Coming:

We believe that Christ will return in this same body to fulfill all the Scriptures pertaining to the events surrounding His Second Coming **(Acts 1:9-11)**; that He will come first in the Rapture of the Church before the Tribulation of seven years **(1 Thessalonians 4:13-18; 5:6-10; 1 Corinthians 15:50-57; Acts 1:10-11; Titus 2:11-14)**; that He will then return in power and glory to set up the Millennial reign and to execute judgment upon the ungodly nations before the inauguration of His earthly millennial reign **(Zechariah 14:4; Matthew 24:29-31; 25:31-36; 2 Thessalonians 1:7-8; Jude 1:14-15; Revelation 1:7; 3:21)**. The Lord will then cast the Antichrist and the false prophet into the lake of fire, send Satan into the abyss, and establish His earthly Davidic throne. The Lord Jesus Christ will reign one thousand years, this literally fulfilling the covenant promises made to a believing remnant of Israel through the Patriarchs of the Old Testament. **(Isaiah 11:1-16; Revelation 19:19-21; 20:1-6).** After the earthly reign of one thousand years, Jesus will bring all the unsaved dead to the judgment of the Great White Throne and all who stand before that Throne will be cast into the lake of fire forever. Satan will also be cast into the lake of fire at that time **(Revelation 20:7-15; Matthew 7:21-23)**.

IV. GOD THE HOLY SPIRIT

A. His Person And Presence:

We believe that the Holy Spirit, proceeding from the Father and the Son, is of one substance, majesty, and glory, with the Father and the Son, very and eternal God; that the Holy Spirit is a Divine Person, equal with God the Father and God the Son and of the same nature; that He was active in creation **(Genesis 1:1-3)**; that the Holy Spirit, the Third Person of the blessed Trinity, though omnipresent from all eternity, took up His abode in the world in a special sense on the day of Pentecost according to the Divine promise; that He dwells in every believer; that, as the Indwelling One, He is the source of all power and all acceptable worship and service; that He never takes His departure from the church, nor from the feeblest of the saints **(John 14:16-17; 16:7; 1 Corinthians**

6:19; Ephesians 2:22); that He is ever present to testify of Christ, seeking to occupy believers with Him and not with themselves nor with their experiences **(John 16:14)**; that His abode in the world in this special sense will cease when Christ comes to receive His own at the completion of the church in the Rapture **(2 Thessalonians 2:7)**.

B. His Ministries:

We believe that, in this age, certain well-defined ministries are committed to the Holy Spirit, and that it is the duty of every Christian to understand them and to be adjusted to them in his own life and experience; that He restrains evil in the world to the measure of the divine will; that He convicts the world respecting sin, righteousness, and judgment **(John 16:7-11)**; that He regenerates all believers **(John 3:6)**; that He indwells and anoints all who are saved **(Matthew 28:20; John 14:16-17; Acts 5:32; Romans 8:9, 15, 23; 1 Corinthians 6:19; 1 John 2:20-27)**; that He seals believers unto the day of redemption **(Ephesians 1:13-14; 4:30)**; that He baptizes into the one body of Christ of all who are saved **(Mark 1:8; John 1:33; Acts 11:16; 1 Corinthians 12:13)**; that He intercedes for the believers **(Romans 8:26-27)**; and that He fills for power, leading, bearing witness, teaching, and service those among the saved who are yielded to Him and who are subjects to His will **(Luke 24:49; Acts 1:8; John 14:26; Acts 4:8, 31; Romans 8:14, 16; Ephesians 5:18)**.

C. His Temporary Gifts:

We believe that some gifts of the Holy Spirit such as speaking in tongues and miraculous healings were temporary; that speaking in tongues was never the common or necessary sign of the baptism or the filling of the Spirit; and that the deliverance of the body from sickness or death awaits the consummation of our salvation in the resurrection **(1 Corinthians 13:8-12)**.

D. His Counterfeit:

We believe the *Charismatic Tongues Movement* is an unscriptural error relating to God the Holy Spirit and is not of God; that genuine tongues in the New Testament were authentic languages rather than the present ecstatic utterances which are counterfeit and spurious; that the sign gifts such as speaking in tongues, interpretation of tongues, special knowledge, and others, were all sign gifts which were manifested during the Apostolic age; that all such sign gifts ceased with the completion of the New Testament canon around 90 or 100 A.D. **(1 Corinthians 13:8-12)**; that this movement seeks to unite apostates with believers in an unscriptural, ecumenical movement; and that true believers should separate from the Charismatic Tongues Movement immediately and completely **(2 Corinthians 6:14-7:1; Ephesians 5:11)**.

V. THE CREATION OF THE UNIVERSE

We believe the Biblical account of the creation of the physical universe, angels, and man *ex nihilo* **(Genesis 1-2; Colossians 1:16-17; John 1:3)** and that this account is neither allegory nor myth, but a literal, historical account of the direct, immediate creative acts of the Triune God in six literal solar days without any evolutionary process, either naturalistic or theistic. **(Genesis 1:5, 8, 13, 19, 23, 31)**. We reject the theory of evolution in any form. This rejection necessarily includes the so-called theistic evolution and the gap theory to be contradictory to the clear teaching of Scripture.

VI. THE CREATION AND FALL OF MAN

We believe that man was created by a direct work of the Triune God and not from previously existing forms of life **(Genesis 1:1-2, 26-27; 2:7)**; and that all men are descended from the historical Adam and Eve, the first parents of the entire human race; that man fell through sin **(Genesis 2:17; 3:6)**; that, as a consequence of his sin, man lost his spiritual life and innocence, becoming dead in trespasses and sins **(Genesis 6:5; Psalm 14:1-3; 51:5; Jeremiah 17:9; John 3:6)**; that he became susceptible to the power of the devil; that this spiritual death, or total depravity of human nature, has been transmitted to the entire human race of man, the Man

Christ Jesus alone being excepted; and that every child of Adam is born into the world with a nature, which not only possesses no spark of divine life, but is essentially and unchangeably bad apart from divine grace and faith in Christ. We believe in the universality and exceeding sinfulness of sin **(Romans 3:10-19; 8:6-7; Ephesians 2:1-3, 8-10; 1 Timothy 5:6)**.

VII. THE CHRISTIAN'S TWO NATURES

We believe that a saved person has two natures, the old nature (the flesh), and the new nature (the indwelling Holy Spirit) **(1 Corinthians 6:19-20; 2 Corinthians 5:17-18; Romans 7:15-25; Galatians 5:16-17)**; that we are called with an holy calling, to walk not after the flesh, but after the Spirit **(Romans 8:1-2, 4)**; that we should live in the power of the indwelling Spirit so that we will not fulfill the lust of the flesh **(Romans 6:11-13; 8:12-13; Galatians 5:16-23; Ephesians 4:22-24)**; that the flesh, with its fallen, Adamic nature, in this life is never eradicated **(Galatians 5:16-17; John 3:6)**; that it is with us to the end of our earthly pilgrimage **(John 3:6; 1 John 1:8, 10)**; and that it needs to be kept by the Spirit constantly in subjection to Christ, or it will surely manifest its presence in our lives to the dishonor of our Lord **(1 Peter 1:14-16; 1 John 3:5-9)**.

VIII. THE CHRISTIAN'S SERVICE

A. We believe that Divine, enabling gifts for service are bestowed by the Holy Spirit upon all who are saved **(Romans 12:6-8; 1 Corinthians 12:4-11)**; that, while there is a diversity of gifts, each believer is energized by the same Spirit; that each believer is called to his own divinely appointed service as the Spirit may will; that in the Apostolic church there were certain gifted men—apostles, prophets, evangelists, pastors and teachers—who were appointed by God for the perfecting of the saints unto their work of the ministry **(Ephesians 4:11-15)**; that today there are no apostles or prophets, but there are still some men who are especially called of God to be evangelists, pastor-teachers; and that it is to the fulfilling of His will and to His eternal glory that these gifted men shall be sustained and encouraged in their service for God; and that these gifts of evangelists and pastor-teachers are not given to children and women **(1 Corinthians 14:34-35; 1 Timothy 2:11-14)**.

B. Women are allowed by Scripture to teach other women and children **(Titus 2:4)**.

IX. SATAN AND FALLEN AND UNFALLEN ANGELS

A. Satan's Creation And Fall:

We believe that God created an innumerable company of spiritual beings, known as angels; that one, "Lucifer, son of the morning"—the highest in rank—sinned through pride, thereby becoming Satan **(Isaiah 14:12-17; Ezekiel 28:11-19; 1 Timothy 3:6)**; that a great company of the angels followed him in his moral fall; that some of them became demons and are active as his agents and associates in the prosecution of his unholy purposes; and that others who fell are "reserved in everlasting chains under darkness unto the judgment of the great day" **(2 Peter 2:4; Jude 1:6)**. Although fallen angels are referred to in the masculine gender, they are spirit beings and unable to reproduce **(Psalm 104:4; Hebrews 1:14; Matthew 22:30; Mark 12:25)**.

B. Satan's Influences:

We believe that Satan is the originator of sin **(Genesis 3:1-19; 5:12-14)**; that, under the permission of God, he, through subtilty, led our first parents into transgression, thereby accomplishing their moral fall and subjecting them and their posterity to his own power **(2 Corinthians 4:3-4; Ephesians 6:10-12)**; that he is the enemy of God and the people of God, opposing and exalting himself above all that is called God or that is worshiped **(2 Thessalonians 2:4)**; that he who in the beginning said, "I will be like the most High," in his warfare appears as an angel of light **(2 Corinthians 11:13-15)**; that he counterfeits the works of God by fostering religious movements and systems of doctrine **(1 Timothy 4:1-3)**; and that these systems in every case are characterized by a denial of the efficacy of the Blood of Christ and of salvation by grace alone. Satan is actively opposing the cause of Christ on every hand and is the archenemy of every true believer. His warfare incorporates the deception of mixing error and truth as well as that which is flagrantly vile and evil **(2 Corinthians 11:1-15; 1 Peter 5:8-9; Ephesians 6:10-13; Revelation 12:9-11; Matthew 4:1-11; John 8:21-24)**.

C. Satan's Judgment:

We believe that Satan was judged at the cross, though not then executed **(Colossians 2:15)**; that he, as usurper, now rules as the "god of this world" **(2 Corinthians 4:3-4)**; that at the second coming of Christ, Satan will be bound and cast into the abyss for a thousand years **(Revelation 20:1-3, 10)**; that after the thousand years, he will be loosed for a little season **(Revelation 20:7)**; and that he will then be "cast into the lake of fire and brimstone, where he *"shall be tormented day and night for ever and ever"* **(Revelation 20:10)**.

Unfallen Angels:

We believe that a great company of angels kept their holy estate and are before the throne of God **(Luke 15:10; Ephesians 1:21; Revelation 7:11-12)**; and that they are sent forth from God as ministering spirits to minister to them who shall be heirs of salvation **(Hebrews 1:14)**.

D. Man Lower Than The Angels:

We believe that man was made lower than the angels **(Hebrews 2:6-7)**; that, in His incarnation, Christ took for a little time this lower place that He might lift the believer to His own sphere above the angels **(Hebrews 2:6-10)**.

E. Fallen Angels:

We believe Satan marshals a host of fallen angels that can also serve to deceive the unsuspecting by "transforming themselves into...apostles of Christ and ministers of righteousness..." **(2 Corinthians 11:13, 15).** These false spirits can influence the unfaithful servant to say helpful and even true things and can also themselves energize people to do the miraculous. Therefore, every experience and teaching must be examined in light of the Words of God to determine its true source **(Isaiah 8:19-22; 1 John 4:1-3)**.

X. THE FALL OF MAN

We believe that man was created in innocence, in the image and likeness of God, and under the law of his Maker **(Genesis 1:26)**; that by voluntary transgression Adam fell from his state of innocence **(Genesis 3:1-6)**; that all men sinned in him **(Romans 5:12, 19)**; and that because of this all men are totally depraved, are partakers of Adam's fallen nature, are sinners by nature and conduct **(Romans 3:10-19)**, and that all men are under just condemnation without defense or excuse **(Romans 1:18, 20)**.

XI. THE RIGHTEOUS AND THE WICKED

We believe that there is a radical and essential difference between the righteous and the wicked **(Proverbs 14:32; Malachi 3:18; Genesis 18:23; Romans:1:17-18)**; that only those who are justified by faith in our Lord Jesus Christ and sanctified by the Spirit of our God are truly righteous in His sight **(John 8:32; Romans 6:23)**; that all such as continue in impenitence and unbelief are in His sight wicked and under the curse **(1 John 5:19)**; that this distinction holds among men both in and after death; that the saved will enter into the joys of heaven **(John 14:1-3; Philippians 1:23; 2 Corinthians 5:6-8)**; and that the lost will undergo everlasting conscious suffering in hell's lake of fire **(Matthew 25:41; Revelation 20:14-15)**.

XII. SALVATION ONLY THROUGH CHRIST

A. The Basis Of Salvation:

We believe that the salvation of sinners is Divinely initiated and wholly of grace through the mediatorial offices of Jesus Christ, the eternal Son of God **(Jonah 2:9)**; that Christ, by the appointment of the Father, voluntarily took upon Himself our nature, yet without sin **(Matthew 18:11; Philippians 2:7-8; Hebrews 2:14-17)**; that He honored the Divine law by His personal obedience, thus qualifying Himself to be our Savior; that He shed His incorruptible Blood in His death **(Leviticus 17:11; 1 Peter 1:18-19)**; that He fully satisfied the just demands of a holy and righteous God regarding sin **(Galatians 3:13)**; that His Blood sacrifice consisted not in setting us an example by His death as a martyr **(Matthew 26:28)**; and that this sacrifice was a voluntary substitution of Himself in the sinner's place, the Just dying for the unjust, Christ the Lord bearing our sins in His own body on the tree **(Isaiah 53:4-7; Romans 3:25; 1 Corinthians 15:3; 2 Corinthians 5:21; 1 Peter 2:24; 3:18; 1 John 4:10)**.

B. The Means Of Salvation:

We believe that, owing to universal death through sin, no one can enter the kingdom of God unless born again; that no degree of reformation however great, no attainments in morality however high, no culture however attractive, no baptism or other ordinance however administered, can help the sinner to take even one step toward heaven **(Isaiah 64:6; John 3:5, 18; Galatians 6:15; Philippians 3:4-9)**; that a new nature imparted from above, a new life implanted by the Holy Spirit through the Word, is absolutely essential to salvation **(John 3:16; Acts 15:11; 1 Peter 1:23; Ephesians 2:8-9)**; that only those thus saved are sons of God; that our redemption has been accomplished solely by the Blood of our Lord Jesus Christ **(Leviticus 17:11; Ephesians 1:7; 1 Peter 1:18-19)**; that He was made to be sin and was made a curse for us, dying in our place and stead **(Romans 5:6-9; 2 Corinthians 5:21; Titus 3:5)**; and that no repentance, no feeling, no faith, no good resolutions, no sincere efforts, no "lordship salvation," no submission to the rules and regulations of any church, nor all the churches that have existed since the days of the Apostles, can add in the very least degree to the value of the Blood, or to the merit of the finished work wrought for us by Him who united in His Person true and proper Deity with perfect and sinless humanity **(Ephesians 2:8-9; Titus 3:5; James 1:18)**.

C. The Reception Of Salvation:

We believe that the new birth of the believer comes only through faith in Christ **(John 1:12; 3:16, 18, 36; 5:24; 6:29; Acts 13:39; 16:31; Romans 1:16-17; 3:22, 24-26; 4:5; 10:4; Galatians 3:22)**; that repentance is a vital part of believing; that repentance is in no way, in itself, a separate and independent condition of salvation; and that no other acts, such as confession, "lordship salvation," baptism, prayer, or faithful service, is to be added to believing as a condition of salvation.

XIII. THE NEW BIRTH

A. The Definition Of The New Birth:

We believe that in order to be saved, sinners must be born again **(John 3:3, 5; Ephesians 2:1, 5; 1 John 5:1)**; that the new birth is a new creation in Christ Jesus **(2 Corinthians 5:17; Colossians 2:13; John 3:8)**; that it happens the instant a person believes on and receives the Lord Jesus Christ as personal Savior **(Acts 16:30-31)**; that it is instantaneous and not a process **(John 5:24)**; that in the new birth the one dead in trespasses and in sins is made a partaker of the divine nature and receives eternal life, the free gift of God **(Romans 3:23; 6:23)**; that the new creation is brought about by our sovereign God when we exercise personal faith in the Lord Jesus Christ; that this faith comes about under the convicting power of the Holy Spirit in connection with our voluntary faith in the gospel of Christ; that its proper evidence appears in a transformed and holy life.

B. The Results Of The New Birth:

We believe that when an unregenerate person exercises faith in Christ which is illustrated and described as such in the New Testament, he passes immediately out of spiritual death into spiritual life, and from the old creation into the new **(John 5:24; 2 Corinthians 5:17)**; that, being justified from all things, accepted before the Father according as Christ His Son is accepted, loved as Christ is loved, having his place and portion as linked to Him and one with Him forever **(John 17:23)**; that, though the saved one may have occasion to grow in the realization of His blessings and to know a fuller measure of divine power through the yielding of his life more fully to God; that he is, as soon as he is saved, in possession of every spiritual blessing and absolutely complete in Christ **(Acts 13:39; Romans 5:1; 1 Corinthians 3:21-23; Ephesians 1:3; 2 Peter 1:4; Colossians 2:10; 1 John 5:11-12)**; and that the believer is in no way required by God to seek a so-called "second blessing" or a "second work of grace."

XIV. JUSTIFICATION

A. We believe that justification is that judicial act of God whereby He declares the believer righteous upon the basis of the imputed righteousness of Christ **(Romans 3:24; 4:5; 5:1, 9; Galatians 2:16; Philippians 3:9; Titus 3:5)**; and that it is bestowed, not in consideration of any work of righteousness which we have done, but solely through faith in the Redeemer's incorruptible shed Blood **(Acts 20:28; 1 Peter 1:18-19)**.

B. The all-sufficient and "finished" work of Redemption is accomplished through the death, burial, and resurrection of Jesus and all benefits of the redemption are positionally appropriated at the moment of receiving Christ by faith. Salvation is a free gift offered to "whosoever" through faith in the one true Gospel. Adding Moralism or other religious "works" such as baptism, sacraments, or any other condition to obtain God's gift of salvation by faith alone in the finished work of Christ is a "another gospel, that is not another" that causes those trusting therein to misplace their faith and remain under God's curse **(Galatians 1:6-9; Galatians 5:2-9; Romans 1:16-17; 1 Corinthians 15:1-11; John 5:24-27)**.

XV. SANCTIFICATION

We believe that sanctification, which is a setting-apart unto a holy God, is threefold **(2 Corinthians 1:10)**; this setting apart is already complete for every saved person because his position toward God is the same as Christ's position **(Hebrews 3:1; 10:10-14; 1 Corinthians 1:30)**; that, since the believer is in Christ, (1) he is set apart unto God in the measure in which Christ is set apart unto God; that he retains his sin nature, which cannot be eradicated in this life; that, while the standing of the Christian in Christ is perfect, his present state is no more perfect than his experience in daily life; (2) that there is a progressive sanctification wherein the Christian is to *"grow in grace,"* and to *"be changed"* by the Word of God, by the unhindered power of the Spirit, by confession of sin, and by the *"Blood of Jesus Christ His Son [that] cleanseth [him] from all sin"* **(John 17:17; 1 John 1:7, 9; 2 Corinthians 3:18; 7:1; Ephesians 4:24; 1 Thessalonians 4:3-4; 5:23; Hebrews 12:10)**; (3) that the child of God will yet be fully sanctified in his state as he is now sanctified in his standing in Christ when he shall see his Lord and shall be *"like Him"* **(Ephesians 5:25-27; 1 John 3:2; Jude 1:24-25)**.

XVI. THE ETERNAL SECURITY OF BELIEVERS

We believe that all who are truly born again are kept by God the Father and God the Son; that, because of the eternal purpose of God toward the objects of His love, because of His freedom to exercise grace toward the meritless on the ground of the propitiatory Blood of Christ **(Romans 5:9; Ephesians 1:7)**, because of the very nature of the divine gift of eternal life, because of the present and unending intercession and advocacy of Christ in heaven **(Hebrews 7:25; 1 John 2:1-2)**, because of the immutability of the unchangeable covenants of God, because of the regenerating, abiding presence of the Holy Spirit in the hearts of all who are saved **(1 Corinthians 6:19-20)**, we and all true believers everywhere, once saved shall be kept saved forever **(Philippians 1:6; 2:12-13; John 10:27-30; Romans 8:35-39; Jude 1:1; John 5:24; 13:1;**

14:16-17; 17:11; Romans 8:29-30; 1 John 5:13; Jude 1:24); that God is a holy and righteous Father; that, since He cannot overlook the sin of His children, He will, when they sin, chasten them and correct them in infinite love **(Hebrews 12:5-7)**; and that, having undertaken to save them and keep them forever, apart from all human merit, He, Who cannot fail, will in the end present every one of them faultless before the presence of His glory and conformed to the image of His Son **(Romans 8:29)**. We believe that once a lost sinner has become a "new creature in Christ," he can never lose that new relationship in the family of God which is based upon Christ's imparted righteousness **(2 Peter 1:4)** and not his own. The life that God imparts to the believing sinner is "eternal life" and by its nature cannot be terminated **(John 10:27-30; 11:25-26; 14:19-20; Romans 8:1; 35-39; Galatians 4:6-7; Hebrews 13:5; Colossians 2:9-10; Joshua 24:17; Job 7:20; Psalm 37:28; 97:10; 145:20; Proverbs 2:8; Luke 17:33; 1 Thessalonians 5:23; 2 Timothy 4:18; Jude 1:1).** Texts that supposedly teach one can lose his salvation are speaking of loss of reward, not the loss of salvation, or they speak to the right to be called a child of God. **(1 Corinthians 3:5-15; 2 John 1:7-9; Revelation 3:11-13; 1 Timothy 1:12-17; Ephesians 1:7-14; 4:20-32).**

XVII. THE ASSURANCE OF THE BELIEVERS

We believe it is the privilege, and not only of some, but of all who are born again by the Spirit through faith in Christ as revealed in the Scripture, to be assured of their salvation from the very day they take Him to be their Saviour **(Luke 10:20; 2 Corinthians 5:1, 6-8; 2 Timothy 3:12; 1 John 5:13)**; and that this assurance is not founded upon any fancied discovery of their own worthiness or fitness, but wholly upon the testimony of God in His written Word, exciting within His children filial love, gratitude, and obedience **(Luke 22:32; Hebrews 10:22)**.

XVIII. THE CHURCH

A. Definition Of The Church:

We believe that a local church is an organized congregation of immersed believers, associated by covenant of faith and fellowship of the gospel, observing the ordinances of Christ, governed by His laws, and exercising the gifts, rights and privileges invested in them by His Word **(1 Corinthians 11:2; Acts 2:41-42; 20:17-28)**; that its officers are pastors and deacons, whose qualifications, claims and duties are clearly defined in the Scriptures **(1 Timothy 3:1-13; Titus 1:5-11)**; that the true mission of the church is the faithful witnessing of Christ to all men as we have opportunity rather than the social gospel or social action **(Romans 15:26)**; that the local church has the absolute right of self-government free from the interference of any hierarchy of individuals or organizations; that the one and only Superintendent of the church is Christ through the Holy Spirit; that believers should not sue one another in secular courts **(1 Corinthians 6:1)**; that it is Scriptural for true churches to help one another, and to cooperate with each other in contending for the faith and for the furtherance of the gospel; and that each local church is the sole judge of the measure and method of its cooperation; that on all matters of membership, of polity, of government, of discipline, and of benevolence, the will of the local church is final. We believe God has ordained the ministry of the local, independent, indigenous assemblies of believers to accomplish His work in this dispensation. The local church's membership is to be composed of *"born again,"* water-baptized believers.

The church, as both a local assembly and the *"general assembly"* are Christ's body. They both exist as an organization and as a living organism consisting of all those who, in the present dispensation, truly believe and accept Jesus Christ as Saviour and confess Him as Lord. The Church as an organization and an organism exists always in local churches during the Church Age. The Church as the "general assembly" will be the organization and organism of Christ during the Kingdom Age to rule the Kingdom with Christ. Although Christ is building this Church throughout the Church Age, the "general assembly" does not become a functional entity until the rapture, which is her first call to assemble **(Romans 8:14-28; Hebrews 12:18-29; James 1:16-18; 1 Corinthians 1:1-9; Matthew 16:13-20; Revelation 2:26-27)**.

B. Beginning Of The Church:

We believe the Church Age, or the Dispensation of Grace began on the day of Pentecost **(Acts 2:1)**; and that there is a unity of all New Testament believers in the Church which is the Body of Christ as members of the family of God **(1 Corinthians 12:12-13; Ephesians 1:22-23; 3:1-6; 4:11; 5:23; Colossians 1:18; Acts 15:13-18)**.

XIX. THE CHURCH'S GREAT COMMISSION

We believe that it is the explicit message of our Lord Jesus Christ to those whom He has saved that they are sent forth by Him into the world even as He was sent forth by His Father into the world **(John 20:21)**; that after they are saved they are divinely reckoned to be related to this world as strangers and pilgrims, ambassadors and witnesses **(2 Corinthians 5:18-20; 1 Peter 1:17; 2:11)**; and that their primary purpose in life should be to make Christ known to the whole world, by means of both home and foreign missions **(Matthew 28:18-19; Mark 16:15; John 17:18; Acts 1:8)**.

XX. THE CHURCH'S TWO ORDINANCES: BAPTISM AND THE LORD'S SUPPER

A. Baptism:

We believe that Christian baptism is the single backwards immersion of a believer in water to show forth in a solemn and beautiful emblem our identification with the crucified, buried and risen Savior, through Whom we died to sin and rose to a new life **(Matthew 3:16; 28:18-20; John 3:23; Acts 8:36-39; Romans 6:3-5; Colossians 2:12)**; that baptism is to be performed under the authority of the local church; and that it is prerequisite to the privileges of church membership.

B. The Lord's Supper:

We believe that the Lord's Supper is the commemoration of Christ's death until He come **(Acts 2:41-42; 1 Corinthians 11:23-28)**; that it should be preceded by solemn self-examination; that the Biblical order of the ordinances is baptism first and then the Lord's Supper; and that participants in the Lord's Supper should be immersed believers.

We believe the church's two ordinances are to be continued until Jesus returns. The church is to be missionary and evangelistic in spreading the Gospel into all ethnicities and people groups. It is not the mission of the church to usher in the Kingdom, work for political or economic justice, major on social improvement, or Christianize society. The ministry of the Church is to strive together in faithfulness to the Gospel, *"contend earnestly for the faith,"* proclaim and maintain purity of doctrine and practice, and worship and serve the Lord in *"spirit and truth."* Scripture testimony to the truthfulness of these statements can be found in the following Scriptures: **(Acts 2:41-47; 20:17-32; Matthew 28:16-20; Ephesians 4:11-16; 1 Corinthians 11:23-34; Jude 1:3).**

C. Foot-washing is not an ordinance.

We do not believe Foot-washing is an ordinance of the church. The account in the gospel of John is the Lord's example of being humble and serving.

XXI. BIBLICAL SEPARATION

A. We believe Biblical separation is an important Bible doctrine; that we should obey the Biblical commands to separate ourselves wholly and completely unto God **(2 Corinthians 6:14-7:1; 1 Thessalonians 1:9-10; 2 John 1:9-11)**; that evil, false doctrine, and spiritual compromise are all contagious **(1 Corinthians 15:33)**; that separation from such evil is the only dependable Biblical safeguard to remain spiritually clean **(2 Corinthians 6:17)**; that we should therefore separate ourselves from worldliness, modernism, ecclesiastical apostasy, Neo-evangelicalism, the Charismatic Movement, immorality,

Biblical compromises, and "disorderly" brethren; that obedient believers should not have close fellowship either with unbelievers or with "disorderly" brethren **(2 Thessalonians 3:6, 11, 14-15; 1 Timothy 6:3-5; Romans 16:17)**; that we should repudiate cooperation with men or movements, such as the emerging church, which attempt to unite true Bible believers and apostates in evangelistic or other cooperative spiritual efforts; that we should be in sympathy with, and have close fellowship with only those organizations or movements whose speakers, associates, leaders or sponsors are NOT connected in any way with religious apostasy, neo-evangelical compromise, or charismatic confusion; that we should be in sympathy with, and have close fellowship with only those persons who speak on the platforms of men, churches, organizations or movements whose other speakers, associates, leaders or sponsors are NOT in any way connected with religious apostasy, neo-evangelical compromise, or charismatic confusion; and that we should have the above principles of Biblical separation not only stated on paper, but also put into practice. We may speak or teach at a wayward church if we are not told what to say or teach. Stated another way:

B. We believe that all Christians are to be wholly separated unto the Lord, and as a necessary result, they must be:

1. ***Separated from worldly and sinful practices.***

   They are to be holy, even as He is holy, and this desired behavior will always be diametrically opposed to the course of this present age. **(1 Peter 1:13-16; 1 Corinthians 6:19-20; Romans 12:1-3; 1 John 2:15-17.)**

2. ***Separated from apostasy and unbelief.***

   A believer must not be "unequally yoked together with unbelievers," thereby being identified with unbelief by association, whether in ministry, worship, marriage, or by joint religious activities. **(2 Corinthians 6:11-18; 1 Timothy 6:3-5; 2 Timothy 2:19-26; 2 Timothy 3:1-5; Amos 3:1-3).**

3. Separated from disobedient brethren and doctrinal compromise.

This is with respect to all ministry and service. A believer sounds an uncertain trumpet when he identifies himself with, or fellowships with, those holding to corrupted doctrinal positions and practices, thereby leading others astray. Separation from those who are not walking according to truth deters the leavening effect of compromise, and gives a faithful warning to the erring brother. **(Romans 16:17; 2 Thessalonians 3:6, 14-15; 2 John 1:10-11; Galatians 2:11; 1 Corinthians 15:33-34).**

4. We believe in total abstinence from alcohol.

The Scripture is very clear concerning this admonition, but many have corrupted the warnings in Scripture by 'claiming' Jesus made fermented wine at the wedding feast in Cana and by using a verse which has nothing to do with alcohol. Someone said: "There are many Christians who believe that you can partake in anything as long as you do it in moderation. Of course, they are thinking of things like eating, drinking (alcohol), etc. As long as you do not overindulge, then you are doing fine." They claim Philippians 4:5 indicates "everything in moderation" including alcohol. However, the cited passage concerns the control of an individual's emotions when dealing with relationships. The verses that should be used concerning the alcohol issue are those which proclaim *"be sober."* In 1 Timothy 3:2, the Bible uses the word, "vigilant." A pastor, elder, bishop must be "vigilant" (the Greek word is NEPHALOS from NEPHO). NEPHALOS and NEPHO mean "sober, temperate, **abstaining from wine, be sober**); that is NO alcohol. There are 6 other verse where these Greek words occur and include **ALL** Christians: **1 Thessalonians 5:6 ("sober"); 5:8 ("sober"); 1 Timothy 3:2 ("vigilant"); 1 Timothy 3:11 ("sober");**

2 Timothy 4:5 ("watch"); Titus 2:2 (sober"); 1 Peter 1:13 ("sober").

*1 Thessalonians 5:6 Therefore let us not sleep, as do others; but let us watch and **be sober**.*

*1 Thessalonians 5:8 But let us, who are of the day, **be sober**, putting on the breastplate of faith and love; and for an helmet, the hope of salvation.*

*1 Timothy 3:2 A bishop then must be blameless, the husband of one wife, **vigilant**, sober, of good behaviour, given to hospitality, apt to teach;*

*1 Timothy 3:11 Even so must their wives be grave, not slanderers, **sober**, faithful in all things.*

*2 Timothy 4:5 But **watch** thou in all things, endure afflictions, do the work of an evangelist, make full proof of thy ministry.*

*Titus 2:2 That the aged men **be sober**, grave, temperate, sound in faith, in charity, in patience.*

Furthermore, Jesus could not have made alcoholic wine or He would have broken the commandment in Proverbs 31:4 *"It is not for kings, O Lemuel, it is not for kings to drink wine; nor for princes strong drink:"* In addition, Jesus is called the *"King of Kings"* in Revelation 19:16. Additionally, Jesus is called the *"Prince of Peace"* in Isaiah 9:6. Again, he would have been made a sinner if he made and drank alcohol.

5. Good Works

A. We believe that all followers of the Lord Jesus Christ should maintain good works; a "good work" being that which is done in obedience to the will of God as revealed in the Word of God. Works will determine the reward or loss of reward at the **Judgment Seat of Christ before**

which every Christian will stand. Every believer must realize his responsibility before God to "maintain good works," i.e., walk in the light of the Word of God. The Bible is the believer's absolute Standard of faith and practice; his perfect Counsel. The Word provides him with "all things that pertain unto life and godliness" **(2 Peter 1:3-4)**. The Bible (Nouthetic Counseling), not any form of psychological counseling or therapy, is the answer. **(Ephesians 2:8-10; Titus 2:11-14; Titus 3:1-11; 1 Corinthians 1:18-29; 1 Corinthians 3:5-15; 2 Corinthians 5:9-11).**

B. We establish lines of demarcation by avoiding the following specific false teachings:

a. We reject as false doctrine the teaching of Monergism or Pretemporal Reprobation as part of Soteriology.

b. We reject as false doctrine the teaching of any position other than Pre-tribulation rapture of the Church.

c. We reject as false doctrine the teaching of any position on church polity other than Congregational Polity.

d. We reject as false doctrine the teaching of any degree of Covenant (Replacement) Theology.

e. We reject as false doctrine the teaching of any form of Pentecostalism, Second Blessing Theology, Sinless Perfectionism, continuation of "tongues," or continuation of revelatory knowledge in ongoing prophecy.

f. We reject as false doctrine the teaching of any form of cooperation with Apostate churches or Ecumenical Evangelism.

g. We reject as false doctrine the teaching of any form of Theistic Evolution or Long Day Proponents seeking to justify God creating through Process Evolution.

h. We reject as false doctrine the teaching of any form of Mysticism such as Contemplative Prayer or Cataphatic Imaging (imagining an image of God to which one prays, seeking visions of God or from God, or seeking religious ecstasism).

XXII. CIVIL GOVERNMENT

We believe that civil government is of divine appointment for the interests and good order of human society **(Exodus 18:18, 21-22)**; that it began in **Genesis 9:6** after the universal flood of Noah; that capital punishment for premeditated murder must be a part of Biblical government **(Genesis 9:6; Romans 13:3-4)**; and that magistrates are to be prayed for, and those fulfilling the definition of Biblical government **(2 Samuel 23:3; Romans 13:1-7)** should be conscientiously honored, and obeyed, except in those things opposed to the will of our Lord Jesus Christ Who is the only Lord of the conscience, and the coming King of kings **(Daniel 3:17-18; Matthew 22:21; Acts 4:19-20; 5:29; 23:5)**.

XXIII. ISRAEL

We believe in the sovereign selection of Israel as God's eternal covenant people **(Genesis 13:14-17)**; that she is now dispersed because of her disobedience and rejection of Christ **(Romans 11:1-32)**; that she will be regathered in the Holy Land in belief **(Ezekiel 37)**; that, after the completion of the Church, Israel will be saved as a nation at the second advent of Christ; and that she will be blessed above all people during the thousand year Millennial reign of Christ her Messiah. We do not believe in Replacement Theology.

XXIV. THE RAPTURE—THE BLESSED HOPE

We believe that, according to the Word of God, the next great event in the fulfillment of prophecy will be the coming of Christ in the air to receive to Himself into heaven both His own who are alive and remain unto His coming, and also all who have fallen asleep in Jesus **(John 14:1-3; 1 Thessalonians 4:16-18; 1 Corinthians 15:42-44, 51-54)**; that this event will be premillennial (before the Millennium) and pretribulational (before any part of the seven year Tribulation) **(Revelation 3:10)**; that it may occur at any moment; that this event is the blessed hope set before us in the Scripture, for which we should be constantly looking **(Titus 2:11-14)**; and that at that moment the dead in Christ shall be raised in incorruptible, glorified bodies, and the living in Christ shall be given immortal, glorified bodies without tasting death **(1 Corinthians 15:42-44, 51-54; Philippians 3:20-21)**.

XXV. THE TRIBULATION

We believe that the translation or rapture of the church will be followed by the Tribulation of seven years, which is the fulfillment of Daniel's seventieth week for Israel **(Daniel 9:25-27; Revelation 6:1-19:21)**; that, during the seven year Tribulation, the church, the body of Christ, will be in heaven; that the whole period of Daniel's seventieth week will be a time of judgment on the whole earth; that at the end of the tribulation the times of the Gentiles will be brought to a close; that the latter half of this period will be the time of Jacob's trouble **(Jeremiah 30:7)**, which our Lord called the Great Tribulation **(Matthew 24:15-21)**; that universal righteousness will not be realized previous to the second coming of Christ; that the world is day by day ripening for judgment; and that the age of Grace will end with a fearful apostasy **(1 Timothy 4:1-3; 2 Timothy 3:1-5)**.

XXVI. THE SECOND COMING OF CHRIST

We believe that the seven-year period of Tribulation in the earth will be climaxed by the return of the Lord Jesus Christ to the earth as He went, in person, on the clouds of heaven, and with power and great glory **(Daniel 9:25-27; Matthew 24:29-31; 24:15-25:46; Acts 1:9-11; 15:16-17)**; that He will then sit upon the throne of David, establish His literal thousand-year millennial kingdom, bind Satan, place him in the abyss, and lift the curse which now rests upon the whole creation **(Psalm 72:8; Isaiah 9:6-7; 11:1-9; 32:1; Luke 1:30-33; Acts 2:29-30; 1 Corinthians 15:25; Revelation 20:1-4, 6, 14)**; that He will restore Israel to her own land and give her the realization of God's covenant promises **(Ezekiel 37:21-28; Romans 8:19-23; 11:25-27; Revelation 20:13)**; and that He will bring the whole world to the knowledge of God **(Deuteronomy 30:1-10; Isaiah 11:9)**.

XXVII. THE ETERNAL STATE

We believe that at death the spirits and souls of those who have trusted in the Lord Jesus Christ for salvation pass immediately into His presence in heaven and there remain in conscious bliss until the resurrection of their glorified bodies when Christ comes for His own **(Luke 23:42; 2 Corinthians 5:8; Philippians 1:23)**; that at this time, their bodies will be resurrected and, reunited with their spirits and souls, they will be with Christ forever in the glories and blessings of heaven **(1 Corinthians 15:51-57)**; that the spirits and souls of the unbelieving remain after death conscious of condemnation and in misery until the final judgment of the Great White Throne at the close of the millennium **(Luke 16:19-26; Revelation 20:11-15)**; that at this time, their bodies will be resurrected and, reunited with their spirits and souls, they will be cast into the lake of fire along with death and hell **(Revelation 20:11-15)**; and that they will not be annihilated, but punished with everlasting destruction from the presence of the Lord, and from His power **(2 Thessalonians 1:7-9; Jude 1:6-7)**.

A. HEAVEN

We believe Heaven is a real, literal place of eternal blessedness prepared by God for those who have been clothed in the righteousness of Christ through faith in the shed blood of "the Lamb of God." **(John 14:1-6; 2 Corinthians 5:1-10; Revelation 7:13-17; 21:22-27).**

B. HELL

We believe Hell is a real, literal place of eternal suffering for those whose names are not written in the "book of life." There is no intermediate state of existence in which the unsaved can do penance to pay for his own sins **(Revelation 20:11-15; 21:22-27; Luke 16:19-31)**.

XXVIII. THE BIBLICAL DISPENSATIONS

Definition.

We believe that the dispensations are stewardships by which God administers His purpose on the earth through man under varying responsibilities; that the changes in the dispensational dealings of God with man depend upon changed conditions or situations in which man is successively found with relation to God, and that these changes are the result of the failures of man and the judgments of God; that different administrative responsibilities of this character are manifest in the Biblical record; that they span the entire history of mankind; that each ends in the failure of man under the respective test and in an ensuing judgment from God; that three of these dispensations or rules of life are the subject of extended revelation in the Scripture (see below), namely, (1) the Dispensation of the Mosaic Law, (2) the present Dispensation of Grace **(John 1:17)**, and (3) the future Dispensation of the Millennial Kingdom; that these are distinct and are not to be intermingled or confused, as they are chronologically successive; and that so-called "Covenant Theology" as found in "Reformed Theology" is unscriptural. Three of these dispensations—the Law, the Church, and the Kingdom—are the subjects of detailed revelation in Scripture **(Genesis 1:28; 1 Corinthians 9:17; 2 Corinthians 3:9-18; Galatians 3:13-25;**

Ephesians 1:10; 3:2-10; Colossians 1:24-25, 27; Revelation 20:2-6).

A. Not Ways Of Salvation.

We believe that the dispensations are not ways of salvation, nor different methods of administering the so-called Covenant of Grace; that they are not in themselves dependent on covenant relationships; that they are ways of life and responsibility to God which test the submission of man to His revealed will during a particular time; that, if man trusts in his own efforts to gain the favor of God or salvation under any dispensational test, because of inherent sin, his failure to satisfy fully the just requirements of God is inevitable and his condemnation sure.

B. Salvation By The Blood of Christ.

We believe that according to the "eternal purpose" of God **(Ephesians 3:11)** salvation in the divine reckoning is always "by grace, through faith" **(Ephesians 2:8-9)**; that it rests upon the basis of the shed Blood of Christ **(Ephesians 1:7)**; that God has always been gracious, regardless of the ruling dispensation; and that man has not at all times been under an administration or stewardship of grace as is true in the present dispensation **(1 Corinthians 9:17; Ephesians 3:2, 9; Colossians 1:25)**.

C. Salvation By Faith.

We believe that it has always been true that "without faith it is impossible to please" God **(Hebrews 11:6)**; that the principle of faith was prevalent in the lives of all the Old Testament saints; that it was historically impossible that they should have had as the conscious object of their faith the incarnate, crucified Son, the Lamb of God **(John 1:29)**; that it is evident that they did not comprehend as we do that the sacrifices depicted the person and work of Christ; that they did not understand the redemptive significance of Christ; that they did not understand the redemptive significance of the prophecies or types concerning the sufferings of Christ **(1 Peter 1:10-12)**; that their faith toward God was manifested in other ways as is shown by the long record in **Hebrews 11:1-40**; and that their faith thus manifested was counted unto them for righteousness **(Cf.**

Romans 4:3 with Genesis 15:6; Romans 4:5-8; Hebrews 11:7).

XXIX. Civil Government.

A. We believe that God has ordained and created all authority consisting of three basic institutions: (1) the home, (2) the church, and (3) the state. Every person is subject to these authorities, but all (including the authorities themselves) are answerable to God and governed by His Word. God has given each institution specific Biblical responsibilities and balanced those responsibilities with the understanding that no institution has the right to infringe upon the other.

B. The home, the church, and the state are equal and sovereign in their respective Biblically assigned spheres of responsibility under God **(Romans 13:1-7; Ephesians 5:22-24; Hebrews 13:17; 1 Peter 2:13-14)**.

XXX. Human Sexuality.

A. We believe that God has commanded that no intimate sexual activity be engaged in outside of a marriage between one man and one woman. We believe that any form of homosexuality, lesbianism, bisexuality, bestiality, incest, fornication, adultery, and pornography are sinful perversions of God's gift of sex. We believe that God disapproves of and forbids any attempt to alter one's gender by surgery or appearance **(Genesis 2:24; Genesis 19:5, 13; Genesis 26:8-9; Leviticus 18:1-30; Romans 1: 26-29; 1 Corinthians 5:1; 6:9; 1 Thessalonians 4:1-8; Hebrews 13:4)**.

B. We believe that the only Scriptural marriage is the joining of one man and one woman **(Genesis 2:24; Romans 7:2; 1 Corinthians 7:10; Ephesians 5:22-23)**.

XXXI. Family Relationships.

A. We believe that men and women are spiritually equal in position before God but that God has ordained distinct and separate spiritual functions for men and women in the home and the church. The husband is to be the leader of the home, and men are to be the leaders (pastors, deacons, choir leader or minister) of the church. Accordingly, only men are eligible for licensure and ordination by the church **(Galatians 3:28; Colossians 3:18; 1 Timothy 2:8-15; 3:4-5, 12)**.

B. We believe that God has ordained the family as the foundational institution of human society. The husband is to love his wife as Christ loves the church. The wife is to submit herself to the Scriptural leadership of her husband as the church submits to the headship of Christ. Children are an heritage from the Lord. Parents are responsible for teaching their children spiritual and moral values and leading them, through consistent lifestyle example and appropriate discipline, including Scriptural corporal correction **(Genesis 1:26-28; Exodus 20:12; Deuteronomy 6:4-9; Psalm 127:3-5; Proverbs 19:18; 22:15; 23:13-14; Mark 10:6-12; 1 Corinthians 7:1-16; Ephesians 5:21-33; 6:1-4; Colossians 3:18-21; Hebrews 13:4; 1 Peter 3:1-7)**.

C. We believe that polygamy is prohibited by Scripture (**Genesis 2:22-24; Deuteronomy 24:5; Proverbs 5:18-19; 12:4; 18:22; 19:14; 20:6-7; 30:18-19; Matthew 19:4-6; Mark 10: 6-9; 1 Corinthians 7:1-16; Ephesians 5:22-23; Colossians 3:18-19; Hebrews 13:4-7)**.

XXXII. Divorce and Remarriage.

We believe that God disapproves of and forbids divorce and intends marriage to last until one spouse dies. Divorce and remarriage is regarded as adultery except on the grounds of fornication. Although divorced and remarried persons or divorced persons may hold positions of service in the church and be greatly used of God for Christian service, they may not be considered for the offices of pastor or deacon. **(Malachi 2:14-17; Matthew 19:3-12; Romans 7:1-3; 1 Timothy 3:2, 12; Titus 1:6)**

XXXIII. Abortion.

We believe that human life begins at conception and that the unborn child is a living human being. Abortion constitutes the unjustified, unexcused taking of unborn human life. Abortion is murder. We reject any teaching that abortions of pregnancies due to rape, incest, birth defects, gender selection, birth or population control, or the physical or mental well being of the mother are acceptable. **(Job 3:16; Psalm 51:5; 139:14-16; Isaiah 44:24; 49:1, 5; Jeremiah 1:5; 20:15-18; Luke 1:44)**

XXXIV. Euthanasia.

We believe that the direct taking of an innocent human life is a moral evil, regardless of the intention. Life is a gift of God and must be respected from conception until natural death. Thus we believe that an act or omission which, of itself or by intention, causes death in order to eliminate suffering constitutes a murder contrary to the will of God. Discontinuing medical procedures that are extraordinary or disproportionate to the expected outcome can be a legitimate refusal of over-zealous treatment **(Exodus 20:13, 23:7; Matthew 5:21; Acts 17:28)**.

XXXV. Love.

We believe that we should demonstrate love for others, not only toward fellow believers, but also toward both those who are not believers, those who oppose us, and those who engage in sinful actions. We are to deal with those who oppose us graciously, gently, patiently, and humbly. God forbids the stirring up of strife, the taking of revenge, or the threat or the use of violence as a means of resolving personal conflict or obtaining personal justice. Although God commands us to abhor sinful actions, we are to love and pray for any person who engages in such sinful actions. **(Leviticus 19:18; Matthew 5:44-48; Luke 6:31; John 13:34-35; Romans 12:9-10; 17-21; 13:8-10; Philippians 2:2-4; 2 Timothy 2:24-26; Titus 3:2; 1 John 3:17-18)**

XXXVI. Lawsuits Between Believers.

We believe that Christians are prohibited from bringing civil lawsuits against other Christians or the church to resolve personal disputes. We believe the church possesses all the resources necessary to resolve personal disputes between members. We do believe, however, that a Christian may seek compensation for injuries from another Christian's insurance company as long as the claim is pursued without malice or slander **(1 Corinthians 6:1-8; Ephesians 4:31-32)**.

XXXVII. Missions.

We believe that God has given the church a great commission to pro- claim the Gospel to all nations so that there might be a great multitude from every nation, tribe, ethnic group, and language group who believe on the Lord Jesus Christ. As ambassadors of Christ, we must use all available means to go to the foreign nations and not wait for them to come to us **(Matthew 28:19-20; Mark 16:15; Luke 24:46-48; John 20:21; Acts 1:8; 2 Corinthians 5:20)**.

XXXVIII. Giving.

We believe that every Christian, as a steward of that portion of God's wealth entrusted to him, is obligated to financially support his local church. We believe that God has established the tithe as a basis for giving, but that every Christian should also give other offerings sacrificially and cheerfully to the support of the church, the relief of those in need, and the spread of the Gospel. We believe that a Christian relinquishes all rights to direct the use of his tithe or offering once the gift has been made. **(Genesis 14:20; Proverbs 3:9-10; Acts 4:34-37; 1 Corinthians 16:2; 2 Corinthians 9:6-7; Galatians 6:6; Ephesians 4:28; 1 Timothy 5:17-18; 1 John 3:17)**

SECTION 2.02—AUTHORITY OF STATEMENT OF FAITH

The Statement of Faith does not exhaust the extent of our faith. The Bible itself is the sole and final source of all that we believe. We do believe, however, that the foregoing Statement of Faith accurately represents the teaching of the Bible and, therefore, is binding upon all members. All literature used in the church shall be in complete agreement with the Statement of Faith.

SECTION 2.03—COVENANT

Having been led, as we believe, by the Spirit of God, to receive the Lord Jesus Christ as our Savior, and on profession of our faith, having been baptized in the name of our Father, and of the Son, and of the Holy Ghost, we do now, in the presence of God, angels, and this assembly, most solemnly and joyfully enter into covenant with one another, as one body in Christ.

We engage, therefore, by the aid of the Holy Spirit, to walk together in Christian love; to strive for the advancement of this church in knowledge, holiness and comfort; to promote its prosperity and spirituality; to sustain its worship, ordinances, discipline and doctrines; to give it a sacred preeminence over all institutions of human origin; and to contribute cheerfully and regularly to the support of the ministry, the expenses of the church, the relief of the poor, and the spread of the Gospel through all nations.

We also engage to maintain family and private devotions; to religiously educate our children; to seek the salvation of our kindred, acquaintances, and all others; to walk circumspectly in the world; to be just in our dealings, faithful to our engagements, and exemplary in our deportment; to avoid all tattling, backbiting, and excessive anger; to abstain from such worldly amusements as watching ungodly movies, gambling, rock music, and dancing; to be free from all oath-bound secret societies and partnerships with unbelievers; to abstain from the sale or use of tobacco in any form, narcotic drugs, or intoxicating drink as a beverage; and to be zealous in our efforts to advance the Kingdom of our Savior.

We further engage to watch over one another in brotherly love; to remember each other in prayer; to aid each other in sickness and distress; to cultivate Christian sympathy in feeling and courtesy of speech; to be slow to take offense, but always ready for reconciliation, and mindful of the rules of our Savior, and to secure reconciliation without delay.

We moreover engage, that when we remove from this place, we will as soon as possible unite with some other church where we can carry out the spirit of this covenant and the principles of God's Word.

ARTICLE 3—MEMBERSHIP

SECTION 3.01—QUALIFICATIONS FOR MEMBERSHIP

Those seeking membership should evidence a genuine experience of regeneration through faith in and acceptance of the Lord Jesus Christ as personal Savior. Candidates for membership will be encouraged to read the Statement of Faith, Covenant, and Bylaws of this church, general church practices, and expectations of members. A member of the pastoral staff will meet with the candidate prior to presenting them to the church for membership to answer any questions and to ensure their qualification for and understanding of church membership. Upon the recommendation of the pastor, membership will be granted upon a majority vote of the members present at any church service or meeting, and upon compliance with any one of the following conditions:

A. By baptism (immersion) at this local church following a profession of faith as a believer in Christ Jesus as personal Savior;

B. By letter of transfer from another Bible-believing church of like faith and practice, or other written statement of good standing from the prior church if the applicant has been baptized by immersion subsequent to a profession of faith;

C. By testimony of faith, having been baptized by immersion in another Bible-believing church of like faith and practice; or

D. By restoration, if having been removed from membership, upon majority vote of the congregation after confession is made publicly before the church membership of the sin or sins involved, and satisfactorily evidencing repentance to the pastor (or the board of deacons if the office of pastor is vacant).

SECTION 3.02—DUTIES OF A MEMBER

On becoming a member of this church, in addition to the covenant contained in Section 2.03, each member further covenants to love, honor, and esteem the pastor; to pray for him; to recognize his authority in spiritual affairs of the church; to cherish a brotherly love for all members of the church; to support the church in prayer, tithes, offerings and with other financial support as the Lord enables; and in accordance with Biblical commands, to support through a lifestyle walk affirming the beliefs and practices of the church.

SECTION 3.03—PRIVILEGES OF MEMBERSHIP

A. Only members, at least eighteen years of age, who are physically present at a duly-called meeting of the church, and who are in good standing shall be entitled to vote. There shall be no proxy or absentee voting. The eligible membership of the church has certain limited areas to exercise a vote. Members may not vote to initiate any church action; rather the vote of a member is to confirm and ratify the direction of the church as determined by the pastor and the board of deacons.

B. This congregation functions not as a pure democracy, but as a body under the headship of the Lord Jesus Christ and the direction of the pastor as the under-shepherd with the counsel of the board of deacons. Determinations of the internal affairs of this church are ecclesiastical matters and shall be determined exclusively by the church's own rules and procedures. The pastor shall oversee and/or conduct all aspects of ministry for this church. The board of deacons shall give counsel and assistance to the pastor as requested by him.

C. Membership in this church does not afford the members with any property, contractual, or civil rights based on principles of democratic government. Although the general public is invited to all of the church's worship services, the church property remains private property. The pastor (or in his absence, an individual designated by the board of deacons) has the authority to suspend or revoke the right of any person, including a member, to enter or remain on church property. If after being notified of such a suspension or revocation, the person enters or remains on church property, the person may, in the discretion of the pastor (or in his absence, an individual designated by the board of deacons), be treated as a trespasser.

D. A member may inspect or copy the prepared financial statements of the church and the minutes of the proceedings of church meetings and of board meetings, provided he shall have made a written request upon the church and the church has received the written request at least five business days before the requested inspection date.

> **1.** A member may not, under any circumstances, inspect or copy any record relating to individual contributions to the church, the list of names and addresses of the church members, or the accounting books and financial records of the church.
>
> **2.** The church may impose a reasonable charge, covering the costs of labor and material, for copies of any documents provided to the member before releasing the copies to the member.

SECTION 3.04—DISCIPLINE OF A MEMBER

A. There shall be a discipline committee consisting of the pastor and the board of deacons. These men shall have sole authority in determining heretical deviations from the Statement of Faith and violations of the church covenant. If the pastor or a deacon is the subject of a disciplinary matter, he shall not sit as a member of the discipline committee. The pastor and deacons shall be entitled to the same steps as other church members and be subject to the same discipline.

B. Members are expected to demonstrate special loyalty and concern for one another. When a member becomes aware of an offense of such magnitude that it hinders spiritual growth and testimony, he is to go alone to the offending party and seek to restore his brother. Before he goes, he should first examine himself. When he goes, he should go with a spirit of humility and have the goal of restoration.

C. If reconciliation is not reached, a second member, either a deacon or the pastor, is to accompany the one seeking to resolve the matter. This second step should also be preceded by self-examination and exercised in a spirit of humility with the goal of restoration.

D. If the matter is still unresolved after the steps outlined in *Subsections (B) and (C)* have been taken, the discipline committee, as the church representatives Biblically responsible for putting down murmuring, shall hear the matter. If the matter is not resolved during the hearing before the discipline committee, the committee shall recommend to the members of the church that they, after self-examination, make an effort personally to go to the offending member and seek that member's restoration.

E. If the matter is still unresolved after the steps outlined in *Subsections (B), (C), and (D)* have been taken, such members who refuse to repent and be restored are to be removed from the membership of the church upon a majority vote of the membership present at a meeting called for the purpose of considering disciplinary action.

F. No matter may be heard by the discipline committee or the church unless the steps outlined in *Subsections (B) and (C)* have been taken, except in the case of a public offense.

G.If an unrepentant offending party is removed from the church membership, all contact with him from that point forward (except by family members) must be for the sake of restoration.

H.The procedures provided in this section are based on **Matthew 18:15-20; Romans 16:17-18; 1 Corinthians 5:1-13; 2 Corinthians 2:1-11; Galatians 6:1; 1 Thessalonians 5:14; 2 Thessalonians 3:6, 10-15; 1 Timothy 5:19-20; and Titus 3:10-11.**

SECTION 3.05—TRANSFER OF MEMBERSHIP

Members not under the disciplinary process of *Section 3.04* may request that letters of transfer be sent to another church.

SECTION 3.06—TERMINATION OF MEMBERSHIP

A. The membership of any individual member shall automatically terminate without notice if the member in question has not attended a regular worship service of the church in the preceding six months. Upon good cause being shown to the pastor, this provision for termination may be waived in the case of any individual member at the discretion of the pastor.

B. No member of this church may hold membership in another church. The membership of any individual member shall automatically terminate without notice if the member unites in membership with another church.

C. The membership of any individual member shall automatically terminate without notice if the member states that he or she is actively involved in any conduct described in *Section 2.01(XXX)* or files a lawsuit in violation of *Section 2.01(XXXVI)*.

D. No provision contained in this section shall be subject to or governed by the procedures regarding discipline of members set forth in *Section 3.04.*

E. A member may resign at any time, but no letter of transfer or written statement of good standing will be issued upon such resignation, except at the discretion of the pastor.

F. The membership of an individual will automatically terminate upon his or her death.

G. The membership of any individual member shall be automatically terminated as determined and recommended by the pastor and board of deacons without notice if the member openly, aggressively, and unashamedly disagrees with any provision found in the Statement of Faith.

H. The membership of any individual member shall automatically terminate without notice if the member in a spirit of dissension actively engages in secretive discussions and/or intentionally organized, secretive meetings in a concerted effort to overthrow the pastor or present church leadership.

SECTION 3.07—AFFILIATED CO-LABORER

Those desiring fellowship, accountability and opportunities for service with this assembly on a temporary basis but who maintain active membership in a like body of believers outside this city, may be granted affiliated co-laborer status with this church. The affiliated co-laborer may be eligible to serve in certain capacities determined by the pastor and deacons, and may attend fellowship events granted for members.

In no way, however, does this affiliation grant membership or the rights of membership to the individual(s) so granted. Affiliated co-laborers shall not be entitled to hold any office, vote in or have any say in any church matter, and shall not be counted for quorum purposes. A person wishing to become an affiliated co-laborer with this assembly must request so of the pastor, who will, in consultation with the deacons if necessary, decide if affiliated co-laborer status may be granted to the individual. If the pastor so determines, the person may be granted such upon a majority vote of the church membership at any public service or church administration meeting.

ARTICLE 4—OFFICERS

SECTION 4.01—CHURCH OFFICERS

A. The church officers are pastor *(See Section 5.01)*, deacon *(See Section 5.02)*, minister of records or church clerk *(See Section 5.03)*, financial secretary (or minister of finance) *(See Section 5.04) or* other positions of the church determined by the pastor or Board of Deacons in the absence of a pastor. One person may hold two or more offices, except that of pastor. The pastor, from time to time as he deems appropriate, may appoint other church officers, subject to a majority confirmation vote by present, voting church members at any regular or special church administrative meeting. The pastor may appoint a woman to hold a committee chairmanship or office as long as the position exercises no authority over a man.

B. All church officers will have a background check; the background check will include finger-printing for any church position that includes working with children or the finances of the church. Furthermore, the pastor my require fingerprinting for any church officer position he deems necessary.

C. Any person having a prior criminal history at any time in his life may not serve in any official capacity at the church without a thorough background check and explicit approval by the pastor.

SECTION 4.02—DESIGNATION OF CORPORATE OFFICERS

As an accommodation to legal relationships outside the church, the pastor shall serve as president of the corporation; the minister of records shall serve as secretary of the corporation; the minister of finances shall serve as treasurer of the corporation; and the chairman of the board of deacons shall serve as vice president of the corporation.

SECTION 4.03—ELIGIBILITY FOR OFFICE

A. The church shall not install or retain an officer who fails to adhere to or expresses disagreement with the Statement of Faith. All church officers, upon request of the pastor, shall affirm their agreement with the Statement of Faith (as set forth in Article 2).

B. All church officers must be approved initially and thereafter annually by the pastor in order for them to commence or continue in their offices.

C. Only church members are eligible for election or appointment to any church office or position with the exception of pastors. Affiliated co-laborers with this ministry are not eligible for such election or appointment. A pastor may be called who is not a member of the church.

SECTION 4.04—TERMS OF OFFICE

A. The relationship between the pastor and the church shall be permanent unless dissolved at the option of either party by the giving of a month's notice, or less by mutual consent. The calling of a pastor or severance of the relationship between the pastor and the church may be considered at any regular church administration meeting, provided notice to that effect shall have been given from the pulpit to the church two Sundays prior to said regular church administration meeting. A three-fourths majority of the eligible members present and voting shall be required to call a pastor or to sever the relationship between the pastor and the church. Disciplinary removal of the pastor from office automatically terminates his membership. A restoration to membership after disciplinary removal will be subject to the requirements of Section 3.01(D).

B. The term of service for all offices and positions in the church, except the pastor and deacons, shall be **one year**, at the expiration of which the officers may be re-elected or re-appointed.

C. A vacancy occurring in any office or board, except in the case of the pastor, may be filled at any regular church administration meeting.

D. All elected and appointed officers shall serve in their respective offices until their successors are duly elected or appointed.

E. Officers and Members of the board of deacons may be removed from office for unbiblical conduct or failure to perform their duties upon a majority vote of the pastor and remainder of the board of deacons, as determined by the other board members, upon a majority vote of the remaining members of the board of deacons.

SECTION 4.05—ELECTION OF OFFICERS AND CALLING A PASTOR

The annual election of officers by the church membership shall occur during the month of December at the annual church administration meeting.

Upon the resignation, death or dismissal of the Pastor, the church shall seek a candidate who subscribes to the Statement of Faith, the Covenant and bylaw provisions of this church, and whose life aligns with the qualifications of a pastor as described in I Timothy 3:1-7 and Titus 1:6-9. The church shall abide by the following guidelines for calling a pastor:

A The ordained members shall select a pulpit committee to consist of all deacons and up to five total members elected by a simple majority of the ordained members. The pulpit committee shall require a Doctrinal Statement, references, and three recordings of preaching or teaching services (if available) from each prospective candidate. All prospective candidates must be married and have a testimony salvation, baptism, and faithful service in a church of like faith. Approved candidates will be invited to the church for at least a complete Sunday. The pulpit committee will interview the candidate, discuss the condition of the church, and allow for the candidate to question the pulpit committee.

B. Prior to being announced to the congregation as a formal candidate, any man being considered for pastoral candidate must preach at least one Sunday service. Preferably, a minimum of three qualified candidates will be considered before any vote is taken. Thereafter, upon a majority vote of the pulpit committee, they shall formally announce the candidates to the church. The church will then vote by secret ballot to bring back one candidate with his family at the expense of the church for further consideration. That candidate must then preach at least two regularly scheduled services and be available to the members for a question and answer time. After the candidate leaves, the church will vote by secret ballot whether or not to accept this candidate. If not selected, the same process will be repeated for additional candidates;

C Notice from the pulpit must be given 2 consecutive Sundays prior to a formal candidate's preaching services, and 2 consecutive Sundays prior to the church congregational vote;

D The candidate must be elected as Pastor by a three-fourths majority vote of qualified, present voting members. The pulpit committee will only present for consideration to the church one candidate at a time, and an up or down vote must be cast prior to consideration of other potential candidates.

SECTION 4.06—PASTORAL OVERSIGHT OF OFFICERS AND STAFF

A. Subject to the approval of the church membership and on the condition that they shall become a member of the church upon assuming their duties, the pastor may hire associates and assistants to assist the him in carrying out his God-given responsibilities.

B. All church staff, whether paid or volunteer, shall be under the supervision of the pastor who has the sole authority to dismiss the same. No employee or volunteer shall be hired, appointed, or retained who fails to adhere to or expresses disagreement with the Statement of Faith.

C. Upon determination of the pastor the pastor can appoint someone to fulfill a position. The pastor will determine accountability of all officers, deacons, employees of the church.

ARTICLE 5—DUTIES AND POWERS OF OFFICERS

SECTION 5.01—THE PASTOR

A. The pastor shall preach the Gospel regularly and shall be at liberty to preach the whole counsel of the Word of God as the Lord leads him. He shall administer the ordinances of the church, act as moderator at all church meetings for the transaction of church matters, supervise the teaching ministries of the church, and tenderly watch over the spiritual interests of the membership.

B. The pastor shall appoint the members of the various committees at the annual church administration meeting. He shall serve as the president of the corporation. He shall publicly inform all newly-elected officers of the particular function and the responsibilities of their respective offices. He shall extend the right hand of fellowship to all new members on behalf of the church, and perform such other duties as generally appertain to such a position. The pastor shall be free to choose the means and methods by which he exercises the ministry that God has given him.

C. All appointments for public worship and Bible study and the arrangements thereof, including time and place and the use of the property belonging to the church for purposes other than the stated appointments, shall be under the control of the pastor, who shall be able to determine the appropriateness of practices as well as persons permitted to use the church property. The pastor shall be responsible to fill the pulpit for each regularly scheduled church service as well as any special services. In the event of his absence, he (or the chairman of the deacon board in the case of a vacancy in the office of pastor or where the pastor is ill and unable to perform his duties) shall be responsible to invite speakers from within the membership or outside the church to preach in a manner consistent with the beliefs articulated in the Statement of Faith.

D.The pastor or his designee shall be in charge of the use of the "Prophets Chamber" in the fellowship (recreation) hall.

E. The pastor or his designee shall be in charge of the cemetery. The pastor shall designate that the cemetery is for members of the church, a spouse, or a child that has not reached the age of accountability.

F. The pastor shall approve fellowship events and approve trips by members of the church. All individuals traveling to fellowships shall sign a release form (see the attached examples from CLA).

G. The pastor shall be responsible, in coordination with the deacons, to establish mandatory safety and security procedures for all ministries and programs involving minors.

SECTION 5.02—THE BOARD OF DEACONS

A. Deacons are servants of the people and serve the people under the direction and oversight of the pastor. The board of deacons shall assist the pastor, in such manner as he shall request, in promoting the spiritual welfare of the church, in conducting the religious services, and in performing all other work of the church. They shall make provision for the observance of the ordinances of the church. They shall, if requested by the pastor, consider applications for church membership. They shall, in cooperation with the pastor, disburse the benevolence fund. They shall assist the pastor in visitation and all other evangelistic efforts of the church. The board of deacons shall assist the pastor in caring for the administrative needs of the church's various ministries as requested by the pastor. They shall provide the pulpit supply and choose a moderator for church meetings if the pastor is unavailable or the office of pastor is vacant. Upon the death, resignation, or dismissal of the pastor, the board of deacons may appoint a pulpit committee.

B. Immediately following the annual church administration meeting, the pastor and board of deacons shall assemble and elect, from their own number, a chairman who shall be vice president of the corporation, a vice chairman, and a secretary.

C. The pastor and the board of deacons shall constitute the board of trustees of the corporation.

The board of trustees shall exercise only the following specific powers, upon authorization by a majority vote of the members present at a duly-called church administration meeting:

1. To purchase, hold, lease, or otherwise acquire real and personal property on behalf of the church, and to take real and personal property by will, gift, or bequest on behalf of the church.

2. To sell, convey, alienate, transfer, lease, assign, exchange, or otherwise dispose of, and to mortgage, pledge, or otherwise encumber the real and personal property of the church, to borrow money and incur indebtedness for the purpose and the use of the church; to cause to be executed, issued, and delivered for the indebtedness, in the name of the church, promissory notes, bonds, debentures, or other evidence of indebtedness; and to secure repayment by deeds of trust, mortgages, or pledges.

3. To exercise all powers necessary for the dissolution of the church corporation.

4. The pastor and Board of Deacons shall establish a benevolent fund as directed by the pastor to be distributed by the pastor or the Board of Deacons.

5. The Chairman of the Deacons shall be responsible for helping the pastor with any personal or ministerial duties or problems.

6. All powers of the directors, (whether deacons or other appointed group) shall be compatible with the laws of the state of Georgia.

SECTION 5.03—THE MINISTER OF RECORDS

The minister of records (or church clerk) shall:

A. Certify and keep at the office of the church, the original bylaws or a copy, including all amendments or alterations to the bylaws.

B. Keep at the place where the bylaws or a copy are kept a record of the proceedings of meetings of the board of deacons, with the time and place of holding, the notice of meeting given, the names of these present at the meetings.

C. Sign, certify, or attest documents as may be required by law.

D. See that all notices are duly given in accordance with the provisions of these by- laws. (In case of the absence or disability of the secretary, or his or her refusal or neglect to act, notice may be given and served by the pastor or by the chairman of the board of deacons.)

E. Be custodian of the records of the church, including the membership roll, baptisms, and certificates of ordination, licenses, and commissions.

F. See that the reports, statements, certificates, and all other documents and records required by law are properly kept and filed.

G. Exhibit at all reasonable times to proper persons on terms provided by law the bylaws and minutes of proceedings of the board of deacons or the minutes of the meetings of the church members.

H. Keep an account of any special events in the life of the church which are of historical interest and give a report at the annual church administration meeting of the status of the church membership roll in the past year.

I. Keep all records at the office of the church and deliver them to any successor upon leaving office.

J. Serve as the secretary of the corporation and be a member in good standing.

SECTION 5.04—THE MINISTER OF FINANCE (TREASURER)

The minister of finance shall:

A. Have charge and custody of, and be responsible for, all funds of the corporation, and deposit all funds in the name of the church in banks, trust companies, or other depositories as shall be selected by the pastor or the board of deacons.

B. Receive, and give receipt for all contributions, gifts, and donations to the church.

C. Disburse, or cause to be disbursed, the funds of the church as may be directed by the pastor, the board of deacons, or the budget adopted by the members of the church at the annual church administration meeting, taking proper vouchers for the disbursements. Write, sign, record, and mail checks in payment of church bills and routine expenses approved by the pastor and/or deacons as well as disburse funds and salaries as directed by the church.

D. Keep and maintain adequate and correct accounts of the church's properties and business transactions including account of its assets, liabilities, receipts, disbursements, and capital.

E. Make all expenditures of the church (except miscellaneous petty cash disbursements) by check.

F. When and as requested, render to the pastor and the board of deacons accounts of all his transactions as minister of finance and of the financial condition of the church.

G. Present a written report of itemized disbursements at the regular quarterly church administration meetings and make a general report for the year at the annual church administration meeting.

H. Keep all church financial records at the office of the church and deliver them to any successor upon leaving office.

I. Serve as treasurer of the corporation.

J. Be responsible for issuing form 1099 and W2 forms (see the attached examples).

K. Must never allow the offering plates to be out of the sight of at least two (2) church members appointed for counting the offering. He shall direct that two (2) people are to count the money separately, and then sign and date the 'offering-slip.'

L. Must arrange for individuals who can sign checks for the church. At least two directors of this corporation shall be authorized to sign church checks in the treasurer's absence. No persons shall be permitted to sign checks written to themselves, and no expenditures of the church (except miscellaneous petty cash disbursements) shall be made by cash.

M. Arrange for a credit card account for the church for the pastor, associate pastor, and chairman of the board.

N. He shall demand receipts for all expenditures by petty cash, credit cards, or credit account. Any receipts **<u>not</u>** turned into the treasurer by the pastor, associate pastor, or chairman of the board will not be paid.

O. Tithing amounts (the record) by members of the church is a private matter, and shall not be released to anyone, including the pastor, chairman of the board, any officer of the church.

SECTION 5.05—FINANCIAL SECRETARY

The financial secretary shall:

A. Count, along with two other persons so appointed, and record in a permanent record all the monies received in offerings for the church. This shall be done following each service or day of services of the church.
B. Convey in a timely manner all funds received to the treasurer for verification and deposit in the bank, including moneys received from outside sources, and shall provide the treasurer with a record of all monies received, specifying the distribution into various funds as designated. A copy shall be provided to the pastor each week or upon request.
C. Maintain a permanent weekly record of individual giving for all donations, offerings, contributions and gifts, and shall guard said records confidentially as a sacred trust. The financial secretary shall issue an official receipt to each contributor upon request at the end of the fiscal year, or upon special request at another time.
D. The chairman of the deacons may assume the duties of the financial secretary in the absence of a financial secretary, unless already serving in the capacity of the treasurer.

SECTION 5.06—ASSOCIATE PASTORS

Under the direction and guidance of the pastor, the associate pastor(s) of the church shall assist the pastor in carrying out the ministries of the church.

SECTION 5.07—DUTIES OF ALL OFFICERS

A. All officers shall prepare a written report of their work for the annual church administration meeting and shall surrender all records in their possession to the minister of records at the close of their term of office to be filed as a permanent record of the work of the church. All records are the property of the church and must be kept in the church office.

B. Any officer who neglects his duties as outlined in the bylaws may be removed from his office, at the discretion of the pastor, and another may be appointed by the pastor to serve the unexpired term.

SECTION 5.08—INSTALLATION OF OFFICERS

A. Public installation service in which all newly-elected officers of the church are to be dedicated to their respective offices and the ordination of newly-elected deacons shall be held at a public church service following their election at the annual church administration meeting.

ARTICLE 6—MEETINGS

SECTION 6.01—MEETINGS FOR WORSHIP

Unless otherwise determined by the pastor, the church shall meet each Sunday for public worship, both morning and evening, and at least once during the week for Bible study and prayer. Except when circumstances forbid it, the ordinance of the Lord's Supper shall be observed on the first Sunday evening of each month or as it seems appropriate to the pastor, but not less than quarterly.

SECTION 6.02—MEETINGS FOR CHURCH ADMINISTRATION

A. The annual church administration meeting shall be held within the first two weeks of December as determined by the pastor, at which time the regular church administration shall be considered. A quorum shall consist of the members present. Public notice of the meeting shall be given from the pulpit for two successive Sundays immediately preceding the meeting.

B. All church administration meetings shall be opened and closed with prayer for divine guidance and blessing.

C. The moderator shall determine the rules of procedure according to his sense of fairness and common sense, giving all members a reasonable opportunity to be heard on a matter. The moderator is the final authority on questions of procedure, and his decision is final and controlling. The following order shall be observed at the regular church administration meetings:

1. Devotions & prayer
2. Reading of minutes
3. Reception of members
4. Dismissal of members
5. Report of officers
6. Reports of standing committees
7. Reports of special committees
8. Unfinished matters
9. Election of officers
10. New matters
11. Adjournment
12. Benediction

D. The pastor can call a business meeting at his discretion in coordination with the deacons, but no later than quarterly. A quarterly business meeting at which time the financial reports will be reviewed, if not reviewed monthly.

E. At the annual meeting, election of officers and similar business will be conducted.

F. For any meeting under this article, the moderator, in his sole discretion, shall have full and unilateral authority to require nonmembers to leave the meeting room and to order the immediate removal of any member or other person present who is deemed by the moderator to be disruptive to the proceedings by act or presence. The moderator shall have full authority to order the removal of all children (ages to be determined by the moderator) if the moderator determines, in his sole discretion, that circumstances so warrant. If the moderator determines that compliance with his order of removal is unsatisfactory, the moderator may, in his sole discretion, revoke the disruptive person's right to remain on the premises in accordance with Section 3.03(C) and treat the person as a trespasser.

SECTION 6.03—SPECIAL MEETINGS

A. The pastor (or deacons if the office of pastor is vacant or the pastor is the subject of possible disciplinary action) may call a special meeting by giving notice of such a meeting and the purpose for which it is called to the church from the pulpit at least one Sunday and not less than one week prior to said meeting. A meeting for the calling of a pastor or the severance of the relationship between the church and pastor shall be called in accordance with the provision of *Section 4.04(A)*.

B. Bible conferences, missionary conferences, and revivals may be held as the pastor deems beneficial.

C. Any TRIPS by members of the church for fellowship must be approved by the Pastor, if he is in good standing, or chairman of the deacons if the pastor is disqualified by Section 2.01 or 4.03.

SECTION 6.04—MOTIONS

Members who desire that a certain motion be made or subject matter be discussed during an annual, regular, or special business meeting must file a written recommendation with the pastor and deacons two weeks prior to the set meeting. The church leadership will then consider the proposal and proceed according to their conscience and what they understand to be in the best interests of the church. All other motions will be presented by the pastor and/or chairman of the board of deacons (or other moderator if the office of pastor is vacant) unless the pastor and/or deacons has delegated authority to another member and/or officer to raise certain motions.

SECTION 6.05—FISCAL YEAR

The fiscal year of the church shall begin January 1st and end December 31st.

ARTICLE 7—MINISTRY OF EDUCATION

SECTION 7.01—PURPOSE

The church believes that it is to provide the members' children with an education, which is based upon and consistent with Biblical teachings. The church believes that the home and church are responsible before God for providing a Christian education. To this end, the church shall engage in ministries in education in keeping with the following dictates.

SECTION 7.02—CHURCH PARTICIPATION

All educational programs or courses of instruction formulated and offered by the church shall be primarily for the benefit of the members of the church; however, the pastor may permit non-church members to participate in church educational programs or courses of instruction if he deems it in the best interest of the church.

SECTION 7.03—STAFF MEMBERSHIP

All instructors, teachers, and administrators shall be members of this church. This provision shall not apply to visiting missionaries, evangelists, or preachers engaged for the purpose of delivering sermons, conducting revivals, or other special meetings on a temporary basis.

SECTION 7.04—STATEMENT OF FAITH ACCORD

All educational programs or courses of instruction shall be taught and presented in full accord with the Statement of Faith of the church. The church shall not hire, appoint, or retain any employee or volunteer for its educational programs who fails to adhere to or expresses disagreement with the Statement of Faith.

SECTION 7.05—UNITY

All educational programs or courses of instruction shall be conducted as an integral and inseparable ministry of the church.

SECTION 7.06—TEACHING

All educational programs or courses of instruction shall be conducted consistent with the teaching of the inerrant Word of God. Sunday School shall be conducted for children and adults with an effort to bring in people from the community. Any assertion or belief which conflicts with or questions a Bible truth is a pagan deception and distortion of the truth which will be disclaimed as false. It is the responsibility of every instructor or teacher to present the inerrant Word of God as the sole infallible source of knowledge and wisdom.

SECTION 7.07—CHRISTIAN WALK

All administrators, instructors, and teachers shall continue or adopt a lifestyle consistent with the precepts which they teach, whether in or out of the classroom; but especially in compliance with the Statement of Faith.

ARTICLE 8—ORDINATION

SECTION 8.01—ORDINATION QUALIFICATIONS

A. Only male member of this church or its mission churches, who gives evidence of a genuine call of God into the work of the ministry and possesses the qualifications stated in **1 Timothy 3:1-7** and **Titus 1:6-9**, may be considered for ordination as a minister of the Gospel or ordained as deacons **(1 Timothy 3:8-13)** under the direction of the pastor and Scripture.

B. The candidate must have an experience of conversion, a divine call to the ministry, a consistent Christian walk, a vital concern for the souls of men and for the edification of the church at home and abroad.

C. The candidate must affirm his unequivocal adherence to the Statement of Faith set forth in Article 2 of these bylaws. His doctrinal position on matters not specifically addressed in the Statement of Faith must be based on the Scriptures as the Word of God.

D. Graduation from a four-year Bible college, or its equivalent, is recommended. Any uncertainty as to call or other obvious disqualifications should bar a man from ordination regardless of educational attainments.

E. All persons licensed or ordained by this church must be convinced Baptists who accept the historic Baptist distinctives in all matters pertaining to church order and practice.

F. A Bible college or seminary graduate should spend at least one year after graduation engaged exclusively in preaching and pastoral work before being considered for ordination. Exceptions to this rule will be made when the candidate has had adequate pastoral experience before and during his formal biblical education, or when he must seek early ordination to satisfy requirements for pastoral service of a mission church, missionary service or chaplaincy.

SECTION 8.02—ORDINATION PROCEDURE

A. Upon a conference with the pastor, and after the pastor has approved the candidate for ordination as a pastor or deacon, the pastor shall call a council to examine and pass on the qualification of the candidate. The ordination council may consist of ordained ministers of like faith invited to participate in the examination of the candidate. The council should take its responsibility seriously and examine the candidate carefully. The outcome of the examination will be a recommendation to the church whether or not to ordain. If the council recommends ordination, the church shall vote to adopt or reject the council's recommendation at a duly noticed church administration meeting.

B. If the candidate is found worthy of ordination by the council, the church shall vote to adopt or reject the council's recommendation at a duly noticed church administration meeting.

C. The pastor and the chairman of the deacons shall arrange for the ordination service. The following parts are usually included in the ordination service: Introduction consisting of the reading of Scripture relating to the qualifications for ordination, prayer, special music and reading of the determination of the examining council; Ordination charge to the church; Ordination prayer accompanied by laying on of hands by the council; Charge to the candidate; Benediction by the newly ordained minister.

D. Deacons selected for ordination will agree with the Statement of Faith, Bylaws, and other procedures deemed necessary for successful operation of the church under the authority of the pastor and Board of Deacons.

SECTION 8.03—REVOCATION OF ORDINATION

A. Should a minister ordained by the church be found living a life unbecoming a servant of the Lord or preaching and teaching contrary to the Word of God, the pastor may call a council to hear the charges and the minister's defense.
B. The reviewing council shall consist of the board of deacons and ordained ministers of like faith invited to participate in the hearing of the charges and the minister's defense.
C. Upon a recommendation by a majority vote of the council, the church will then revoke the minister's ordination certificate.

SECTION 8.04—LICENSE

A. Those who desire to prepare for the gospel ministry may be issued a license to preach by this church after the pastor and board of deacons have examined the candidate's divine call and qualifications.
B. The pastor and the board of deacons may license an associate or assistant pastor as a preliminary step to ordination at a later date.
C. A license to the ministry shall be considered the equivalent to ordination, but shall be considered probationary in nature. It is expected that the licensed minister will be considered for ordination within four years of being licensed.

ARTICLE 9—INDEMNIFICATION

SECTION 9.01—ACTIONS SUBJECT TO INDEMNIFICATION

The church will indemnify any person who was or is a party or is threatened to be made a party to any threatened, pending or completed action, suit, or proceeding, whether civil, criminal, administrative, or investigative, including all appeals (other than an action by or in the right of the church) by reason of the fact that the person is or was a pastor, deacon, officer, employee, or agent of the church, against expenses, including attorneys' fees, judgments, fines, and amounts paid in settlement actually and reasonably incurred by him in connection with the action, suit, or proceeding; and if that person acted in good faith and in a manner he reasonably believed to be in or not opposed to the best interests of the church and, with respect to any criminal action or proceeding, had no reasonable cause to believe his conduct was unlawful. The termination of any action, suit, or proceeding by judgment, order, settlement, conviction, or on a plea of nolo contendere or its equivalent, shall not, of itself, create a presumption that the person did not act in good faith and in a manner that he reasonably believed to be in or not opposed to the best interests of the church and, with respect to any criminal action or proceeding, had no reasonable cause to believe that his or her conduct was unlawful.

SECTION 9.02—EXPENSES SUBJECT TO INDEMNIFICATION

To the extent that a pastor, deacon, officer, employee, or agent has been successful on the merits or otherwise in defense of any action, suit, or proceeding referred to in this Article, or in defense of any claim, issue, or matter in that action, suit, or proceeding, he or she will be indemnified against expenses, including attorneys' fees, actually and reasonably incurred by him or her in connection with the action, suit, or proceeding.

SECTION 9.03—LIMITATIONS OF INDEMNIFICATION

Any indemnification made under this Article, may be made by the church only as authorized in the specific case on a determination that indemnification of the pastor, deacon, officer, employee, or agent is proper in the circumstances because he has met the applicable standard of conduct set forth in *Section 9.01*. The determination shall be made (a) by a majority vote of a quorum consisting of the pastor and deacons who were not and are not parties to or threatened with the action, suit, or proceeding; (b) if the described quorum is not obtainable or if a majority vote of a quorum of disinterested deacons so directs, by independent legal counsel in a written opinion; or (c) by a majority vote of the members of the church.

SECTION 9.04—TIMING OF INDEMNIFICATION

Expenses of each person seeking indemnification under this Article, may be paid by the church as they are incurred, in advance of the final disposition of the action, suit, or proceeding, as authorized by the board of deacons in the specific case, on receipt of an undertaking by or on behalf of the pastor, deacon, officer, employee, or agent to repay the amount if it is ultimately determined that he or she is not qualified to be indemnified by the church.

SECTION 9.05—EXTENT OF INDEMNIFICATION

The indemnification provided by this Article shall be deemed to be discretionary unless otherwise required as a matter of law or under any agreement or provided by insurance purchased by the church, both as to action of each person seeking indemnification under this Article in his official capacity and as to action in another capacity while holding that office, and may continue as to a person who has ceased to be a pastor, deacon, officer, employee, or agent and may inure to the benefit of the heirs, executors, and administrators of that person.

SECTION 9.06—INSURANCE

The church will purchase and maintain insurance on behalf of any person who is or was a pastor, deacon, officer, employee, or agent of the church against any liability asserted against him and incurred by him in that capacity, or arising out of his status in that capacity, whether or not the church would have the power to indemnify him against liability under the provisions of this Article.

ARTICLE 10—COMMITTEES

SECTION 10.01—STANDING COMMITTEES

The pastor (or the board of deacons if the office of pastor is vacant) shall appoint standing committees and designate a chairperson for each standing committee and, except when otherwise specifically provided in these bylaws, shall determine the membership of each standing committee. In addition to the discipline committee, the pastor may appoint other standing committees as he deems appropriate.

SECTION 10.02—SPECIAL COMMITTEES

The pastor, and at his discretion the board of deacons under his guidance, may create special committees to provide them with advice and information regarding matters submitted to the committee for consideration. The committee shall have no authority to act on behalf of the corporation. The members of the committee shall be approved by and serve solely at the pleasure of the pastor and board of deacons. The special committee shall be subject to the control and direction of the pastor and board of deacons at all times.

SECTION 10.03—ACTIONS OF COMMITTEES

Committees, whether standing or special, have no authority to act on behalf of the corporation. Their primary function is to research and recommend. Committees shall make available upon request all records and materials to the pastor or deacons, who shall have the right to overrule any plans or decisions made by the committee. Each committee shall have a secretary that keeps minutes of each meeting and shall timely submit the minutes to the pastor and church clerk to be filed with church records. If deemed appropriate by the pastor and deacons, the committee secretary, in conjunction with the chairman, shall submit an annual report to the church of the decisions and plans of the committee.

ARTICLE 11—DESIGNATED CONTRIBUTIONS

From time to time the church, in the exercise of its religious, educational, and charitable purposes, may establish various funds to accomplish specific goals. Contributors may suggest uses for their contributions, but all suggestions shall be deemed advisory rather than mandatory in nature. All contributions made to specific funds or otherwise designated shall remain subject to the exclusive control and discretion of the pastor and the board of deacons. No fiduciary obligation shall be created by any designated contribution made to the church other than to use the contribution for the general furtherance of any of the purposes stated in Section 1.02.

ARTICLE 12—BINDING ARBITRATION

SECTION 12.01—SUBMISSION TO ARBITRATION

Believing that lawsuits between believers are prohibited by Scripture, all members of this church agree to submit to binding arbitration any matters which cannot otherwise be resolved, and expressly waive any and all rights in law and equity to bringing any civil disagreement before a court of law, except that judgment upon the award rendered by the arbitrator may be entered in any court having jurisdiction thereof.

SECTION 12.02—NOTICE OF ARBITRATION

In the event of any dispute, claim, question, or disagreement arising out of or relating to these bylaws or any other church matter, the parties shall use their best efforts to settle such disputes, claims, questions, or disagreement as befits Christians. To this effect, they shall consult and negotiate with each other in good faith and, recognizing their mutual interests not to disgrace the name of Christ, seek to reach a just and equitable solution. If they do not reach such solution within a period of sixty (60) days, then upon notice by either party to the other, disputes, claims, questions, or differences shall be finally settled by arbitration as described in *Section 12.01*, above, and such Procedures for Arbitration as are adopted pursuant to *Section 12.04*, below.

SECTION 12.03—LIMITATIONS ON ARBITRATION DECISIONS

A. Should any dispute involve matters of church discipline, the arbitrators shall be limited to determining whether the procedures for church discipline as outlined under *Section 3.04*, were followed.

B. Should any dispute involve the removal from office of the pastor or any church officer, the arbitrators shall be limited to determining whether the procedures set forth in *Sections 4.04 or 5.06* were followed.

SECTION 12.04—ARBITRATION PROCEDURES

The Procedures for Arbitration shall be as adopted by the pastor and the board of deacons.

ARTICLE 13—CONFLICT OF INTEREST

SECTION 13.01—PURPOSE

The purpose of this conflict of interest policy is to protect the church's interest when it is contemplating entering into a transaction or arrangement that might benefit the private interest of an officer or director of the church or might result in a possible excess benefit transaction. This policy is intended to supplement but not replace any applicable state or federal laws governing conflicts of interest applicable to nonprofit and charitable organizations.

SECTION 13.02—DEFINITIONS

A. Interested Person:

Any director or officer who has a direct or indirect financial interest.

B. Financial interest:

A person has a financial interest if the person has, directly or indirectly, through business, investment, or family:

(1) An ownership or investment interest in any entity with which the church has a transaction or arrangement,

(2) A compensation arrangement with the church or with any individual or entity with which the church has a transaction or arrangement, or

(3) A potential ownership or investment interest in, or compensation arrangement with, any entity or individual with which the church is negotiating a transaction or arrangement.

(4) A financial interest is not necessarily a conflict of interest. A person who has a financial interest may have a conflict of interest only if the board of directors decides that a conflict of interest exists.

C. Compensation:

Compensation includes direct and indirect remuneration as well as gifts or favors that are not insubstantial.

D. Board:

The term "board" refers to the board of directors of the church.

SECTION 13.03—PROCEDURES

A. In connection with any actual or possible conflict of interest, an interested person must disclose the existence of the financial interest and be given the opportunity to disclose all material facts to the directors considering the proposed transaction or arrangement.

(B) After disclosure of the financial interest and all material facts, including any presentations by and discussion with the interested person, he shall leave the board meeting while the determination of a conflict of interest involving the transaction or arrangement is discussed and voted upon. The remaining board members shall decide if a conflict of interest exists by a majority vote.

(1) The chairman of the board shall, if appropriate, appoint a disinterested person or committee to investigate alternatives to the proposed transaction or arrangement.

(2) After exercising due diligence, the board or committee shall determine whether the church can obtain with reasonable efforts a more advantageous transaction or arrangement from a person or entity that would not give rise to a conflict of interest.

(3) If a more advantageous transaction or arrangement is not reasonably possible under circumstances not producing a conflict of interest, the board shall determine by a majority vote of the disinterested directors whether the transaction or arrangement is in the best interests of the church, for its own benefit, and whether it is fair and reasonable. In conformity with the above determination it shall make its decision as to whether to enter into the transaction or arrangement.

(C) If the board has reasonable cause to believe a member has failed to disclose actual or possible conflicts of interest, it shall inform the member of the basis for such belief and afford the member an opportunity to explain the alleged failure to disclose.

(D) If, after hearing the member's response and after making further investigation as warranted by the circumstances, the board determines the member has failed to disclose an actual or possible conflict of interest, it shall take appropriate disciplinary and corrective action.

SECTION 13.04—RECORDS OF PROCEEDINGS

(A) The minutes of the board shall contain the names of the persons who disclosed or otherwise were found to have a financial interest in connection with an actual or possible conflict of interest, the nature of the financial interest, any action taken to determine whether a conflict of interest was present, and the board's decision as to whether a conflict of interest in fact existed.

(B) The minutes of the board also shall contain the names of the persons who were present for discussions and votes relating to the transaction or arrangement, the content of the discussion, including any alternatives to the proposed transaction or arrangement, and a record of any votes taken in connection with the proceedings.

SECTION 13.05—COMPENSATION

A voting member of the board who receives compensation, directly or indirectly, from the church for services rendered may not vote on matters pertaining to that member's compensation.

ARTICLE 14—AMENDMENTS

These bylaws may be revised or amended by a majority vote of the members present and voting at any regular church administration meeting or other scheduled meeting called by the pastor, provided that said revision or amendment has been submitted in writing and announced from the pulpit seven (7) days before the vote is taken.

AMENDMENT #1

Facility Use Policy

It is a nonnegotiable matter of policy that Zion Hill Baptist Church does not rent, lease, or allow its facilities to be used by individuals, organizations, or any other group outside of its current active members, unless such other use is specifically sponsored and/or approved by the Pastor. In any and all cases church facilities will only be used for purposes which are in agreement with all policies, procedures, and beliefs as set forth in the Statement of Faith, Covenant, and Bylaws, ZHBC 2013, and all amendments thereto.

ADOPTION

These bylaws were adopted by a two-thirds majority vote of the members present and voting at a duly called meeting of the church in which a quorum was present.

These bylaws supersede any other bylaws of ____________ BAPTIST CHURCH.

Date: ______________ Minister of Records: ______________

ARTICLE 15—TAX-EXEMPT PROVISIONS

SECTION 15.01—PRIVATE INUREMENT

No part of the net earnings of the church shall inure to the benefit of or be distributable to its members, trustees, officers, or other private persons, except that the church shall be authorized and empowered to pay reasonable compensation for the services rendered and to make payments and distributions in furtherance of the purposes set forth in *Section 1.02* hereof.

SECTION 15.02—POLITICAL INVOLVEMENT

No substantial part of the activities of the church shall be the carrying on of propaganda or otherwise attempting to influence legislation. The church shall not participate in, or intervene in (including the publishing or distribution of statements) any political campaign on behalf of any candidate for public office.

SECTION 15.03—DISSOLUTION

Upon the dissolution of the church, the trustees shall, after paying or making provision for payment of all the liabilities of the church, dispose of all of the assets of the church to such organization or organizations formed and operated exclusively for religious purposes as shall at the time qualify as an exempt organization or organizations under Section 501(c)(3) of the Internal Revenue Code of 1986 (or the corresponding provision of any future United States Internal Revenue Law), as the trustees shall determine. Assets may be distributed only to tax-exempt organizations which agree with the church's Statement of Faith.

SECTION 15.04—RACIAL NONDISCRIMINATION

The church shall have a racially nondiscriminatory policy and, therefore, shall not discriminate against members, applicants, students, and others on the basis of race, color, sex, or national or ethnic origin with exception of sections above that state only men are qualified for pastor, deacon, or other offices of the church.

SECTION 15.05—LIMITATION OF ACTIVITIES

Notwithstanding any other provision of these bylaws, the church shall not, except to an insubstantial degree, engage in any activities or exercise any powers that are not in furtherance of the purposes stated in *Section 1.02.*

ARTICLE 16—PROCEDURES FOR ARBITRATION

SECTION 16.01—SCOPE OF ARBITRATION

The parties must, prior to the selection of arbitrators, agree to the scope of the matters to be considered by the arbitrators. In doing so the parties must conduct themselves with the utmost courtesy as befits believers in Jesus Christ. If the parties cannot agree upon the scope of the dispute for arbitration, the scope shall be determined by the arbitrators.

SECTION 16.02—SUBMISSION TO ARBITRATION

A. The parties, as Christians, believing that lawsuits between Christians are prohibited by Scripture, and having agreed, according to *Article 12* of the church bylaws, to submit disputes to binding arbitration, and to waive any legal right to take the dispute to a court of law, will refer and submit any and all disputes, differences, and controversies whatsoever within the agreed scope of arbitration to a panel of three arbitrators, to be selected as follows:

> **1.** All arbitrators must be born-again Christians of good reputation in the community and who affirm the church's Statement of Faith in its entirety.
>
> **2.** Each party shall submit a list of three proposed arbitrators to the other party, and the other party will choose one of the three proposed arbitrators to serve on the panel.
>
> **3.** The third arbitrator will be selected by mutual agreement of the other two arbitrators.
>
> **4.** In selecting the arbitrators, each party shall act in good faith in choosing Christian arbitrators who have no prior knowledge of the facts leading up to the dispute, are not

related to or close friends with the selecting party, and who will act impartially and with fundamental fairness.

5. No arbitrator may be an attorney.

6. No arbitrator may be employed or ever have been employed by, or under the authority of, either party or any other arbitrator.

7. The arbitrators will be selected as soon as possible but no later than 30 days after the parties have agreed to the scope of the arbitration.

8. The arbitration will be held at a neutral site agreed to by the arbitrators.

B. The arbitrators shall, subject to the provisions of these procedures, arbitrate the dispute according to the terms of these procedures, the Bible as interpreted by the church's Statement of Faith, and any applicable church documents.

C. Each party may be represented by counsel throughout the process at the party's own expense. Discovery will be allowed as needed, as determined in the discretion of the arbitrators. Formal rules of evidence shall not apply.

SECTION 16.03—TERMS AND CONDITIONS OF ARBITRATION

A. The arbitrators shall have full power to make such regulations and to give such orders and directions, as they shall deem expedient in respect to a determination of the matters and differences referred to them.

B. The arbitrators shall hold the arbitration hearing as soon as possible, but no later than thirty (30) days after the selection of the third arbitrator.

C. There shall be no stenographic record of the proceedings, and all proceedings shall be closed to the media and any other individuals not directly involved in the proceedings.

D. Normally, the hearing shall be completed within three (3) hours. The length of the hearing, however, may be extended by the arbitrators in their discretion or an additional hearing may be scheduled by the arbitrators to be held promptly.

E. There will be no post-hearing briefs.

F. The arbitrators are to make and publish their award, in writing, signed by each of them concerning the matters referred, to be delivered to the parties no later than 48 hours from the conclusion of the hearing, unless otherwise agreed by the parties. The arbitrators may, in their discretion, furnish an opinion.

SECTION 16.04—CONDUCT AND RULES OF HEARING

A. The arbitrators may, in their absolute discretion, receive and consider any evidence they deem relevant to the dispute, whether written or oral, without regard to any formal rules of evidence.

B. The parties and their respective witnesses must, when required by the arbitrators, attend and submit to examination and cross-examination under oath as to all or any of the matters referred to in the proceedings and to produce and deposit with the arbitrators all or any evidence within their possession or control concerning such matters.

C. If a party defaults in any respect referred to in *Subsection 4(B)*, above, the arbitrators may proceed with the arbitration in their discretion as if no such evidence were in existence, insofar as it may be favorable to the party in default.

D. All presentations shall be controlled by the arbitrators. Any disputes regarding procedure shall be decided solely by the arbitrators.

SECTION 16.05—DUTIES OF ARBITRATORS

A. The arbitrators are to receive all evidence, prayerfully consider such evidence in an impartial manner, and render a decision which, based upon Scriptural principles, is fair to all parties.

B. The arbitrators have full power to order mutual releases to be executed by the parties, and either of the parties failing, such orders shall have the effect of a release, and may be duly acknowledged as such.

C. In the event that either party or a witness for either party shall fail to attend the arbitration hearing, after such written notice to such party as the arbitrators shall deem reasonable, the arbitrators may proceed in the absence of such party or witnesses without further notice.

SECTION 16.06—DECISION OF ARBITRATORS

A. It is preferred that the arbitrators reach a unanimous decision, but if a unanimous decision cannot be obtained, a majority decision will be accepted. The written decision of a majority of the arbitrators shall be final and binding on all parties, and judgment upon the award rendered by the arbitrators may be entered in any court having jurisdiction thereof. There is no appeal from the decision of the arbitrators.

B. The decision of the arbitrators is to be kept confidential by all parties for a period of one year. For purposes of these procedures, the church membership may be informed of the decision if the church or any church pastors, officers, trustees, employees, or board members were a party to the proceeding.

C. Should any party commence legal proceedings against another party with respect to the agreed scope of the dispute or the binding decision of the arbitrators, with the exception of an action to enforce the decision of the arbitrators, that party shall pay to the other party all expenses of said proceedings, including reasonable attorneys' fees. In the event it becomes necessary for one party to commence legal proceedings to enforce the decision of the arbitrators, the non-prevailing party must bear all of the costs of said proceedings, including reasonable attorneys' fees.

SECTION 16.07—PARTIES TO COOPERATE

No party shall unreasonably delay or otherwise prevent or impede the arbitration proceedings. No party will involve the news media in the dispute in any way. No party shall publicize the dispute in any way to anyone not a party to the proceedings, except as permitted by the arbitrators and except that a party may disclose the proceedings of this arbitration to his or her spouse, legal counsel, accountants, insurance carrier, and as otherwise required by law.

SECTION 16.08—COSTS AND EXPENSES

Each party shall pay his or her own costs and expenses related to presenting the party's case to the arbitrators. The costs of the arbitration, including any fees for the arbitrators is to be shared equally by both parties.

SECTION 16.09—AMENDMENTS

These Procedures for Arbitration may be revised or amended by a majority vote of the board of deacons present and voting at any regular board meeting.

SECTION 16.10—ADOPTION

A. These Procedures for Arbitration were adopted by a majority vote of the church at which a quorum was present.

B. These Procedures for Arbitration supersede any other Procedures for Arbitration previously adopted by the board of deacons, if any exist.

Date Approved: ________________ Pastor: ________________

SUGGESTED FORMS AND DOCUMENTS TO USE FOR THE MINISTRY

The Christian Law Association (CLA) performs a great service to churches to help them resolve difficult issues, which aids them to be proper in their administration of ministerial duties. Their website is:

http://www.christianlaw.org/cla/

A. Examples of Resources (Documents) from CLA.

These are examples of very helpful materials for ministries that are available from CLA:

1. *"Sample Staff Handbook."*
2. *"From Offering Plate to Disbursement."*
3. *"Ministry Leadership Series: Audit of Documents."*
4. *"Audit of Finances."*
5. *"Payroll Primer."*
6. *"Ministry Vehicles."*

There are many other books available from CLA that may be of help to ministry leaders in a church.

Attached to this document are a few of CLA's forms for perusal. They are used with permission from CLA.

B. Liability Release Forms for Christian Ministries

1. There is no document that will entirely release a church from all liability, but a waiver signed by a parent for a child or a waiver signed by an adult on a trip with other church members for fellowship and educational purposes will suffice. The document must contain an accurate description of the activity that will be participated in by a child or adult.
   a. A form signed a year ago is not a valid document for a current trip.
   b. Do not allow an adult or child to participate in an event if a form has not been signed.

c. Be certain that the waiver form signed by individuals or parents contains a notice that it is a legal document.

d. The form must be signed by someone who has the legal capacity to act on behalf of a child. A minor or someone adjudicated to be mentally incompetent cannot act as the signee.

C. Suggested Financial Report Form:

Sample General Fund
Statement of Revenue and Expense
for the Month and Year-to-Date Ending (Current Month)

Support and Revenue	**Month**	**Year-to-Date**	**Budget**	**Budget Remaining**	**% of Budget Rec'd/Spent**
Contributions	26,417	247,123	305,000	57,877	81.02%
Interest Income	623	5,112	5,000	(112)	102.24%
Workshops/Events Income	214	600	1,000	400	60.00%
Total Support and Revenue	27,254	252,835	311,000	58,165	81.30%
Expenses (by Program)					
Worship	9,000	77,845	100,000	22,155	77.85%
Education	2,403	9,453	10,000	547	94.53%
Care/Fellowship	925	8,766	10,000	1,234	87.66%
Evangelism	1,613	8,453	10,000	1,547	84.53%
Resources	2,543	28,488	50,000	21,512	56.98%
Community Relief	800	2,475	3,000	525	82.50%
Youth	865	2,776	3,000	224	92.53%
Administration	10,325	111,457	125,000	13,543	89.17%
Total Expenses	28,474	249,713	311,000	61,287	80.29%
Excess of Support and Revenue over Expenses	(1,220)	3,122	-	(3,122)	

LIST OF SCRIPTURE REFERENCES IN THIS ACTUAL SOF AND BYLAWS

Genesis 1:1 14, 18, 20
Genesis 1:1-2; 26-27; 2:7 20
Genesis 1:1-3 18
Genesis 1:5, 8, 13, 19, 23, 31 20
Genesis 1:26 14, 23, 38
Genesis 1:26-28 38
Genesis 1:28 36
Genesis 2:17; 3:6 20
Genesis 2:22-24 38
Genesis 2:24 37
Genesis 3:1-6 23
Genesis 3:1-19; 5:12-14 21
Genesis 3:15 15
Genesis 6:5 20
Genesis 9:6 33
Genesis 13:14-17 33
Genesis 14:20 40
Genesis 15:6 37
Genesis 18:23 23
Genesis 19:5, 13 37
Exodus 12:6-7 16
Exodus 18:18, 21-22 33
Exodus 20:12 38
Exodus 20:13, 23:7 39
Exodus 20:2-3 14
Leviticus 16:6, 14, 15 16
Leviticus 16:14-15, 17 17
Leviticus 17:11 16, 17, 23, 24
Leviticus 18:1-30 37
Leviticus 19:18 39
Deuteronomy 6:4 14, 38
Deuteronomy 6:4-9 38
Deuteronomy 24:5 38
Deuteronomy 30:1-10 34
Joshua 24:17 27
2 Samuel 23:3 33
Job 3:16 38
Job 7:20 27
Psalm 12:6-7 12, 13
Psalm 12:6-7; 78:1-8; 119:89, 111, 152, 160 13
Psalm 14:1-3; 51:5 20
Psalm 19:7-11 12
Psalm 37:28; 97:10, 145:20 27
Psalm 51:5; 139:14-16 38
Psalm 72:8 34
Psalm 104:4 21
Psalm 127:3-5 38
Psalm 138:2 12
Proverbs 2:8 27
Proverbs 3:9-10 40
Proverbs 5:18-19; 12:4; 18:22; 19:14; 20:6-7; 30:18-19 38
Proverbs 14:32 23
Proverbs 19:18; 22:15; 23:13-14 38
Ecclesiastes 3:14 13
Isaiah 7:14 15
Isaiah 8:19-22 23
Isaiah 9:6-7;11:1-9 34
Isaiah 11:1-16 18
Isaiah 11:9 34
Isaiah 14:12-17 21
Isaiah 30:8, 40:6-8 13
Isaiah 40:8 12

Isaiah 44:24; 49:1, 5 38
Isaiah 53:4-7 24
Isaiah 64:6 24
Jeremiah 1:5; 20:15-18 38
Jeremiah 17:9 20
Jeremiah 30:7 34
Ezekiel 28:11-19 21
Ezekiel 37 34
Ezekiel 37:21-28 34
Daniel 3:17-18 33
Daniel 9:25-27 34
Amos 3:1-3 30
Jonah 2:9 23
Zechariah 14:4 18
Malachi 2:14-17 38
Malachi 3:18 23
Matthew 1:18-25 15
Matthew 3:16; 28:18-20 29
Matthew 4:1-11 22
Matthew 4:4; 5:17-18; 24:35; 28:20 13
Matthew 5:21 39
Matthew 5:44-48 39
Matthew 7:21-23 18
Matthew 9:4; 14:15-21 15
Matthew 16:13-20 28
Matthew 18:11 23
Matthew 18:15-20 44
Matthew 19:3-12 38
Matthew 19:4-6 38
Matthew 21:18 1153
Matthew 22:21 33
Matthew 22:30 21
Matthew 24:15-21 34
Matthew 24:29-31; 24:15-25:46 34
Matthew 24:29-31; 25:31-36 18
Matthew 25:41 23
Matthew 26:28 16, 24
Matthew 28:6-7 17
Matthew 28:16-20 29
Matthew 28:18-19 14, 29
Matthew 28:19 14, 40
Matthew 28:19-20 40
Matthew 28:20 19
Mark 1:8 19
Mark 10:6-9 38
Mark 10:6-12 38
Mark 12:25 21
Mark 12:26 12
Mark 12:29 14
Mark 16:6 17
Mark 16:15 29, 40
Mark 16:19 17, 18
Luke 1:30-33 34
Luke 1:35 15
Luke 1:44 38
Luke 2:40 15
Luke 4:2 15
Luke 4:30 15
Luke 6:31 39
Luke 10:20 27
Luke 15:10 22
Luke 16:19-26 35
Luke 16:19-31 35
Luke 17:33 27
Luke 22:32 27
Luke 23:42 35
Luke 24:2-7, 39-40 17
Luke 24:13-28 12
Luke 24:27, 44 12
Luke 24:46-48 40

Luke 24:49 19
Luke 24:51 17
John 1:1-2; 10:30 15
John 1:3 14 19, 20
John 1:12; 3:16, 18, 36; 5:24; 6:29 24
John 1:11 14
John 1:14 14, 15
John 1:14, 10:30 15
John 1:14, 18 15
John 1:14; 16:7-18 14
John 1:17 36
John 1:29 16, 17, 36
John 1:33 19
John 2:7-11 15
John 3:3, 5 24
John 3:5, 18 24
John 3:6 19, 20
John 3:8 25
John 3:16 24
John 3:23 29
John 5:24 25, 26
John 5:24-27 26
John 5:24; 13:1; 14:16-17; 17:11 26
John 5:39 12
John 8:21-24 22
John 8:32 23
John 10:27-30 26
John 10:27-30, 11:25-26, 14:19-20 27
John 10:35 13
John 11:35 15
John 13:34-35 39
John 14:1-3 23, 33
John 14:1-6 35
John 14:10, 26 14
John 14:16-17 19
John 14:16-17; 16:7 18
John 14:26 19
John 16:7-11 19
John 16:12-16 12
John 16:14 18
John 17:17 12 13, 26
John 17:18 29
John 17:23 25
John 20:17 17
John 20:20, 27 17
John 20:21 28, 40
Acts 1:8 19, 29, 40
Acts 1:9-11 17, 18 34
Acts 1:9-11; 15:16-17 34
Acts 1:10-11 18
Acts 1:16 12
Acts 2:1 28
Acts 2:23 16
Acts 2:27-31; 5:30; 13:34-37 17
Acts 2:29-30 34
Acts 2:41-42 27, 29
Acts 2:41-42; 20:17-28 27
Acts 2:41-47, 20:17-32 29
Acts 4:8, 31 19
Acts 4:19-20; 5:29; 23:5 33
Acts 4:34-37 40
Acts 5:3-4 14
Acts 5:32 29
Acts 11:16 19
Acts 13:39 24, 25
Acts 13:39; 16:31 24
Acts 15:11 24
Acts 15:13-18 28
Acts 16:30-31 25

Acts 17:2-3; 18:28; 26:22-23; 28:23 12
Acts 17:2-3 12
Acts 17:28 39
Acts 20:28 16, 25
Romans 1:16-17 24, 26
Romans 1:16-17; 3:22, 24-26; 4:5; 10:4 24
Romans 1:18, 20 23
Romans 1: 26-29 37
Romans 3:10-19 20, 23
Romans 3:10-19; 8:6-7 20
Romans 3:23; 6:23 25
Romans 3:24; 4:5; 5:1, 9 25
Romans 3:25 17, 24
Romans 3:25-26 17
Romans 4:3 37
Romans 4:5-8 37
Romans 5:1 16, 23, 25
Romans 5:1, 9 16
Romans 5:6-9 24
Romans 5:9 26
Romans 5:12, 19 23
Romans 6:3-5 29
Romans 6:11-13; 8:12-13 20
Romans 6:23 23
Romans 7:1-3 38
Romans 7:2 37
Romans 7:15-25 20
Romans 8:1-2, 4 20
Romans 8:1, 35-39 26
Romans 8:9, 15, 23 19
Romans 8:14, 16 19
Romans 8:14-28 28
Romans 8:19-23; 11:25-27 34
Romans 8:26-27 19
Romans 8:29 26
Romans 8:29-30 26
Romans 8:34 15
Romans 8:35-39 26
Romans 11:1-32 33
Romans 12:1-3 30
Romans 12:6-8 21
Romans 12:9-10; 17-21; 13:8-10 39
Romans 13:1-7 33, 37
Romans 13:3-4 33
Romans 15:26 28
Romans 16:17 30, 31, 44
Romans 16:17-18 44
1 Corinthians 1:1-9 28
1 Corinthians 1:18-29 32
1 Corinthians 1:30 26
1 Corinthians 2:13 12
1 Corinthians 3:5-15 27, 32
1 Corinthians 3:21-23 25
1 Corinthians 5:1; 6:9 37
1 Corinthians 5:1-13 44
1 Corinthians 6:1 18, 19, 20, 26, 28, 30, 39
1 Corinthians 6:1-8 39
1 Corinthians 6:19 18, 19, 20, 26, 30
1 Corinthians 6:19-20 20, 26, 30
1 Corinthians 7:1-16 38
1 Corinthians 7:10 37
1 Corinthians 8:6 14
1 Corinthians 9:17 36
1 Corinthians 11:2 27, 29
1 Corinthians 11:23-28 29
1 Corinthians 11:23-34 29
1 Corinthians 12:4-11 21

1 Corinthians 12:12-13 28
1 Corinthians 12:13 19
1 Corinthians 13:8-12 19
1 Corinthians 14:34-35 21
1 Corinthians 15:1-11 26
1 Corinthians 15:3 24, 30, 31
1 Corinthians 15:4 17, 33
1 Corinthians 15:25 34
1 Corinthians 15:33 30, 31
1 Corinthians 15:33-34 31
1 Corinthians 15:42-44, 51-54 33
1 Corinthians 15:50-57 18
1 Corinthians 15:51-57 35
1 Corinthians 16:2 40
2 Corinthians 1:10 26
2 Corinthians 2:1-11 44
2 Corinthians 3:9-18 36
2 Corinthians 3:18; 7:1 26
2 Corinthians 4:3-4 22
2 Corinthians 5:1, 6-8 27
2 Corinthians 5:1-10 35
2 Corinthians 5:6-8 23
2 Corinthians 5:8 35
2 Corinthians 5:9-11 32
2 Corinthians 5:10 13
2 Corinthians 5:14 17
2 Corinthians 5:17 15, 20, 35
2 Corinthians 5:17-18 20
2 Corinthians 5:17-21 15
2 Corinthians 5:18-20 29
2 Corinthians 5:20 40
2 Corinthians 5:21 15, 24
2 Corinthians 6:11-18 30
2 Corinthians 6:14-7:1 19, 30
2 Corinthians 6:17 30
2 Corinthians 9:6-7 40
2 Corinthians 11:1-15 22
2 Corinthians 11:13, 15 22
2 Corinthians 11:13-15 22
2 Corinthians 13:14 14
Galatians 1:6-9 26
Galatians 2:11 31
Galatians 2:16 25
Galatians 3:13 23, 36
Galatians 3:13-25 36
Galatians 3:22 24
Galatians 3:28 38
Galatians 4:6-7 27
Galatians 5:2-9 26
Galatians 5:16-17 20
Galatians 5:16-23 20
Galatians 6:1 24, 44
Galatians 6:6 40
Galatians 6:15 24
Ephesians 1:3 25
Ephesians 1:7 16, 24, 26, 36
Ephesians 1:7-14, 4:20-32 27
Ephesians 1:10; 3:2-10 36
Ephesians 1:13-14; 4:30 19
Ephesians 1:21 22
Ephesians 1:22-23, 3:1-6, 4:11, 5:23 28
Ephesians 2:1-3, 8-10 20
Ephesians 2:1, 5 24
Ephesians 2:8-9 24, 36
Ephesians 2:8-10 32
Ephesians 2:13 16
Ephesians 2:22 18
Ephesians 3:2, 9 36
Ephesians 3:11 36
Ephesians 4:11-15 21

Ephesians 4:11-16 29
Ephesians 4:22-24 20
Ephesians 4:24 26
Ephesians 4:28 40
Ephesians 4:31-32 39
Ephesians 5:11 19
Ephesians 5:18 19
Ephesians 5:21-33; 6:1-4 38
Ephesians 5:22-23 37, 38
Ephesians 5:22-24 37
Ephesians 5:25-27 26
Ephesians 6:10-12 22
Ephesians 6:10-13 22
Philippians 1:6, 2:12-13 26
Philippians 1:23 23, 35
Philippians 2:2-4 39
Philippians 2:5-8 15
Philippians 2:7-8 23
Philippians 3:4-9 24
Philippians 3:9 25
Philippians 3:20-21 17, 34
Colossians 1:14 16
Colossians 1:15-16 14
Colossians 1:16-17 20
Colossians 1:17 13
Colossians 1:18 28
Colossians 1:20 16
Colossians 1:24-25, 27 36
Colossians 1:25 36
Colossians 2:9-10 27
Colossians 2:10 25
Colossians 2:12 29
Colossians 2:13 25
Colossians 2:15 22
Colossians 3:18 38
Colossians 3:18-19 38
Colossians 3:18-21 38
1 Thessalonians 1:9-10 30
1 Thessalonians 2:13 12
1 Thessalonians 4:1-8 37
1 Thessalonians 4:3-4; 5:23 26
1 Thessalonians 4:13-18 18
1 Thessalonians 4:16-18 33
1 Thessalonians 5:6; 5:8 31
1 Thessalonians 5:6-10 18
1 Thessalonians 5:14 44
1 Thessalonians 5:23 27
2 Thessalonians 1:7-8 18
2 Thessalonians 1:7-9 35
2 Thessalonians 2:4 22
2 Thessalonians 2:7 19
2 Thessalonians 3:6 30, 31, 44
2 Thessalonians 3:6, 10-15 44
2 Thessalonians 3:6, 11, 14-15 30
2 Thessalonians 3:6, 14-15 31
1 Timothy 1:12-17 27
1 Timothy 2:5 15, 18
1 Timothy 2:6 16
1 Timothy 2:8-15; 3:4-5, 12 38
1 Timothy 2:11-14 21
1 Timothy 3:1-13 27
1 Timothy 3:2 31, 38
1 Timothy 3:2, 12 38
1 Timothy 3:6 21
1 Timothy 3:11 31
1 Timothy 4:1-3 22, 34
1 Timothy 5:6 20
1 Timothy 5:17-18 40

1 Timothy 5:19-20 44
1 Timothy 6:3-5 30
2 Timothy 2:19-26 30
2 Timothy 2:24-26 39
2 Timothy 3:1-5 30, 34
2 Timothy 3:12 27
2 Timothy 3:16-17 12, 13
2 Timothy 4:5 31, 32
2 Timothy 4:18 27
Titus 1:5-11 27
Titus 1:6 38, 48, 58
Titus 2:2 31, 32
Titus 2:4 21
Titus 2:11-14 18, 32, 34
Titus 3:1-11 32
Titus 3:2 39
Titus 3:5 24, 25
Titus 3:10-11 44
Hebrews 1:1-3 14
Hebrews 1:3 17, 18
Hebrews 1:3; 2:17; 5:9-10 7:25; 9:25; 12:2 18
Hebrews 1:14 21, 22
Hebrews 2:6-7 22
Hebrews 2:6-10 22
Hebrews 2:14-17 23
Hebrews 3:1; 10:10-14 26
Hebrews 4:15 15
Hebrews 7:24-25 15
Hebrews 7:25 26
Hebrews 9:7, 12-14, 22, 24 12:22-24 17
Hebrews 9:12-14, 18-24 10:19-22 16
Hebrews 9:14 16
Hebrews 9:22-23 16
Hebrews 10:5-14 17
Hebrews 10:19 16
Hebrews 10:22 27
Hebrews 11:1-40 37
Hebrews 11:6 36
Hebrews 11:7 37
Hebrews 12:5-7 27
Hebrews 12:10 26
Hebrews 12:18-29 28
Hebrews 12:22-24 16
Hebrews 13:4 37, 38
Hebrews 13:4-7 38
Hebrews 13:5 27
Hebrews 13:17 37
Hebrews 13:20-21 16
James 1:16-18 28
James 1:18 24
1 Peter 1:10-12 36
1 Peter 1:13 30, 31
1 Peter 1:13-16 30
1 Peter 1:14-16 21
1 Peter 1:17; 2:11 29
1 Peter 1:18-19 16, 23, 24, 25
1 Peter 1:23 13, 24
1 Peter 1:23-25 13
1 Peter 2:13-14 37
1 Peter 2:24; 3:18 24
1 Peter 3:1-7 38
1 Peter 3:18 17
1 Peter 5:8-9 22
2 Peter 1:3-4 32
2 Peter 1:4 25, 27
2 Peter 1:16-21 12
2 Peter 1:20-21 13
2 Peter 1:21 12
2 Peter 2:4 21
1 John 1:7, 9 26

1 John 1:8, 10 20
1 John 1:10 17
1 John 2:1 15, 18, 26, 30
1 John 2:1-2 15, 26
1 John 2:15-17 30
1 John 2:20-27 19
1 John 3:2 26
1 John 3:5 17, 21
1 John 3:5-9 21
1 John 3:17 39, 40
1 John 3:17-18 39
1 John 4:1-3 23
1 John 4:10 24
1 John 5:1 14, 23, 25, 26, 27
1 John 5:1-8 14
1 John 5:11-12 25
1 John 5:13 26, 27
1 John 5:19 23
2 John 1:2 13
2 John 1:7-9 27
2 John 1:9-11 30
2 John 1:10-11 31
Jude 1:1 26, 27
Jude 1:3 12, 13, 29
Jude 1:6 21, 35
Jude 1:6-7 35
Jude 1:24 26
Jude 1:24-25 26
Jude 1:14-15 18
Revelation 1:4-6 14
Revelation 1:5; 7:14 16
Revelation 1:7; 3:21 18
Revelation 2:26-27 28
Revelation 3:10 34
Revelation 3:11-13 27
Revelation 4:11 14
Revelation 5:9 16
Revelation 6:1-19:21 34
Revelation 7:11-12 22
Revelation 7:13-17, 21:22-27 35
Revelation 12:9-11 22
Revelation 12:11 16
Revelation 19:19-21, 20:1-6 18
Revelation 20:1-3, 10 22
Revelation 20:1-4, 6, 14 34
Revelation 20:2-6 36
Revelation 20:7 18, 22
Revelation 20:7-15 18
Revelation 20:10 22
Revelation 20:11-15 35
Revelation 20:11-15, 21:22-27 35
Revelation 20:12 13
Revelation 20:13 34
Revelation 20:14-15 23

INDEX OF WORDS AND PHRASES IN THIS ACTUAL SOF AND BYLAWS

Abortion, 5, 38
absentee, 42
abyss, 18, 22, 34
acceptance, 17, 41
Adam, 20, 23
Adamic nature, 20
administer, 49
administers, 35
administration, 36, 46, 47, 51, 53, 55, 59, 67, 73
admonition, 31
adultery, 37, 38
advent, 33
Advocate, 17
age of accountability, 50
age of Grace, 34
alcohol, 5, 31, 32
all-sufficient and, 25
alter one's gender, 37
ambassadors, 28, 39
amended, 67, 72
angels, 20-22, 40
annihilated, 35
annual church administration meeting, 48-50, 52-55
annual meeting, 56
another church, 44, 45
Antichrist, 18
Apocrypha, 12
apostates, 16, 19, 30
apostles, 3, 13, 21, 22
Apostolic age, 19
appoint, 46, 49, 50, 57, 62, 66
appointment of the Father, 23
arbitration, 64, 69-72
arbitrators, 64, 68-72
archenemy, 22
arose from the dead in the same body, 17
ascended into Heaven, 17
assets, 52, 68
associate, 53, 54, 60
assured of their salvation, 27
attorney, 69
attributes, 14
authority, 12, 29, 37, 41-43, 49, 55-57, 60, 62, 63, 69
authority and sufficiency of the Holy Bible, 12
autographs, 12, 13
backbiting, 41
background, 46
backwards, 29
banks, 52
Baptist forefathers, 13
baptizes, 19
basis, 25, 36, 40, 45, 57, 66, 68
basis of race, color, sex, or national or ethnic origin, 68
be sober, 31, 32
benevolence, 28, 50
benevolence fund, 50
bestiality, 37
Bible-believing church, 42
binding, 40, 63, 69, 71
binding arbitration, 63, 69

bisexuality, 37
blessed hope, 34
Blood, 5, 16, 17, 23-26, 36
board of deacons, 42, 43, 47, 50, 51, 52, 56, 60-64, 72
body of Christ, 19, 34
Body of Christ, 28
brotherly love, 41, 42
building, 11, 28
by grace, through faith, 36
bylaws, 41, 51, 52, 54, 58, 62, 64, 67-69
camps, 11
Cana, 31
candidate, 41, 48, 58, 59, 60, 68
canon, 19
capital, 33, 52
capital punishment, 33
captivity captive, 17
cast into the lake of fire, 18, 22, 35
Cataphatic Imaging, 33
cemetery, 50
chains, 21
Chairman, 51
Charismatic Movement, 30
Charismatic Tongues Movement, 19
charitable, 11, 63, 64
check, 46, 52, 53
cheerfully, 40
child, 20, 26, 27, 38, 50, 73
children, 21, 27, 38, 41, 46, 56, 57, 58
Christ known, 29
Christian education, 11, 57
Christian unity, 13
chronology, 12
church, 2, 11, 13, 18, 21, 24, 27-30, 32, 34, 37-69, 71, 72, 73
Church Age, 28
circumstances, 43, 55, 56, 61, 66
civil government, 33
civil lawsuits, 39
claims, 27, 64
cleanses, 16
commemoration, 29
committee, 43, 44, 48, 62, 63, 66
completed revelation, 12
conception, 39
confession, 24, 26, 42
Congregational Polity, 32
conscience, 16, 33, 56
conscious, 23, 35, 36
conscious suffering, 23
consequences, 16
consummation, 19
Contemplative Prayer, 33
contend earnestly for the faith, 29
contradictory, 20
contributions, 43, 52, 54, 63
convicts, 19
cooperate, 28
coordination, 50, 55
corporal correction, 38
corrupted, 31
costs, 43, 71, 72
counseling, 32
counterfeits, 22

covenant, 18, 27, 34, 36, 40-43
Covenant (Replacement) Theology, 32
covenant of faith, 27
Covenant Theology, 36
covenants of God, 26
creation, 12, 18, 20, 25, 34
credit card, 53
cross-examination, 70
curse, 23, 24, 26, 34
custodian, 51
Davidic throne, 18
Day of Atonement, 17
day of Pentecost, 18, 28
daycare centers, 11
dead in trespasses and sins, 20
death, 16, 17, 19, 23, 25, 29, 34, 35, 39, 45, 48, 50
December, 48, 55, 57
defense of any claim, 61
Deity, 14, 15, 24
deposit, 52, 53, 70
descended, 17, 20
determined by the pastor, 13, 42, 45, 46, 55
devotions, 41
dies, 38
direction of the church, 42
disagreement, 47, 49, 58, 63, 64
disbursements, 52, 53
disciplinary, 43, 44, 47, 56, 66
discipline, 28, 38, 40, 43-45, 62, 64
Discovery, 69
discretion of the pastor, 43, 45, 54, 63
disobedience, 33
Dispensation, 28, 36
Dispensation of Grace, 28, 36
dispensational, 35, 36
dispensations, 35, 36
disputes, 39, 64, 69, 71
dissolved, 47
divorce, 38
doctrinal, 5, 12, 31, 58
doctrines, 40
donations, 52, 54
duplicated, 12
ecclesiastical apostasy, 30
ecstasism, 33
ecstatic utterances, 19
ecumenical, 19
educate, 41
educational, 11, 57-59, 63, 73
efficacy of the Blood of Christ, 22
eighteen years of age, 42
emblem, 29
enemy of God, 22
English Authorized Version of 1611, 13
equal, 14-16, 18, 37
equality, 14
erring, 31
error, 19, 22
eternal covenant people, 33
eternal suffering, 35
eternity, 14, 18
Euthanasia, 5, 39
evangelists, 21, 57

Eve, 20
events, 18, 45, 50, 52
every experience and teaching must be examined, 23
evolutionary process, 20
ex nihilo, 20
exalting himself above all that is called God, 22
examined, 60
example by His death, 23
examples, 50, 53, 73
exclusively for religious purposes, 68
exhaust, 40
expenses, 40, 52, 60, 61, 71, 72
explicit message, 28
extended revelation, 36
EXTENT OF INDEMNIFICATION, 7, 62
extent of our faith, 40
fails to adhere, 47, 49, 58
faith, 12, 13, 16, 17, 20, 23-25, 27, 28, 31, 32, 35, 36, 40-42, 59, 60, 64, 69
fallen angels, 21, 22
false prophet, 18
family of God, 27, 28
fellowship of the gospel, 27
felony, 46
financial statements, 43
fiscal year, 54, 57
Foot-washing, 5, 29
form 1099, 53
forms, 20, 73
fornication, 37, 38
free from any error, 12
functions, 37, 43
funds, 52, 53, 63
gap theory, 20
gender, 38
gender selection, 38
general assembly, 28
general public, 43
geography, 12
gift of sex, 37
gifts, 19, 21, 27, 52, 54, 65
giving, 40, 47, 54-56
glorified, 17, 34, 35
glorified bodies, 34, 35
God chose every Word, 12
God the Son, 14, 15, 18, 26
good works, 32
gospel of Christ, 25
governed by His laws, 27
government, 28, 33, 43
grammatical-historical meaning, 13
great day, 21
Great High Priest, 17
Great Tribulation, 34
Great White Throne, 18, 35
Greek Traditional Text, 12
guidance, 54, 55, 62
heaven, 16, 17, 23, 24, 26, 33-35
Heaven, 17, 35
Hebrew Masoretic Text, 12
Hell, 35
His person and work, 12
history, 12, 35, 46
holiness, 14, 40
holy estate, 22
holy men of God, 12

Holy Spirit, 12, 14, 15, 18-20, 21, 24-26, 28, 40
home, 29, 37, 57, 58
homosexuality, 37
human life begins at conception, 38
immersed, 27, 29
immersion, 29, 42
immorality, 30
immutable, 14
impenitence and unbelief, 23
imputed, 25
incarnation, 22
incest, 37, 38
incorruptible, 16, 23, 25, 34
indemnify, 60, 62
independent, indigenous assemblies of believers, 28
Indwelling, 18
inerrant Word of God, 58
infallible, 12, 58
infinite power, 14
influence legislation, 68
initiate, 42
initiate any church action, 42
innocence, 20, 23
innocent human life, 39
innumerable company of spiritual beings, 21
inspiration, 12
inspiration of God, 12
installation, 54
insurance, 39, 62, 72
insurance company, 39
intercede, 18
Internal Revenue Law, 68
interpreted, 13, 69
intoxicating drink, 41
Israel, 16, 18, 33, 34
just for the unjust, 17
justice, 14, 29, 39
justification, 25
justified, 23, 25
kept in the church office, 54
King of kings, 33
Kingdom Age, 28
knowledge of God, 34
lake of fire, 18, 23
Lamb, 16, 17, 35, 36
LaVinka, 2
Law, 2, 11, 36, 73
lawsuits, 63, 69
leavening, 31
lesbianism, 37
letter of transfer, 42, 45
letters of transfer, 44
liabilities, 52, 68
liability, 62, 73
liberty, 49
licensure, 38
lifestyle, 38, 41, 42, 58
LIMITATION OF ACTIVITIES, 8, 68
literal, 20, 34, 35
literature, 14, 40
London Baptist Confession, 13
Long Day Proponents, 33
lordship salvation, 24
lose his salvation, 27
loss of reward, 27, 32
love, 17, 26, 27, 31, 38-40, 42
loyalty, 44
Lucifer, 21

lust of the flesh, 20
majority vote of the members, 42, 44, 51, 61, 67
Maker and Preserver, 14
malice, 39
manifest God, 15
marriage, 30, 37, 38
Mary, 15
masculine gender, 21
Mediator, 15
mediatorial offices, 23
MEETINGS, 6, 7, 54-56
members, 11, 28, 39-50, 52, 53, 55-57, 62, 63, 65, 67, 68, 71, 73
membership, 28, 29, 41, 42, 44-52, 62, 71
mental well being, 38
mercy seat, 16
Mercy Seat, 17
Messiah-King, 16
Millennial reign, 18, 33
ministry, 2, 18, 21, 28-32, 40, 43, 47, 49, 58, 60, 73
minor, 73
miraculous, 15, 19, 23
mission, 28, 29, 58, 59
mission of the church, 28, 29
moderator, 49, 50, 55-57
modernism, 30
Monergism, 32
moral fall, 21
Moralism, 25
mortgage, 51
most accurate and faithful translation, 12
most High, 22
mother, 38
moved, 12
movements, 22, 30
murder, 38, 39
murmuring, 44
mutual releases, 71
Mysticism, 33
narcotic drugs, 41
nature, 14, 15, 18, 20, 23, 25, 26, 60, 63, 66
Neo-evangelicalism, 30
NEPHALOS, 31
NEPHO, 31
neutral site, 69
new birth, 24
new life, 24, 29
new nature, 20, 24
New Testament, 12-14, 19, 25, 28
no apostles or prophets, 21
no other acts, 24
Noah, 33
nolo contendere, 61
nondiscriminatory, 68
not ways of salvation, 36
notices, 51
obedience, 14, 23, 27, 32
offerings, 40, 42, 53, 54
offering-slip, 53
officers, 27, 46-49, 54-56, 67, 71
officers are pastors and deacons, 27
old nature, 20
Old Testament, 12, 13, 16-18, 36
Old Testament saints, 17, 36

omnipresent, 18
once delivered, 3, 12, 13
one substance, 14, 15, 18
one thousand years, 18
one year, 47, 59, 71
ongoing prophecy, 32
only to tax-exempt organizations, 68
ordained, 28, 37, 38, 58-60
ordinances, 27, 29, 40, 49, 50
ordinances of Christ, 27
ordination, 38, 51, 54, 58-60
ORDINATION, 7, 58-60
ordination by the church, 38
organism, 28
organization, 28, 68
organized congregation, 27
original, 12-14, 51
original bylaws, 51
originator of sin, 21
overindulge, 31
paid, 49, 53, 60, 61
paid by the church, 61
Paradise, 17
pastor, 21, 31, 38, 41-64, 68
Patriarchs, 18
pattern, 17
penance, 35
perfect human body, 15
perfecting of the saints, 21
perfections, 14
period of sixty (60) days, 64
personal Savior, 25, 41, 42
plenary, 12
Plenary inspiration, 12
policy, 64, 68
political, 29, 68
polity, 28, 32
polygamy, 38
population control, 38
pornography, 37
power of the devil, 20
practical instruction, 12
preaching, 14, 48, 59, 60
preannounced, 15
premeditated murder, 33
presence of the Lord, 35
preserved, 12, 13, 14
Pretemporal Reprobation, 32
Pre-tribulation rapture, 32
pride, 21
print shops, 11
PRIVATE INUREMENT, 8, 67
privileges, 27, 29
procedures, 39, 43-45, 50, 60, 64, 69, 71
Procedures for Arbitration, 64, 72
Process Evolution, 33
progressive sanctification, 26
prohibited by Scripture, 38, 63, 69
promised, 13
propaganda, 68
property, 43, 49, 51, 54
prophecies, 15, 36
prophets, 3, 12, 13, 21
Prophets Chamber, 50
prosperity, 40
Providential care, 13
proxy, 42
psychological, 32
public office, 68
pulpit, 47-50, 55, 56, 67

pulpit committee, 48, 50
pulpit supply, 50
pure, 13, 43
pure democracy, 43
purpose, 26, 29, 35, 36, 44, 51, 53, 56, 57, 64
purposes, 11, 21, 46, 49, 63, 67, 68, 71, 73
quarterly, 53-55
quorum, 46, 55, 61, 67, 72
racially, 68
radio, 11
ransom, 16
rape, 38
Rapture, 18, 19
Received Text, 12
reconciliation, 16, 41, 44
record, 35, 37, 43, 46, 51-54, 66, 70
redeeming work, 17
redemption has been accomplished solely, 24
redemptive, 36
re-elected, 47
regenerates, 19
regular, 45-47, 53, 55, 56, 67, 72
regularly, 40, 48, 49
reign, 18
rejection, 20, 33
remnant, 18
repentance, 24, 42
repentance is a vital part of believing, 24
Replacement Theology, 33
reproduce, 21
rescue missions, 11
responsibility, 32, 36, 37, 58, 59
restoration, 42, 44, 47
restore his brother, 44
resurrection, 17, 19, 25, 35
resurrection body, 17
return, 14, 18, 34
reunited, 35
revelatory knowledge, 32
revenge, 39
revised, 67, 72
rules of procedure, 55
sacrifice, 16, 23
salvation by grace alone, 22
sanctification, 26
Satan, 4, 16, 18, 21, 22, 34
saved, 17-21, 23-26, 28, 33
Savior, 17, 23, 29, 40, 41
schools, 11
science, 12
Scriptural marriage, 37
Scriptures center, 12
seals, 19
second blessing, 25
second coming, 12, 22, 34
Second Coming, 3, 18
second member, 44
second work of grace, 25
self-examination, 29, 44
separation, 30
servants, 50
seven-year period of Tribulation, 34
sexual, 37
sign gifts, 19
sin, 15-17, 19, 20, 23, 24, 26, 27, 29, 36, 41, 42

sin of the world, 16, 17
sinful perversions, 37
sinless, 15, 24
Sinless Perfectionism, 32
six literal solar days, 20
sixty-six books, 12
slander, 39
sober, 31
social action, 28
social gospel, 28
Son of God, 15, 23
son of the morning, 21
sovereign God, 25
special meeting, 56, 57
Spirit, 18-21, 23, 26, 27, 40
spirit beings, 21
spiritual blessing, 25
spiritual death, 20, 25
spiritual welfare, 50
spirituality, 40
standing committees, 55, 62
Statement of Faith, 40, 41, 43, 45, 47-50, 57, 58, 60, 68, 69
stewardships, 35
substitutionary, 17
suit, 60, 61
Superintendent, 28
Superintendent of the church, 28
supernaturally superintended, 12
supervision, 49
tabernacle, 16
tattling, 41
television, 11
term of service, 47
terminate, 45
test, 35, 36
testify, 18
testimony, 27, 29, 42, 44
testimony of God, 27
theistic evolution, 20
Theistic Evolution, 33
theory of evolution, 20
these Three are one God, 14
Third Person, 18
three basic institutions, 37
Three Persons, 14
Throne, 18
times of the Gentiles, 34
tithe, 40
tobacco, 41
tongues, 19, 32
totally depraved, 23
transfer, 51
transforming, 22
transgression, 21, 23
translation, 12-14, 34
trespasser, 43, 56
tribe, 39
Tribulation, 18, 34
Trinity, 15, 18
trips, 50
Triune God, 14, 20
two ordinances, 29
two-thirds majority vote, 67
uncertain trumpet, 31
underlying original **language Texts**, 14
under-shepherd, 43
unequally yoked, 30
ungodly, 18, 41
unilateral, 56

unilateral authority, 56
united, 15, 24
unity, 14, 28
universal death through sin, 24
universal flood, 33
universality and exceeding sinfulness of sin, 20
unlimited inerrancy, 12
unregenerate person, 25
unsaved, 11, 18, 35
unscriptural, 19, 36
vacancy, 47, 50
valid document, 73
verbal, 12
verbally inspired, 12
vigilant, 31
vile, 22
violations, 43
violence, 39
virgin, 15
visible and invisible, 14
visitation, 50
voluntarily, 17, 23
vote, 42, 46, 48, 59-61, 63, 65-67, 72
W2 forms, 53
walking according to truth, 31
warfare, 22
washes, 16
will, 12, 16-23, 26-28, 30, 32, 33-36, 39, 41, 45-49, 51, 53, 56, 58-60, 62, 69-73
will of the local church, 28
Williams, 2
wine, 31, 32
wisdom, 14, 15, 58
without faith, 36
without spot, 16
witnessing, 28
Women, 21
Word, 12, 13, 24, 26, 27, 32, 33, 37, 41, 49, 58-60
WORD OF GOD in English, 14
work, 2, 14, 16, 20, 21, 24-26, 28, 29, 32, 36, 46, 50, 54, 58, 59
worldliness, 30
worship, 11, 18, 29, 30, 40, 43, 45, 49, 55
written report, 53, 54

SAMPLE GUIDELINES FOR NURSERY WORKERS

The nursery should be considered a ministry to the Lord and to the parents of the little ones. The nursery workers should understand that by caring for the infants in a clean, caring environment they are allowing the parents to participate in and enjoy the worship services and classes of the church ministry, without distractions.

1. Very small children and infants can disrupt and serve as a distraction, not only to the parents but also to others in the services.
   a. The little ones often draw the attention of those about them to themselves. They are so cute. Right?
   b. They make noises and often are not able to sit quietly.
2. Parents are often embarrassed because of their children and most often are not able to pay attention to the service.
3. There are differing opinions concerning whether children should be allowed in the auditorium during a worship service. Great care should be exercised to not offend the parents. Children do need to learn at an early age that they can be quiet and sit still. A key to building a great church will be its ability to minister to young families with children and infants.
4. Those who serve in the nursery should be adults and maybe a few older young people. They should members of the church, mature, responsible, and well trained. Now it is necessary, for the protection of the children, to have workers pass a "background check."

5. The facility used for the nursery should have limited access and have a clean, sanitary, attractive, comfortable, safe, ordered, and controlled environment.

    a. A nursery facility that meets these requirements will impress and appeal to the parents and their nursery age children.

    b. A well run and equipped nursery will be a drawing force for church growth.

    c. The activities in the nursery should not "excite" the children in the sense of getting them stirred up physically.

    d. There should be no "running, climbing, fighting or tussles and definitely no throwing of toys or other items. No tantrums.

6. There should be an age limit for the children allowed in the nursery. Thirty-six months of age and younger might be the best standard. It is wise to have at least two divisions in the nursery. The children that can walk should be separate from those which cannot.

    a. Only approved nursery workers should be permitted in the nursery. The nursery should be off limits for older children and most teenagers.

    b. There should be workers trained in CPR, etc.

    c. There must be an identification process in effect. Children and their parents should be registered. Photos of parents with their children are a good idea. Only properly identified persons should be allowed to pick-up a child. Parents should not send someone to get the child in their place, unless pre-arranged with the nursery supervisor.

d. Care should be taken to make note of allergies, illnesses, or health conditions that need guarding.

e. There should be information concerning medications. These should be in a safe place out of the reach of the children, and under lock and key if necessary. This goes for cleaning fluids, etc.

f. The parents must give permission for the children to eat or drink what is provided in the nursery.

7. There should not be a passage way or exit in the nursery so that there are people leaving the facility passing through the nursery.

8. There should be an adult in the nursery for every 3-4 children. One worker with four or five cradle age infants could easily be over whelmed.

9. Nursery workers should be in their places at the very minimum 15 minutes before the service. Thirty minutes would be better. This would allow the workers to make sure everything in the area is in order.

10. Food and snacks should be placed in bug-proof containers. All food droppings should be cleaned up in a timely manner to avoid children eating off of the floor or insects being attracted.

11. Nursery workers should remain in the nursery until the last child has been turned over to its parents.

12. Children with "communicable illnesses" should be care for at home so as to avoid contaminating the other children and the workers.

13. The children should be trained to help "put away" the toys, and materials (Crayolas, printed drawings, etc.). Only child-proof, safe materials should be used.

14. Diapers and other items needed for infants should be stored and available. Dirty diapers should be dumped after each service.

15. Milk and other food items for cradle age infants should be provided by the parents or guardians.

16. The workers should report any problems to the Pastor and Deacons - in that order.

17. Workers need proper training and instruction concerning legal matters.

18. If there is a Nursery Supervisor, she should make sure that these guidelines are observed faithfully.

Guidelines for the Nursery Leader

1. Make up a list of nursery workers for each service. Post this schedule in the nursery on the last Sunday of the month and give a copy to your supervisor.

   a. Try to maintain a ratio of one worker for every three children.

   b. Under most circumstances nursery helpers should be at least 12 years old.

   c. Contact nursery workers to remind them when they are scheduled to be in the nursery.

2. Meet with nursery workers once each quarter.

   a. Impress upon your workers that the nursery is a ministry, both to the parents and to the young children. It is not just a baby-sitting job.

   b. Encourage workers to teach Bible truths to toddlers rather than simply letting them play all the time.

   c. Discuss any problems, equipment needs, or supplies.

   d. Keep your supervisor advised of problems and progress.

3. Check on the nursery each Sunday to be sure it is functioning properly.

   a. Only nursery workers should be allowed in the nursery. Teens, children, and parents are not to be in the nursery unless bringing or picking up children.

   b. Only children 0-36 months should be in the nursery.

4. Be sure all teaching materials are in agreement with the policy and doctrinal position of the church.

5. Remove broken toys and worn-out books. Have safe toys. Keep equipment in good repair. Keep the cabinets neat and well organized.

6. Empty the wastebasket and dispose of dirty diapers after each service.

   a. Sheets should be washed every week, toys every other week and the cribs at least once a month.

   b. Do not leave food in the nursery.

   c. Maintain a supply of fresh water, moist towelettes and plastic bags (for soiled diapers) at all times.

7. Inform your workers that the nursery will be open 15 minutes before and after the services to encourage fellowship among parents and to alleviate possible pressure on any parents who may wish to respond to the invitation.

A Questionnaire for Christian Workers

Please check the areas in which you have had experience:

- ☐ S.S. Teacher ☐ S.S. Superintendent
- ☐ Children's Church ☐ Youth Leader
- ☐ Choir ☐ Visitation
- ☐ Song Leader ☐ Usher
- ☐ Special Music ☐ Bus Ministry
- ☐ Piano/Organ ☐ Bookkeeping
- ☐ Nursery ☐ Electrical Work
- ☐ Deacon ☐ Custodian
- ☐ Artistic Work ☐ Painting
- ☐ Secretarial Work ☐ Carpentry
- ☐ Missionary Leader ☐ Other

Please check the areas of ministry in which you are willing to serve, if asked to do so:

- ☐ S.S. Teacher ☐ S.S. Superintendent
- ☐ Children's Church ☐ Youth Leader
- ☐ Choir ☐ Visitation
- ☐ Song Leader ☐ Usher
- ☐ Special Music ☐ Bus Ministry
- ☐ Piano/Organ ☐ Bookkeeping
- ☐ Nursery ☐ Electrical Work
- ☐ Deacon ☐ Custodian

❑ Artistic Work ☐ Painting

❑ Secretarial Work ☐ Carpentry

❑ Missionary Leader ☐ Other

In some areas of the world this type of questionnaire for Christian workers will be totally impractical.

The church planters should always remember that it is wiser or more prudent to "select workers" and not just ask for volunteers. When a plea for "volunteers" is made there can be individuals that are not qualified respond. It can be detrimental to the ministry and to the individual when a volunteer is rejected for any reason.

APPENDIX SEVEN:

GUIDELINES FOR CALLING A PASTOR

Unless the missionary/pastor plans to remain as pastor indefinitely, the Church will sooner or later be faced with the need of calling a pastor. Generally speaking the missionary guides the new congregation in the matter by helping select a group of mature leaders to form a "Pulpit Committee." This group of church leaders will have the responsibility of praying and seeking God's direction in considering possible candidates for the office of pastor. They should use every means available to gather information on the candidate and his family. This can be accomplished by:

1. If the candidate is a locally known pastor or member of the Church seeking a pastor, some of these steps will not be necessary.

2. Visiting the candidate in several services of the church where he is presently pastoring. A visit of this nature will allow the committee to sense and evaluate the spirit in the church under the candidate's leadership. It also affords the opportunity to experience his preaching ministry.

3. A candidate that is under serious consideration can be invited to spend a few days in the area of the Church. He should be given the opportunity to minister through teaching and preaching.

4. The candidate should be given a copy of the Church's documents (Constitution, Articles of Faith, and By-laws, Missions Policy, etc.) before an interview.

5. There should be a time for the members of the committee to interview him, his wife, and older children if applicable. The candidate and his wife should be permitted to ask questions.

6. It is necessary to ask what the candidate believes concerning:

a. The doctrine of the Church (Baptist/Bible doctrine).

b. The guidelines set forth in the Church's documents. Is he in agreement?

c. How would he change the ministry of the Church?

d. What things would he change – delete or add on?

e. What are his gifts and talents?

f. What type of pastor will he be? One that remains mostly in his office as an administrator? One who gets out and visits the members in their homes?

g. How is the husband/wife relationship? What about the children?

h. Do they have daily family devotions?

i. What is their financial situation? Any large debts?

j. Does he (Do they) meet the qualifications found in Titus and I Timothy 3:1-7?

k. What does he believe concerning:

    1) Divorce and remarriage

    2) The charismatic movement

    3) Neo-evangelicalism

    4) Various Bible versions

    5) Calvinism

    6) Music

    7) Guidelines for church leaders

8) Missions

9) Personal Separation; The use of alcohol, illicit drugs, pornography

10) Ecclesiastical separation

11) How often would he be away from the pulpit?

12) What would he expect from the Church?

13) Other

Once the committee decides to present the individual as a serious candidate, the congregation should also have the opportunity to meet and interview him and his family. Any questions the congregation would like to ask can be written on a piece of paper provided beforehand and given to the chairman of the pulpit committee. This would be helpful in order to avoid embarrassing the candidate or his family with off the wall questions.

Only one candidate at the time should be presented for consideration. Do not make the selection and calling of a pastor a "popularity contest." The candidate must receive a favorable vote by at least 90% of the congregation to be extended a call.

There should be fervent prayer offered before casting a vote. Fasting would be in order as well. The calling of a pastor to be the under-shepherd of the church is one of the most serious and impacting decisions made by the congregation. It should be remembered that it is far easier to call a pastor than it is to "get rid" of one after he has been called. Make sure you know the mind of God.

APPENDIX EIGHT:

A PERSONAL TESTIMONY

In 1969, when Patsy and I left the Spanish Language Institute in San Jose, Costa Rica for Estelí, Nicaragua, I did not know how to start and establish a new church, least of all an indigenous church. Because of my zeal for "doing what we had come to the field to do" we moved almost immediately after language school to Estelí. In my mind it was an ideal location for our ministry. There was no Baptist Church there. It was a population center. It served as a hub for the many ranchers and country folk or "campesinos" living in the province around it. I had also noticed a cobble stone airstrip just north of town that I thought might serve as a base for a village aviation ministry.

My first concern, as it should be for the new missionary arriving on the field, was to get settled into a practical place to live. We were able to rent a new two story apartment from one of the more prominent men in town. Don Chico also owned the electric power plant that provided electricity for the surrounding area. Anytime he was in the apartment we were careful to keep our German shepherd puppy in the wash room. The dog was not dangerous but his name was "Chico." It would have been very offensive to Don Chico to know we had a dog with his nickname. Chico is a common nickname given to men named Francisco. It could very well be argued that by giving our dog a name used by humans *we were insensitive to Latin culture*.

Haste is problematic enough when planting indigenous churches but more damaging is the unintentional insensitivity to the foreign culture that is, more often than not, a matter of *ignorance* . The old adage, "A bear in a china closet" fits many a young missionary to the tee. It is said that ignorance is bliss. I was "charging" ahead blissfully.

It is hard to describe the excitement we felt finally being where we believed the Lord would have us to plant a church, eventually establish a Bible Institute for training national leaders, and of course set up the aviation ministry so I (this should be "we" because it would have been more fruitful to develop this ministry with the assistance of the locales) could plant churches in the many isolated villages in the eastern section of Nicaragua.

It took us several weeks to get settled into our apartment. We didn't have much in the way of household goods. Everything we brought from the States fit in the back of a pickup truck. Patsy and I have come to realize that even the interior decor of one's home can serve to identify with the local people. The nationals can be offended if the missionary's home is too American. Paul felt it important to identify, of course without compromise. This is the evident teaching of:

> *"To the weak became I as weak, that I might gain the weak: I am made all things to all men that I might by all means save some."* I Corinthians 9:22

During our first weeks in Estelí we received an encouraging visit from our pastor's wife, Betty Meadows, her niece, Iva Seacrest, and a Christian businessman, Glen Goad. They were members of Midway Baptist Church in Mt. Airy, North Carolina. Having checked with us about what we might need before making their trip from the States, they brought some new bed sheets for Patsy to use to make curtains for the living room windows. Something simple but with a little fringe they made great curtains. Patsy has always done a wonderful job of decorating our houses. She gave the sheets her special creative touch.

We soon found that renting an apartment was very different from what we had experienced in the States. There was much that had to be done to it before we could move. For security reasons I had to re-hang the front door. I could not imagine why any self-respecting carpenter would hang a door so that the latch could be reached through a jalousie window positioned a few inches from the door. There were other tasks such as building bed frames, cabinets and closets.

My Dad had established his own construction company during my teenage years. Working with him part-time afforded me the opportunity to acquire many valuable skills. I will admit that I was not particularly thrilled at the time about having to work for him but as I have matured I thank God for him every day. A valuable lesson I have learned is that it is far better, if possible, to contract local labor to perform tasks not typically ministerial. By doing so the missionary can provide work and income for a local family, he makes new contacts and ultimately is able to dedicate his time to the task to which he was called of God. The wisdom in this was confirmed many times through the years but especially as we were able to win our first convert in San Miguel, El Salvador. Jose Bonilla, a young electrician's assistant was helping his boss install the light fixtures in our apartment. During a routine break, I was able to lead him to Christ. In Estelí, however, we did not have the income to pay even the meager Nicaraguan wage.

Once settled into our affordable, comfortable, and reasonably secure living quarters we turned our attention to the matter of finding a place to hold services. Though I recommend that every missionary provide for his family first, I am not sure that the best next step is to procure a place to meet. Mostly it seems prudent to begin by winning some converts and then seeking a place to meet. Allowing the new converts to be involved through prayer and helping with the search for a meeting place affords opportunity for maturing and learning. The new converts will recognize soon enough the need for an adequate place to hold Bible studies and services, especially as the number in attendance grows. I did not know then, but later learned that anytime the nationals participate in the recognition of a need, they are more likely to help find the solution... if they own the problem, they will also own the solution. It cannot be emphasized enough that the major task of the missionary church planter is one of, "committing the principles and practices of biblical Christianity" to faithful men (II Timothy 2:2). The church planter should use to advantage every opportunity to give verbal and practical training to his converts.

The decisions I made in the beginning of our ministry and especially the matter of finding a place to hold services accented my ignorance concerning church planting. I made several mistakes, any one of which would have probably led to ultimate failure. I use bold type to highlight them for you.

In my haste to get to the field, we left the States under supported. You may have noticed that I said, "My haste." I accept all responsibility, or should I say "irresponsibility?

Note: Patsy has always been a faithful wife and though I have learned to consider her opinions she has been ready to follow in whatever I have felt was God's will. As my wife she will not be held accountable for my mistakes or bad decisions, only whether she has been willing to follow the Lord's leadership through me. She has the more difficult task and will no doubt receive the greater reward. Because she is willing to allow the Lord to lead through me, I am, for sure, going to take her thoughts into consideration and make sure she knows I have her well-being in mind in every decision. Blessed is the church planter that has a wife like this, but he is a fool if he fails to consider her when making decisions.

The lack of sufficient personal support and no work fund support placed us at a great disadvantage and under a constant financial load. We experienced definite limitations in the areas that depended upon our finances. Having too little support can be a hindrance to church planting but also having an excessive amount of support can undermine the planting of indigenous churches. I will mention this again at the appropriate time.

Haste to get to our place of service in Estelí also kept me from spending a prudent amount of time in Managua to receive mentoring from Dr. Bob Dayton or Dr. Jerry Reece. Both were veterans of at least one term. I had much to learn about the culture, the language, and many other aspects of life and ministry in Nicaragua. There is much wisdom in serving an internship under a veteran missionary for a year or even the first term on the field. The wise servant of God sees the benefits of learning from those that have gone before.

This might be a good place to mention the truth found in Proverbs 9:8b and 9.

> *"...Rebuke a wise man, and he will love thee. Give instruction to a wise man, and he will be yet wiser: teach a just man, and he will increase in learning."*

Our response to correction or instruction shows us to be wise or foolish. Wise constructive criticism from a person that truly loves us and has our best interests at heart can be one of the greatest blessings of our lives. Wise is the Christian that has at least one person in his life to whom he has given the prerogative to point out flaws, problems, or hindrances. I recommend that the missionary carefully select a "confidant" that at the missionary's request has the right to call to the attention of the missionary any and everything that might work against him. I was especially helped in this way as I sought to learn the language and culture.

Note: While we were serving with IBERO, I was helped by having a student or one of the other teachers point out the mistakes I was making when speaking Spanish. Sadly we often "learn our mistakes" and make them a bad habit. Bruce Bell used to say, "It is okay to make a mistake once. When it has been pointed out, do not repeat it."

My desire to have a place to hold services even before we had a single convert and our limited financial resources resulted in our going to the only "affordable" part of town... the lowest of low rent districts... the red light zone (for those unfamiliar with the term, "the red light district", it is used to refer to the area where prostitutes practice their trade) on the very last back street in Estelí. Because of the propensity to live by sight and not by faith I felt the need to have something "tangible" or in this case "visible." Somehow to be able to point to a building with a sign "Iglesia Bautista" made me feel that, at least, I was making progress. I would have bristled at the suggestion that this decision was unwise.

I had given no thought to "how the people of Estelí perceived us or our little building." Most of the people of Estelí would not have been caught dead in our church neighborhood. My actions had isolated us. Because I had no experience ministering to prostitutes, drunkards or the people living in our church neighborhood I could not even reach them.

Generally Roman Catholic people are accustomed to extravagant temples in the center of town, not little one room buildings with holes in the walls, dirt floors, rough wood benches, and a single 40 watt light bulb dangling from an open ceiling. Now that I look back on it I realize how sad it was. Surely the locals must have shaken their heads in disbelief and dismay at the "crazy gringo." (Note: In Nicaragua the word "gringo" carried a very negative connotation. It came into use in the early 1900s as the Nicaraguan people shouted at the green-uniformed American soldiers occupying their land, "green go"!)

The common theory in Central America was that all missionaries were eyes and ears for the CIA. Can anyone possibly believe that the CIA would send an agent to spy on the red light district of a one-horse town? All I can say is that I hope the real agents of the CIA are better prepared for their job than I was for mine.

With a place to meet all prepared we started door-to-door soul winning visitation. If anyone was remotely interested in hearing what we had to say, I am sure they were repulsed as soon as I mentioned where we would be meeting. In all this I had overlooked the importance of winning the confidence of the people of Estelí. Church planting involves and requires <u>the development of "relationships."</u> As long as the missionary stands aloof or is a stranger he will not have much success at winning converts. It seems to me now that it would have been far better to proceed more slowly and to do things that would have allowed the people to get acquainted with us. We could have invited prospects to our house for a meal, or had informal home Bible studies. At times it is necessary to win people to oneself in order to win them to Christ.

The weeks passed slowly. We went each Sunday with the hope that one of the people we had visited during the week would show up. Not even the people who lived near our little church building -- that is really stretching the use of the word "church" -- ventured to one of the services. The little children would come in and look around only to head back out to the street. If prayer alone could plant a church we would have seen one spring to life. If sincerity were the only requisite we would have succeeded. I asked myself over and over again, "what am I doing wrong?" The answer should have been evident.

I can only remember leading one man in the sinner's prayer during the two months that we lived and served in Estelí. Thank God for that one but we never had anyone attend a service, in fact we never really had a service.

In His mercy and grace the Lord Jesus Christ was working on our behalf to give us the opportunity to learn how to plant a church. His plan for us would be fulfilled. How He arranged for me to gain the knowledge and experience necessary to continue to serve Him in church-planting in Central America is a story in itself. To this day I appreciate His goodness in allowing us to live the Estelí experience. We were allowed to go there in fulfillment of His promise in Psalm 37:4. He granted a "desire of our heart" but in the process He showed to me my ignorance concerning planting churches in Nicaragua.

What a relief when the Lord opened the door for us to become involved in the ministry of the Spanish Bible Institute "IBERO." In October of 1969 Dr. Tom Freeney, General Director of BIMI and the newly appointed Central American Director, asked to talk with us and the other missionaries as they traveled through Nicaragua. We were introduced to Bruce Bell at that time. After a brief interview they asked if I would consider working with IBERO as Bruce's assistant. It would mean moving to Mexico, teaching multiple Bible institute courses in Spanish 3 to 4 hours a day and being involved as a member of the church-planting team. You can be assured that I was not chosen for this opportunity because of what I knew about church planting. Our dedication to learning the language well and desire to win souls were our greatest assets. We prayed about the decision, not long, but we did pray. The Lord was seemingly directing.

Since the Lord has burdened me to write this book I am going to take this opportunity to make a statement about God's will that I trust will be helpful. In the previous paragraph I used the expression, "The Lord was seemingly directing." I have learned from the experience of the Apostle Paul as recorded by Luke in Acts 16:10 that it is perfectly okay to express His will in terms that are less than definite. Paul states in this verse that they "endeavored to go into Macedonia, assuredly gathering that the Lord had called us for to preach the gospel to them." As a missionary seeking to do God's will Paul attempted to go toward Asia. The Holy Ghost forbad him to do so. He "thought he knew God's will" but the Lord graciously directed him another way. His expression, "assuredly gathering" reveals that, being forbidden by the Spirit to go in one direction and the vision of the man of Macedonia indicating another, he concluded that God was seemingly leading toward Macedonia. Since God has not recorded His specific will (city, states, subdivision, etc.) for each of us as individuals in the pages of the Holy Bible there is some latitude afforded us concerning where we are to serve. After reading and studying this passage of Scripture I am convinced that my "calling" is to preach the Gospel" – a ministry, not a place. God leads us to the places where we are to preach.

A well-known Pastor was reported to have said that he didn't think God would be upset with us if we went, by some mistake, to what some might consider the wrong place, and started winning souls and building a great church to HIS glory. The "what" (evangelism and church planting) of missions is defined specifically in the Word of God. The "where" is given in general terms... the world. The specific place where God would have each of us to serve as individuals is not always as easy to determine. There may be occasion for us to back up and head in another direction. I am convinced He may lead in one direction only to show us once we are there that He wants us in a different location -- but always doing the same things, evangelism and church planting.

It has been said:

"Abraham didn't know where he was going but he knew what he would do when he got there...

Many missionaries know where they are going but don't know what to do when they get there." Unknown

Understandably there was a certain amount of disappointment upon leaving Estelí. We left without any visible results or fruit remaining. God in His wisdom worked in us and the situation to His glory and our good. I was then ready to learn how to plant an indigenous church.

I am convinced that our ministry was greatly helped by the positive, practical instruction in church planting principles that we received while working with IBERO. My prayer is that the beginning missionaries that study this book will not have to experience the sense of failure, frustration and, yes, discouragement we lived while in Estelí.

INDEX OF WORDS AND PHRASES IN INDIGENOUS CHURCHES

Accountability, 38, 146
Affiliation, 154
Africa, 22, 49, 65
Aggressive, 58
American, 18, 21, 22, 35, 42, 43, 47, 86, 87, 111, 290, 294, 295
Apostle, 32, 33, 84, 88, 141, 296
Australia, 59
Authority, 165
Auxiliary, 27
Aviation, 305, 306
Baptism, 127, 131
Baptist, 5, 15, 16, 25, 28, 38, 39, 50, 52, 57, 66, 84, 87, 100, 103, 106, 114, 121, 127, 131, 132, 136, 137, 139, 146, 148, 150, 151, 154-157, 163, 166, 171, 286, 289, 290, 305
Basics, 52
Bell, 5, 49, 58, 60, 293, 295
Benevolence, 110
Biblical, 2, 26, 85
Body of Christ, 130, 165
Bonilla, 291
Bragg, 65
Brother, 41, 92, 305, 306
Build, 111
By-laws, 285
Calvinism, 286
Carey, 28, 58, 122
Catholicism, 22
Central, 5, 28, 54, 55, 57, 121, 294, 295, 305
Change, 157
Charismatic, 154, 158
Christ, 5, 13, 16, 21, 26, 27, 29, 30, 32-36, 38, 41-45, 52, 53, 55, 57, 58-63, 66, 67, 69, 71, 73, 79, 86-88, 93, 95, 96, 99, 100, 101, 102, 104, 109, 111, 115, 118, 119, 123, 125-131, 137, 138, 141, 142, 146, 147, 159, 162, 163, 165, 168, 169, 291, 294, 295, 306
Christians, 13, 17, 18, 21, 23, 27, 30-32, 36, 38, 50, 51, 59, 60, 62, 63, 69, 70, 75, 88, 89, 94, 96, 98, 109, 114, 119, 141
Church, 5, 17, 26, 38, 52, 57, 69, 83, 84, 87, 99, 100, 106, 117, 121, 125-127, 131, 134, 136, 145, 146, 148-151, 154-158, 165-168, 171, 282, 285-287, 289, 290, 294, 305
City, 19, 50
Civil, 41
Commission, 32, 69, 161

Conditional, 62
Congregation, 145
Constitution, 127, 136-138, 167, 285
Costa Rica, 289, 305
Council, 147, 166-168
Covenant, 84, 131, 137, 138, 165, 167, 168
Deacons, 95, 97, 98, 280
Dean, 50
Decisions, 98, 156
Deitz, 305
Develop, 111
Discipleship, 69, 75
Discipline, 132
Disqualified, 99
Documents, 125, 257
Ecclesiastical, 287
El Salvador, 5, 50, 66, 94, 113, 291, 305
Elders, 95
English, 39, 45, 67, 75, 125, 305
Establish, 25, 105
Europe, 22, 59
Evangelism, 27, 31, 32, 36, 49, 58, 69, 105
Evangelist, 54
Experience, 38, 152
Faithful, 147
Fasting, 287
Father, 13, 34, 44, 75, 125, 128, 129, 159
Faulkner, 121
Fellowship, 103, 117
Freeney, 295
Fruitful, 49
Fuentes, 63, 306
Garlicks, 50
Goad, 290
God, 5, 13, 15, 16, 18, 19, 21, 22, 25-30, 32, 33, 37, 38, 41, 42-45, 47, 48, 50, 56-60, 63-65, 67, 69, 71-73, 75, 76, 79, 83, 86, 87, 88, 91-95, 98-100, 102, 103, 105, 106, 109, 110, 113-115, 118, 120-126, 128-130, 137, 141-143, 145, 146, 159-163, 165, 168, 285, 287, 291, 292, 295-297
Gospel, 17, 21, 52, 53, 130, 137, 146, 149, 159, 161, 296, 305, 306
Grace, 114, 159, 160
Growth, 149
Guatemala, 50, 305
Halsey, 114
Heaven, 23, 129, 130
Hell, 21, 26, 62, 64, 130
Hispanics, 35, 306
Holland, 54
Holy Spirit, 17, 21, 41, 44, 45, 47, 52, 59, 62, 69, 71, 75, 78, 80, 119, 122-126, 128-130, 145, 165, 168
Hope, 105, 106, 129
Human, 109
IBERO, 5, 49, 53, 293, 295, 297, 305
Iglesia, 52, 54, 57, 293, 306
INDEX, 267, 299
Indigenous, 17, 18, 21-23, 25, 31, 37, 49, 67, 69

Institute, 5, 47, 49, 53, 54, 56, 57, 93, 104-106, 122, 289, 290, 295, 305
Islam, 22
Japan, 66
Jesus, 5, 13, 21, 26, 30, 32, 33, 35, 36, 38, 41, 45, 49, 53, 56, 59, 61, 62, 64, 69, 73, 87, 88, 93, 99, 102, 109, 115, 125-127, 129, 130, 131, 137, 138, 141, 146, 147, 159, 162, 165, 168, 169, 295
Jewish, 42
Judas, 57
Judge, 45
Judson, 58
King, 2, 38, 45, 125, 169
KJV, 75
Language, 289
Latin, 22, 35, 49, 87, 289
Leaders, 94, 119, 168
Leadership, 147, 148, 257
Local, 158, 168
Lord, 3, 5, 13, 16, 19, 21, 26, 28, 29, 31-36, 38, 41, 42, 45, 50, 52-57, 59, 60-63, 65-67, 71-73, 75, 77-79, 83, 84, 87, 88, 92-95, 97-99, 101, 102, 104, 109, 111, 113, 114, 119, 120, 122-132, 141, 142, 145, 158, 159, 161, 162, 165, 169, 277, 289, 292, 295, 296, 305
Lost, 84
Loving, 96
Lyons, 73
Maine, 60
Marshes, 49
Martin, 19
Master, 30
Meadows, 290
Member, 148
Mexico, 37, 50, 62, 63, 295, 305
Ministry, 30, 38, 84, 257, 282
Miramonte, 5, 52, 57, 58, 305
Mission, 35, 37, 149-151, 153, 155, 158
Missionary, 37, 94, 114, 122, 149, 151, 155-157, 282, 283, 305
Missions, 5, 17, 37, 114, 145-151, 155-157, 160, 163, 285, 287, 305
Modesty, 43
Money, 37
Music, 42, 282, 286
Nationals, 35, 78, 84, 87, 142
New Testament, 15-19, 26, 27, 34, 36, 40, 69, 101, 105, 113, 117, 125, 127, 128, 166
Nicaragua, 49, 64, 121, 289, 290, 292, 294, 295, 305
Nursery, 279, 280, 282
Omega, 38
Open, 96
Order, 136, 167
Para-church, 25, 28, 29, 154
Pastor, 54, 84, 93, 100, 147, 149-151, 155, 156, 158, 280, 296

Patsy, 3, 5, 49, 289, 290, 292, 305, 306
Payroll, 257
Pedagogy, 105
People, 15, 31, 86, 149
Perfect, 152
Peripheral, 30
Persecution, 18
Policy, 145, 148, 157, 285
Prayer, 167, 168
Principle, 114
Priority, 146
Profile, 157
Promise, 114, 159-161
Provide, 118, 149
Purposes, 83, 128
Qualifications, 95, 150, 151, 153, 154
Relationships, 58, 63
Religion, 2
Repentance, 75
Resources, 257
Responsibility, 148, 155, 156
Rights, 2
Roberson, 99, 121
Role, 30
Salvador, 50, 66, 305
Salvation, 59, 154
Samaritan, 64
San Salvador, 5, 50, 52, 53, 57, 305
San Vicente, 54, 55
Saviour, 26, 34, 61, 63, 66, 71, 94, 119, 129-131
Scholarship, 47
Scripture, 2, 17, 18, 33, 52, 84, 113, 131, 141, 142, 145, 158, 168, 296
Separation, 287
Sisk, 36
Spirit, 44, 69, 76, 94, 95, 99, 100, 119, 120, 126, 129, 165, 296
Spirit-filled, 44, 94, 99, 100, 120
Spiritual, 59, 153
Strategy, 149
Study, 105
Supervisor, 280
Supper, 75, 87, 101, 127, 128, 130
Tabernáculo, 50, 52, 54, 56, 72, 94, 305
Taylor, 30
Teacher, 282
Teaching, 34, 159
Thompson, 19, 77
Train, 76, 78, 79, 112, 120
Translations, 158
Understanding, 148
Underwood, 50
Use, 31, 37, 77, 143, 168
Way, 2
Wilkerson, 100
Will, 87, 91, 110
Wisdom, 112
Woods, 49
Word, 5, 13, 21, 30, 38, 41, 45, 56, 59, 64, 67, 69, 71, 76, 78, 83, 86, 97, 98, 100, 103, 104, 106, 109, 125, 128, 137, 145, 296

ABOUT THE AUTHOR

Dr. Bob C. Green was born in Fort Pierce, Florida in 1943 to Bob and Edris Green. He came to the Lord in 1955 when he was 12 years of age through the ministry of Fairlawn Baptist Church. He surrendered to preach the Gospel when 16 years old. He graduated from Dan McCarty High School in 1961. In 1967 he graduated with a B.A degree with a major in Bible from Tennessee Temple College. Brother Green has since earned a M.A. and two D.Min. Degrees.

He and Patsy (Deitz) of Asheville, North Carolina were married July 15, 1965. In January of 1967 they were approved by Baptist International Missions, Inc. (BIMI) to serve as missionaries in Central America. They served for a number of years doing church planting in Nicaragua, Costa Rica, Guatemala, Mexico and ultimately in El Salvador. Nine of the most productive years were those when they served in El Salvador. They served as a part of the IBERO Bible Institute and as co-founders of the Miramonte Baptist Church in San Salvador. During the nine very productive years they served six years in San Miguel, El Salvador and founded and established the Tabernáculo Bautista de San Miguel. The two churches in El Salvador have reproduced themselves, under national leadership and have planted many dozens of daughter churches, mostly in the eastern sector of the country.

Brother Green is also a pilot and aviation (A&P) mechanic. He used the aircraft as a tool for evangelism, church planting, transportation for Christian workers and emergency medical flights. From 1984 until 1988 Brother Green served as the Director of the recently defunct ministry of Missionary Aviation Institute previously located on the property of the Sugar Valley Airport in Farmington, North Carolina.

The Greens have also served among the millions of Spanish speaking people living in the USA. They have assisted English speaking churches in establishing Spanish ministries to reach Hispanics with the Gospel of Christ. On several occasions they were involved in either establishing autonomous Hispanic churches or assisting other missionaries in the effort. They started and established the Iglesia Bautista Getsemaní in Hendersonville, North Carolina while serving in the USA ministries of BIMI. The church is now pastored by the Rev. Carlos Fuentes.

They continue to serve Christ as missionaries with BIMI. Brother Green is Hispanic Ministries Representative and Aviation Ministries Director. Bob and Patsy live in Harrison, Tennessee.

The Greens have two children, Susan and Timothy and six grandchildren: Hannah (and husband Mitch), Danielle, Joshua, Hunter, Logan, and Natalie.

www.ingramcontent.com/pod-product-compliance
Lightning Source LLC
Chambersburg PA
CBHW062126160426
43191CB00013B/2209

* 9 7 8 0 9 9 6 2 5 9 1 7 0 *